THE RECEPTION
OF UNITED STATES
LITERATURE IN GERMANY

UNIVERSITY OF NORTH CAROLINA
STUDIES IN COMPARATIVE LITERATURE

For Reprints from this Series see page 246.

Foreign Sales through Librairie E. Droz, 11 Rue Massot, Geneva, Switzerland.

UNIVERSITY OF NORTH CAROLINA
STUDIES IN COMPARATIVE LITERATURE
NUMBER THIRTY-NINE

THE RECEPTION
OF UNITED STATES
LITERATURE IN GERMANY

BY

LAWRENCE MARSDEN PRICE

CHAPEL HILL
THE UNIVERSITY OF NORTH CAROLINA PRESS
1966

Printed in the Netherlands by Royal VanGorcum Ltd., Assen

CONTENTS

PREFACE

For several years I have been interested in Anglo-German literary relations and from time to time I have attempted to record the reception of English literature in Germany. Under the name of English literature I rightly included literature in the English language but of American origin. However, after three trials and three errors, 1919, 1935, and 1953,[1] I made the belated discovery that even though American literature was an important if lesser portion of literature in the English language, its relation to German literature was an independent development, and the attempt to include its history led to a break in the continuity of the history of the major element. In 1961 I published a summary which excluded the participation of American literature but achieved uninterrupted continuity in regard to British English literature.[2]

After the completion of this work I felt the need to compile a similar record regarding the reception of United States literature in Germany. I state specifically United States literature in order not to disregard the existence of other American literatures to the north and south of us, but having made this bow, I permit myself in the text, for the sake of brevity and euphony, to use the term "American literature" in the limited sense of United States literature.

A glance at the bibliography of books and essays on which this summary is based will show that the writers speak frequently of German literature and of American literature, which might suggest that nationalistic theories of literature are involved, but this is far from true. The titles simply define the portion of world literature which the investigators proposed to examine more closely. It does not appear that in the period 1775 to 1965 there was anywhere in Western Europe or in North America any literature with distinctive and exclusive national or racial characteristics. It would require many adjectives, several of them contradictory, to enumerate all the qualities of American literature, and these adjectives would be applicable to other literatures of the period as well. If one, for example, should say that a stubborn insistence on political and personal liberty was a constant in American literature, the same would be true of English and German literature. If a racial literature exists anywhere it is rather to be found among primitive tribes, not sophisticated modern societies.

It is not the function of a work of reference such as this to attempt an evaluation of American works of literature or even to suggest that in some instances their receptions in Germany were unduly cold or unduly warm. It was necessary to proceed selectively, and it seemed more advisable to give fuller attention to certain outstanding American men of letters to the relative neglect of other important but still minor authors. The lacunae here are partly filled in by the bibliographical entries, but only partly. Much of the compilation was made in America where certain dissertations, published and unpublished, review journals, and newspapers were not available.

The terminal bibliography serves as a supplement to the text. It is not the result of a futile attempt at all-inclusiveness. Every year over a hundred interesting and important observations on American literature and its authors appear in Germany. They are listed in the frequent bibliographies compiled by such "Fach-journale" as the *Zeitschrift für Anglistik und Amerikanistik*, the *Weimarer Beiträge*, and the *Jahrbuch für Amerikastudien*. This bibliography strives rather to be representative. It includes in largest number monographs, dissertations and other academic publications, but also a few essays and comments of more popular origin. It includes shorter reviews and appraisals from journals of various trends – Protestant, Catholic, Atheistic, Communistic, Socialistic, and Nationalistic. From browsing through these criticisms, the total impression is that, with few exceptions, the German critics are fair and objective in their evaluations of American literature.

No apologies are offered for this one-sided discussion of a two-sided topic. The indebtedness of America to German culture has been fully appreciated by American scholars, most comprehensively by B.Q.Morgan with his *Critical Bibliography of German Literature in English Translation (1481-1927)* 2d ed., Stanford University Press, 1938; 773 pp., and by Henry A. Pochmann, assisted by A.R.Schulze, with their *German Culture in America, Philosophical and Literary Influences, 1600-1900,* University of Wisconsin Press, 1947; 865 pp.

For assistance in compiling this symposium I am indebted to several friends. I wish especially to thank Professors Siegfried Puknat of the University of California at Santa Cruz, B. Q. Morgan of Stanford University, and Dr. Maxwell Knight of the University of California Press.

[1] *English Literature in Germany,* UCP in Modern Philology, XXXVII (1953); 548 pp.
[2] *Die Aufnahme englischer Literatur in Deutschland, 1500-1960,* Bern, Francke, 1961; 496 pp.

PART I

FROM COLONIES TO INDEPENDENCE

I. THE COLONIAL PERIOD

The earliest known reference to America in German literature is to be found in Sebastian Brant's *Narrenschiff*, 1494.

> Ouch hatt man sydt jnn Portigal
> Vnd jnn hispanyen vberall
> Golt / jnslen funden / vnd nacket lüt
> Von den man vor wust sagen nüt.

This was followed by sometimes extensive utilizations of American themes by many well known poets and narrators in Germany. Chiefly references are to the fauna and flora of America, above all to tobacco but also to potatoes, pineapples, aloes, and passion flowers. Of more importance was the confrontation of the unspoiled savage and the corrupt European. The earliest centers of interest were the West Indies, Mexico, and South America, and the references to them lie somewhat aside from the topic here under discussion.[1]

Leaders of the English colonies in America kept in touch with their fellow-mysticists and pietists in Europe. John Winthrop the Younger, long-time Governor of Connecticut, and Johannes Rist were brought together by their common interest in alchemy. The works of John Winthrop's pupil George Stirk or Starkey were well known in Germany, and they also impressed the young Goethe. Peter Streithagen's *Homo Novus*, Heidelberg, 1658, was written under the stimulation of John Cotton's *The Way of*

5

Life, 1641 (German, 1670). The Spener group in Frankfurt read the pamphlets of William Penn before the establishment of Germantown, Pennsylvania, under the leadership of Franz Daniel Pastorius. A common interest in John Eliot's translation of the Bible into one of the Algonquin languages led eventually to a correspondence between August Hermann Francke and Cotton Mather. In his *Vernünftige Gedanken von den Absichten der natürlichen Dinge*, 1724, Christian Wolff especially recommended Cotton Mather's *Christian Philosophy*.

In the German lands of the eighteenth century there was no lack of information regarding America. In his *German Works on America, 1492-1800*, 1952, Palmer lists nearly 900 titles. The greater number of these were translations from the English or other languages. To be sure, Palmer uses the word America in the larger sense, but after 1640 works on the European colonies in North America make up an ever increasing share. To the period 1640 to 1800 belong over seven hundred titles. For the English colonial period, 1640-1775, with which we are at first concerned, there are over four hundred titles.[2] A good comprehensive work was John Oldmixon's *The British Empire in America*, I, II, 1741 (German, 1744). Treatises regarding the various colonies individually come in greater number after 1775, but there were several such during the colonial period. Some of these contributions were in the form of advice to prospective colonists or letters from religious groups to their brethren in Germany, such as Increase Mather's *De successu evangelij apud Indos in Nova Anglia*, 1688 (German, 1696), William Penn's *Some Account of the Province of Pennsilvania*, 1681 (German in the same year), and *Letter from William Penn*, 1683 (German, 1684), Franz Daniel Pastorius' *Umständige geographische Beschreibung der allerletzt erfundenen Provintz Pensilvaniae...* 1700, the Urlesperger reports regarding the Salzburger emigrants, 1731-1767, and Oglethorpe's *A New and Accurate Account of the Provinces of South Carolina and Georgia*, 1732 (German, 1746). From all these works Germans could gain a clear idea of the

6

physical features of the seaboard colonies and their natural resources.

Belletristic works were written, in colonial times, almost exclusively in New England, New York, and Pennsylvania. The total output was not formidable. Had German critics known of any part of it, they would not have been much interested. American literature was still under the shelter of English literature even long after political independence had been attained. German critics, however, should have been interested in the new tendency in the colonies to treat of their heritages with scholarly discrimination. In his "Dissertations on the English Language" (1789), Noah Webster wrote:

> On examining the language and comparing the practice of speaking among the yeomanry of this country, with the style of Shakespeare and Addison, I am constrained to declare that the people of America, in particular the English descendants, speak the most *pure English* now known in the world. There is hardly a foreign idiom in this language; by which I mean a *phrase* that has not been used by the best English writers from the time of Chaucer. They retain a few obsolete *words*, which have been dropt by writers, probably from mere affectation, as those which are substituted are neither more melodious nor expressive. In many instances they retain correct phrases, instead of which the pretended refiners of the language have introduced those which are highly improper and absurd.

By "the best writers from the time of Chaucer" Noah Webster meant the Elizabethans, Sidney, Sir William Temple, Middleton, Bolingbroke, Addison, Swift, Pope, Steele, and Arbuthnot, and as the "Sprachverderber" of more recent times Webster mentioned Garrick, Dr. Johnson, Robertson, Home, Blair, and Gibbon. In the place of the unaffected, clear, and agreeable style of the predecessors these writers had introduced a rhetorical pompous style, offensive to the true nature of the English language.[3]

Webster spoke here not as a rebel against the English language. He assigned to America the mission to defend the English language against the recent innovations. History had reserved

7

this function to the colonists, for the English language had developed for the worse, and the distance from the motherland had protected the colonists from infection. There were a few dissenters, among them Thomas Jefferson, who felt that the English development was in the line of progress and that the American states should assimilate all that was good in it. Meanwhile the English language in America was enriching itself from its situation and drawing upon Dutch, French, German, and Indian contacts and the "Realien" of pioneer life for additions to its vocabulary. The majority of the early men of letters were in agreement with Webster. Benjamin Franklin wrote to Webster a note of approbation. Thus we have at the outset two slightly different programs for a differentiation of the American language, the one conservative, the other progressive, but neither of them pointing toward the development of an American language, to say nothing of an American literature. The "classic" writers of America almost throughout the nineteenth century looked to England for a standard and held it to be the highest compliment when it was said that their style compared favorably with that of the best English writers. An American literary language could only develop from the American grass roots. Leon Kellner regards Lowell's *A Fable for Critics*, 1848, as the earliest call for language freedom. Hemingway may have been slightly in error when he said that Mark Twain was the first to write a whole novel in the American language, but at least he was the first to gain for such a work a place in world literature.

The outbreak of the American War of Independence called the importance of the English colonies in America to the attention of the Germans, who began to take positions in the conflict. The lines were not strictly drawn, with supporters of England and despotism on one side and supporters of freedom-loving Americans on the other side. The primary division was in England. The government was in the hands of the Tories but there was a strong Whig opposition. There were also Tories as well as Whigs in America.

German readers not yet sufficiently informed regarding the issues at stake could soon have full clarification. Edmund Burke's speech on *Conciliation with the Colonies*, 1775, was translated into German, 1777. Burke did not deny the right of England to make laws restricting the commerce of the colonies, but he doubted the feasibility of enforcing the laws, and held that enforcement would lead to harm rather than good.

There was a general distrust in Germany of popular government based in large part on the belief that it would lead to the eventual rise of a tyranny as in previous episodes of history. The most salubrious rule was held to be that by an enlightened hereditary ruler who took counsel with his wisest subjects. Many liberal German political thinkers therefore placed their fondest hopes in the establishment of limited monarchies of the English pattern and regretted to see England's prestige diminished. The rulers of the German courts also, out of their abhorrence of unruly subjects, by censorship and by the giving and withholding of patronage, lent their support to the English cause.

Among the several German cities where the English rule was favored the sentiment was naturally most pronounced in Hanoverian Göttingen. Of the university professors the most distinguished was Georg Christoph Lichtenberg, who had spent many months in England and had talked to the king on the basis of social equality. Even by his like-minded colleagues at the university, Lichtenberg was regarded as an undiscriminating Anglophile. The most influential economist in Göttingen was August Ludwig Schlözer, professor of history and statistics, and one of the earliest authorities on America. His series of journals called *Briefwechsel* was widely read. Schlözer called the participants of the Boston Tea Party "vermummte Strassenräuber" and the rebellious colonists "Verteidiger ihrer faulen Sache."[4]

Literary Göttingen, that is to say the "Göttinger Bund,"

was in near agreement with academic Göttingen. Heinrich Christian Boie, the editor of the *Deutsches Museum*, received and published an article on the rebellion written in England by Helferich Peter Sturz. In England Sturz associated with Tories and with men about the king. Sturz asked for an early publication of a contribution of January 1777, as the interest would soon cool off, for he expected that the arguments of the colonists would shortly be refuted by the canon balls and muskets of General Howe. The people will not long be led astray, he said, by leaders of lowly origin such as Hancock and Adams. The Dutch rebels, he averred, made progress only because they had a prince to lead them.[5]

At the beginning of the war, Friedrich Klopstock, Friedrich Leopold Stolberg, and Johann Heinrich Voss were monarchists. Their defection to republicanism came later. In his poem "Sie und nicht wir," 1790, Klopstock expresses his chagrin that France, not Germany, led the way to freedom, but he accorded to America also its due: "An Amerikas Strömen flammt schon eigenes Licht." In 1792 Klopstock, Pestalozzi, Goethe, Washington, and several others were made citizens of the French Republic. On this occasion Klopstock expressed his pride that he had now become a fellow citizen of Washington.[6]

It would be difficult to maintain that Schiller, "the poet of freedom," showed in his lyric poetry any great enthusiasm for the American causes, although such an attempt has been made on the basis of an early poem and a late fragment. In the early poem, "Der Abend," 1776, Schiller wrote:

> Die Sonne zeigt, vollendend gleich dem Helden,
> Dem tiefen Thal ihr Abendangesicht.
> Für andre, ach! glücksel'gre Welten,
> Ist das ein Morgenangesicht.[7]

and in Schiller's "Nachlass" a fragment of a poem was found:

> Nach dem fernen Westen wollt' ich steuern
> Auf der Strasse, die Kolumbus fand.
> Die Kolumb mit seinem Wanderschiffe
> An die alte Erde band.
> Dort vielleicht ist Freiheit
> Ach, dort ist sie nicht,
> Flieh![8]

In these poems there is no indisputable reference to English America. In the first it is to the whole Western hemisphere lighted up by the sun. In the second poem the distant west of Columbus is a place where freedom is not to be found. For Schiller, as for Goethe, freedom meant peace and the opportunity to cultivate the muses. Another poem of Schiller ends:

> In des Herzens heilig stille Räume
> Musst du fliehen in des Lebens Drang.
> Freiheit ist nur in dem Reich der Träume,
> Und das Schöne blüht nur im Gesang.

Schiller bespoke a nonviolent quest of freedom:

> Wenn sich die Völker selbst befreien,
> Da kann die Wohlfahrt nicht gedeihen.

and again:

> Vor dem Sklaven, wenn er die Kette bricht,
> Vor dem freien Menschen erzittert nicht.

It can, however, be plausibly argued that the American Revolution prefigured to some extent the political action in *Wilhelm Tell:*

> There is a small people that has conquered a difficult terrain and made it hospitable. This people achieved its goal by a peculiar combination of rugged individualism and cooperative effort, personal independence, and spontaneous concern for the general welfare.[9]

There were internal disputes smoothed out by the Rütli oath (cf. The Continental Congress and the Declaration of Independence). Beyond the borders, an outside organizing power seeks to extend its force by assimilating the independent people,

11

which puts up a successful resistance. The author of *Wilhelm Tell* must certainly have rejoiced at the success of the American colonists.

Goethe was interested in the conflict between England and America in 1775, but only mildly. In *Dichtung und Wahrheit* he referred to the uprising in Corsica and the visit of the defeated Paoli to Frankfurt and wrote further:

> Noch lebhafter aber war die Welt interessiert, als ein ganzes Volk sich zu befreien Miene machte,..., man wünschte den Amerikanern alles Glück, und die Namen Franklin und Washington fingen an, am politischen und kriegerischen Himmel zu glänzen und funkeln.

Continuing, Goethe wrote:

> An allen diesen Ereignissen nahm ich jedoch nur insofern teil, als sie die grössere Gesellschaft interessierten. Ich selbst und mein engerer Kreis befassten uns nicht mit Zeitungen und Neuigkeiten; uns war darum zu tun, den ganzen Menschen kennen zu lernen. Die Menschen überhaupt liessen wir gern gewähren.[10]

Goethe then went on to point out that there were checks and balances in the feudal system that still prevailed in Germany, beginning with privileges of the electoral princes. He noted that aristocracy, clergy, military, and mercantile middle class were well content with things as they were. Since Goethe himself belonged to a relatively favored group, his unawareness of any discontent among the lowest and largest groups of subjects is explicable. Goethe took the opportunity to explain that even *Werther* was not intended as a protest of plebeian against aristocrat and that the public did not interpret it in that sense.

Goethe was in accord with the farthest seeing thinkers of the time, among them Wieland, Lessing, Kant, and Herder, who also saw the hope of the future in the leveling upward of humanity as a whole. In 1775, however, Goethe was interested in America for a personal reason. About the year 1830, he recounted in

12

Dichtung und Wahrheit his frustrating relationship with Lili Schönemann in his youth and reported:

> Wohlwollende hatten mir vertraut, Lili habe geäussert,... sie unternähme wohl, aus Neigung zu mir, alle dermaligen Zustände und Verhältnisse aufzugeben und mit nach Amerika zu gehen.

To this Goethe commented: "Amerika war damals vielleicht noch mehr als jetzt das Eldorado derjenigen, die in ihrer augenblicklichen Lage sich bedrängt fanden."[11]

The uprising of the colonies was an event that freed the journals of the time from their provinciality. The humdrum reports of the domestic and social affairs of the ruling houses gave way to the discussions of an event of worldwide significance. Schlözer's series of *Briefwechsel*, (Göttingen), 1762-1782, and his *Staatsanzeiger*, 1782-1793, were outspokenly in favor of the English. Of like conviction was the other leading Göttinger journal, the *Deutsches Museum* of Dohm and Boie, 1776-1788, but to Voss' *Göttinger Musenalmanach*, 1777 ff., Göckingk contributed several poems showing enthusiasm for the cause of the colonials.[12] Friedrich Nicolai's *Allgemeine deutsche Bibliothek*, 1765-1806, published in Prussia, was fairly free from censorship and although pro-monarchical, published reviews that strove to do justice to both sides. Much the same could be said of Wieland's *Teutscher Merkur*, 1773-1789, which, however, was less free from censorship than Nicolai's journal. In 1776 it commented on the colonists' declaration of independence in enthusiastic terms and added: "Diese Zwistigkeiten... verdienen die ernsthafteste Aufmerksamkeit unsers Jahrhunderts und bereiten uns zu den wichtigsten Begebenheiten vor."[13] But too great enthusiasm for the American cause would have occasioned the displeasure of the Weimar court, and Wieland asked his contributors to refrain from controversial subjects. The Swabian journalist Wilhelm Ludwig Weckherlin, editor of *Felleisen* (1778) and *Chronologie* (1779-1781), was as bitter an opponent of the colonies as Schlözer.[14] Two years before the end of the war he prophesied the defeat of the republic.

By far the doughtiest spokesman for the colonies was the Swabian poet Schubart, the editor of the *Deutsche Chronik*, 1774-1777, and again after his ten years imprisonment, 1787-1790. He castigated his fellow journalists for their "wiedergekaute Gewäsche von Alltagsgeschichten und Lobsprüche auf Regenten." None dared to write: "Dieser Fürst legt seinen Unterthanen unerträgliche Lasten auf; jener Staat verkennet die Grundsätze der Menschlichkeit." He admired the prevailing character of the colonists, "eine Art von pietistischem Heroismus, wie wann Herrnhut und Sparta in eins zusammenflössen." Their songs, he said, "sind mistisch, heroisch, Sinzendorfisch, tyrtä-isch."[15] Three months before the declaration of war he prophesied that it would certainly cost the English much money, toil, and blood to bring the provinces of freedom to terms.[16] At the close of the war, when Europe was threatened with upheaval, he called attention to the "dreizehn Pforten... in diesem Freistaate," which were open to the victims of intolerance.[17]

From the foregoing it might fairly be concluded that, at the outbreak of the revolution, favor in Germany was nearly equally divided as between the colonists and England with a considerable neutral element in the middle, and so it might have remained had it not been for the traffic in soldiers.

At best this could only be defended on the grounds of custom and tradition, to which Schlözer added the rather feeble argument that it was not being practiced on a large scale. As a matter of fact, the best estimate is as follows:

Braunschweig	5723 men	3.45% of the population
Hessen-Cassel	16992 men	4.55% of the population
Hessen-Hanau	2422 men	3.95% of the population
Ansbach	1644 men	0.79% of the population
Waldeck	1225 men	1.50% of the population
Anhalt-Herbst	1160 men	5.05% of the population

29,166

Of the men in these contingents more than a third, 11,853, were killed or rendered unfit for service, fighting for a cause to which they were indifferent or hostile. This aroused the indignation of poets of the time. In a picture of the ideal ruler "Der gute Fürst," 1787, Göckingk wrote:

> Er brennt nicht unser Hab' und Gut
> In Feuerwerken auf;
> Nicht auf Maitressen-Gunst beruht
> Der Preis im Wettelauf;
> Auch trägt er unser deutsches Blut
> Den Britten nicht zu Kauf.[18]

In "Die Zukunft," a poem in five "Gesängen," written between 1779 and 1782 but never completed and published, Friedrich Stolberg prophesied the victory of the colonists:

> Frei wird Amerika sein! und kann es
> Euch ein Trost sein,
> Briten, so sei es Euch Trost, dass unter den
> Söhnen der Freiheit
> Eure Brüder die Erstlinge sind.

In this poem the "Genius der Freiheit" promises:

> Auch wird Blut dem Jüngling gegen
> Gold nicht gewogen.
> Um für stolze Nachbarn in fernen
> Welten zu fliessen.[19]

Even Boie, in a poem signed X (1784), tells of the fate of a soldier forced into seven years of service:

> Die hat er treu gedient,
> Und nicht zu mucksen sich erkühnt.
> Die Zeit war um. Nun wollt' er von
> Dem blut- und thränenvollen Frohn
> Zum jungen Weib' und lieben Sohn,
> Allein unsonst war sein Verlangen.
> Er bat, er weint', und Prügel war sein Lohn.

15

Was that er da? Er lief davon,
Ward wieder gefangen
Und in des Königs Namen aufgehangen.[20]

In the *Deutsche Chronik* of 1776, Schubart published a poem by
G. von Koblenz in which a "Hermannssohn" expressed his
humiliation at serving for the pay of foreigners:

Dem Stolz, dem Geist der Britten frohnt
Ein freyer, teutscher Mann!
Ihr Barden leiht mit eure Sprach
(Der Eichenwipfel sausst sie nach)
Klopstock und Ossian –

So sang der Alte und verschwand,
Starr stand ich und schwieg still,
Geh nicht mehr hoch und stolz einher;
Ha! fragt mich einer, wer ich wär'?
Beym Hermann, ich schweig still.[21]

As late as 1787 Schubart expressed his sentiments in his "Kap-
lied", which according to Mattheson was sung from the Limmat
in Switzerland to the Baltic Sea, and from the Moldau in Bohemia
to the banks of the Rhine; and Herder wrote of the victims of the
traffic:

Und doch sind sie in ihrer Herren Dienst
So hündisch-treu! Sie lassen willig sich
Zum Mississippi und Ohio-Strom
Nach Candia und nach dem Mohrenfels
Verkaufen. Stirbt der Sklave, streicht der Herr
Den Sold indess und seine Witwe darbt;
Die Waisen ziehn den Pflug und hungern. Doch
Das schadet nichts; der Herr braucht einen Schatz.[22]

Many verses such as these, more of honest indignation than of
literary merit, appeared at the time. In fact one might speak of
an early emergence of political poetry, a forerunner of that of the
German revolution.

16

The opposition was expressed in other forms of literature as well. Because of his position as librarian in Wolfenbüttel, Lessing was prevented from speaking of the soldier traffic, but in *Minna von Barnhelm*, III, 7, he makes clear his abhorrence of all mercenary soldiering. Hermes made unfavorable mention of the sale of mercenaries in his novel *Sophiens Reise*, 1769-1773. In his journal of the time Schiller refers, with a touch of irony, to the recruits on their way to America, halting a moment to salute "ihren angebeteten Landesvater und Regenten"; and in the "Kammerdiener" scene of *Kabale und Liebe*, II, 2, Schiller makes his boldest and most excoriating attack upon the "Seelenkauf." This scene had to be omitted or modified before the play could be presented. Schiller wrote to Dalberg, 1780: "Iffland wird den Kammerdiener spielen, den ich mit Wegwerfung aller amerikanischen Beziehungen wieder in das Stück hineingeschoben habe."[23]

On the subject of the independence of the colonies, however, Schiller seems to have been indifferent or neutral. He was, nonetheless, one of the European "Bedrängten," who looked upon America as the land of hope and for a short time seriously considered emigration. He wrote to Henriette von Wolzogen, June 8, 1783:

> Ich habe eine Hauptveränderung in meinem Plane gemacht, und da ich anfangs nach Berlin wollte, werde ich mich jetzt vielleicht gar nach England begeben. Doch gewis ist es noch nicht, so grosse Lust ich habe, die Neue Welt zu sehen. Wenn Nordamerika frei wird, so ist es ausgemacht, dass ich hingehe. In meinen Adern siedet etwas. Ich möchte gern in dieser holperichten Welt einige Sprünge machen, von denen man erzählen soll.

To a friend in Stuttgart he wrote on June 19, 1783:

> Ich kanns nicht mehr so leiden. Überall finde ich zwar manche treffliche Leute, und vielleicht könnte ich noch mich an einem Orte niederlassen, aber ich mus fort, ich will nach America und dies soll mein Abschiedsbrief seyn... Ich habe von einem hiesigen

Handelshaus genauen Unterricht von meiner Reise bekommen. Aber wirst Du fragen, was drinnen thun? Das sollen Zeit und Umstände bestimmen. Ich habe meine Medicine nicht vernachlässigt – auch die Philosophie könnte ich dort vielleicht als Professor lehren – vielleicht auch ins politische mich einlassen – vielleicht auch gar nichts von allem... Wenns eine Gelegenheit giebt, sollst Du Nachricht von mir aus America haben.[24]

The "Sturm und Drang" poets of the seventies were less outspoken than might have been expected. A statement that Lenz planned to go to America to fight for the colonists is based on a misinterpretation of certain letters.[25] Klinger once desired to enter the army as an officer, but it is possible that he would have accepted a commission from either side. The scene of his *Sturm und Drang*, 1775, is America, but the action of the play is devoid of political propaganda. There is little doubt, however, that Klinger's sympathies were with the colonies. In a later work, *Geschichte eines Deutschen der neuesten Zeit*, 1797, he described the hardships suffered by the recruits, and adds: "Und liegt nicht schon alles in dem Gedanken begriffen: die Deutschen wurden für Geld nach Amerika verkauft?"

After somewhat protracted negotiations, Baron von Steuben accepted an appointment as an officer in the American army. He was received with acclaim by the troops and the populace and was soon writing with enthusiasm about America:

Welch ein schönes, welch ein glückliches Land ist dieses, ohne Könige, ohne Hohepriester, ohne aussaugende General-Pächter, und ohne müssige Baronen! Armut ist ein unbekanntes Übel.

Schlözer dutifully printed this letter in his *Briefwechsel*,[26] but editorialized that such prosperity presupposed a preceding period of benevolent rule by England. This observation no doubt served to make the publication of the letter more acceptable to Schlözer's most distinguished subscriber, the King of England. Baron von Steuben's greatest difficulty was with foreign officers. He complained:

dass mir hier 6 ausländische Offiziers mer zu schaffen machen als 200 amerikanische... Eine grosse Anzal deutscher Baronen und französischen Marquis sind bereits wider abgesegelt; und ich bin besorgt, wenn sich ein Baron oder Marquis melden lässt. Wir sind hir in einer Republik, und der Hr. Baron gilt nicht Einen Heller mer, als Mstr. Jakob oder Mstr. Peter.[27]

We have also a record of the experience of a Hessian recruit. Johann Gottfried Seume ran away from school, was captured by recruiting agents and held in duress in a prison until he agreed to enlist. After a nauseating voyage, he landed at Halifax, where he suffered chiefly from boredom. He planned with a friend to desert and make his way to Boston, but the declaration of peace anticipated the undertaking. Seume said the recruits were reluctant "sich ohne gegebenes Gutachten mit diesen armen Teufeln von Amerikanern zu schlagen, denen wir alle herzlich gut waren und alles mögliche Glück wünschten."[28]

[1] For these and others see Jantz [13], 146-153.
[2] Palmer [5].
[3] Riese [30] 29.
[4] *Loc. cit.*, I (1776) 53.
[5] King [37] 94: *Deutsches Museum*, 1774; pp. 186 ff.
[6] Klopstock, *Werke*, Leipzig, 1856, IV, 320; X 341.
[7] Schiller, *Werke*, Leipzig, 1910, III, 152.
[8] *Ibid.*, 283; Carruth [47]; King [37], 827.
[9] Jantz [48].
[10] Goethe, *Werke*, Weimar, 1887 ff., I (29), 63 ff.
[11] *Ibid.*, I (29) 156.
[12] King [37] 40-42.
[13] *Loc. cit.*, Oct. 1775, p. 89.
[14] King [37] 121 f.
[15] *Loc. cit.*, II, 386; III, 319.
[16] King [37] 114.
[17] *Loc. cit.*, VIII, 38.
[18] King [37], 27 f., 47 f.
[19] *Archiv für Literaturgeschichte*, XIII (1885) 255.
[20] *Almanach*, 1784, p. 42.

[21] *Loc. cit.*, 1776, 170 f.

[22] Mattheson, *Erinnerungen*, Wien, I, 161; Herder, *Werke*, ed. Suphan, Berlin, 1877 ff. XVIII, 213.

[23] Schiller, *Briefe*, ed. Jonas, Stuttgart, 1896 ff., I, 86.

[24] *Ibid.*, I, 86, 89.

[25] Wertheim [38] 481-483.

[26] *Loc. cit.*, VII (1776), 133.

[27] *Ibid.*, VIII (1779), 385.

[28] Wiener and Reissmann, *Joh. Gottfried Seume.* Leipzig, 1898, p. 27.

The years following the American War of Independence were a period of transition. On the one side there was the unexpectedly steady transforming of thirteen colonies into a well-integrated nation; on the other hand disintegrating forces were at work in France. Schubart wrote in 1787: "Wenn die übrigen Welt-staaten beinah erschlafft sind, so werden hier [in America] noch Thaten geschehen, die der Menschen würdig sind," and a year later:

> Ich glaube der Weissagung, dass nachdem in Asien, Afrika und Europa so erstaunliche Rollen gespielt wurden, auch bald Amerika aufgefordert werde, sich ins grosse Völkerdrama zu mischen und da seine Rolle mitzuspielen.[1]

The reference to the "Weissagung" may have pointed to Bishop Berkeley, who had expressed the same thought many years before (1702) in a moderately good poem containing the often misquoted line "Westward the course of empire takes its way." Herder translated this poem, 1792, but took exception to it. When a new civilization comes into being, it does not follow that the older should pass out of existence, for both may live and benefit each other.[2]

The question arose early in the war, whether the practical, utilitarian colonies could ever participate in the world of literature and other arts. Here Wieland at least was optimistic. Commenting on the Declaration of Independence, he wrote in the *Teutscher Merkur*:

> In jeder Zeile dieser Schrift spricht Patriotismus und Liebe zur Freyheit, und sie verdient würklich, den schönsten Reden des Demosthenes und Cicero an die Seite gesetzt zu werden. Sie ist ein Beweis, dass die schönen Künste und die Beredsamkeit in den englischen Colonien von Amerika nicht weniger als bei uns bleiben und dass die Amerikaner die Feder eben so gut zu führen wissen, als den Degen.[3]

This question continued to be discussed in later decades. Platen wrote in his poem "Columbus Geist":

> Denn nach Westen flüchtet die Geschichte,
> Denn nach Westen wendet sich der Sieg.[4]

On the subject of America as a last potential defender of culture, Friedrich Schlegel wavered, but with gradually increasing doubts.[5] In his discussion "Über die neuere Geschichte," 1810, he called the United States "ein dort in Freiheit aufblühender Staat" and a "Pflanzschule europäischer Menschheit und europäischer Freiheit."[6] In 1829, on the other hand, he called America a "Pflanzschule" of destructive principles.[7] Germany should transplant to America thirty or forty German "Naturphilosophen." In the distant future, then, there might take place a "Wiederaufbau Europas nach der Zerstörung" and a "Reifwerdung der Menschenkultur in Amerika."[8]

The foremost revealer to the Germans of American life with its unlimited possibilities was Benjamin Franklin. The tenth son of a soap maker, he left school at the age of ten to assist his father, became an apprentice printer at the age of thirteen, and left Boston at the age of seventeen to make his fortune in Philadelphia. A year later he found himself stranded in England. At the age of twenty-three he purchased the *Pennsylvania*

22

Gazette and made it an influential newspaper. The series of annuals, *Poor Richard's Almanack*, ran for twenty-five years. They were "a poor man's *Spectator*." Franklin taught himself French, Italian, Spanish, and Latin, but apparently not German to any great extent. He was appointed postmaster of Philadelphia, became clerk of the general assembly, established the first fire and police system in the colonies, and founded an academy which later became the University of Pennsylvania. He was elected a member of the general assembly, later postmaster general of all the colonies, helped to manage the financing of the British in the French and Indian wars, and was sent to England to petition the king for remedies in the government of Pennsylvania. He stayed in England several years and formed useful acquaintances. Meanwhile he had made studies in science which had won for him degrees and distinctions in Scotland, England, the state of Milan, Holland, Germany, and America. At odd moments he had discovered a means to remedy smoking chimneys, by devising a more efficient stove, and to invent the lightning rod, and he argued the cause of the colonies before the British Parliament.

Much of this he had accomplished before the outbreak of the war of the colonies. Such a career could not fail to arouse the astonishment and admiration of the subjects of the German rulers, in view of the limited possibilities open to persons of lowly origin. In 1766 the Germans had their first view of this remarkable American in Göttingen, where Franklin accepted membership in the "Königliche Gesellschaft der Wissenschaften." While he was there, citizens of the city had the opportunity to question him about conditions in America. The following year there appeared a volume entitled: *Einige Anmerkungen über Nord-Amerika und über dasige Grossbrittanische Colonien.* "Aus mündlichen Nachrichten des Herrn Dr. Franklins von Herrn Hofrath Achenwall." A third edition, 1777, contained a translation called: *Schrift von den Streitigkeiten mit den Colonien in Amerika,* written by John Wesley.

Among the other Germans whom Franklin met in Göttingen

were Michaelis and Putter, but probably not Lichtenberg.[9] Less fortunate was his kindly interest in E. R. Raspe, curator of the museum in Kassel and the author of the Baron Münchhausen tales. After Raspe's disgrace for misuse of the museum funds and his subsequent flight to England, Franklin let Raspe's letters remain unanswered.[10] In 1777 at Passy near Paris, where he was representing the colonies before the French, Franklin met several other noted Germans, among them Baron Steuben and Georg Forster.

Most of Franklin's works were translated into German during his lifetime or shortly thereafter, among them *Sämtliche Werke, I-III, aus dem Französischen*, Dresden, 1780 and *Werke I-III*, Weimar, 1794 *(Kleine Schriften meist in der Manier des "Zuschauers" nebst seinem Leben)*.

Of all Franklin's works, his autobiography aroused the greatest interest. A translation into French was commended by Herder. The German translation, *Benjamin Franklins Jugendjahre von ihm selbst für seinen Sohn beschrieben*, Berlin, 1792, was one of the last undertakings of Gottfried August Bürger. After *Robinson Crusoe* it was for a time the most widely read book by the youth of Germany. Herder called Franklin "den edelsten Volksschriftsteller unseres Jahrhunderts"[11] and began his *Briefe zur Beförderung der Humanität* with some comments on Franklin. He spoke particularly of Franklin's "Sinn der Humanität": "Er, der Menschheit Lehrer, einer grossen Menschengesellschaft Ordner sey unser Vorbild."[12] In 1727, Franklin organized in Philadelphia a club called the "Junto," which later developed into the American Philosophical Society. As a preliminary to admission, candidates had to submit written answers to a searching questionnaire. On the model of this club, Herder organized the "Freitag Gesellschaft" in Weimar in 1791. Among the members were Wieland, Bode, Knebel, and Bertuch. Herder read these questions before the "Freitag Gesellschaft" and they were later published under the title *Benjamin Franklin's Rules for a Club established in Philadelphia, übertragen und ausgelegt als Statut für eine Gesell-*

schaft von Freunden der Humanität[13] 1792. Wieland wrote of Franklin's modesty:

> Fiel eine Kron' ihm zu, und es bedürfte nur,
> Sie mit der Hand im Fallen aufzuhaschen,
> Er streckte nicht die Hand. Verschlossen dem Begier,
> Von keiner Furcht, von keinem Schmerz betroffen,
> Ist nur dem Wahren noch die heitere Seele offen,
> Nur offen der Natur, und rein gestimmt zu ihr.[14]

When the letter of admission to the Academy of Sciences of Paris was sent to Franklin in 1777, it was accompanied by a dedication by Turgot: "Eripuit coelo fulmen, septrumque tyrannis," which the poet Schubart translated:

> Er wusste den Strahl der Tyrannen,
> Wie Blitze des Himmels zu bannen.

Johann Jacob Meyen began his epic (in "fünf Gesängen"), 1787:

> Den Philosophen besingt mein Lied,
> der dem neueren Welttheil
> Jenseits der Mar del Nord das Licht
> der Wissenschaft brachte
> Und sein seufzendes Vaterland
> von Tyrannen befreite.[15]

Georg Forster wrote of Franklin later:

> Amerika ist glücklich, dass es so bald nach der Gründung seiner
> gesitteten Staaten aus ihrem Schosse den Weisen hervorgehen sah,
> dessen innere Harmonie ihm gleichsam die Natur unterwarf, ihn
> zur Entdeckung des Wahren in allen ihren Verhältnissen führte,
> und ihn zum Lehrer seiner Brüder bestimmte.[16]

The outbreak of the French Revolution led to a reorientation of many minds. Edmund Burke, for example, who had always sought conciliation with the colonies, now wrote *Reflections on the Revolution in France*, 1790, in which he condemned all revolutions in principle. Many well wishers of America shared his view. Again there were many favorable not only to the American states, but to the democratic uprising in France. Among the more prominent of these were Georg Forster and Christoph Daniel Ebeling in Germany and Thomas Paine in America.

Thomas Paine's personality was in marked contrast to that of the diplomatically restrained Benjamin Franklin. Nearly all of Paine's published works were translated into German. The first two, *Common Sense* and *The American Crisis*, were published anonymously, and Paine's authorship did not become clear until the appearance of *Letter Addressed to the Abbé Raynal on the Affairs of North America, in which the Mistakes of the Abbé's Account of the Revolution in America are Criticized*, Philadelphia, 1782 (French, Amsterdam and Brussels, 1783).

Common Sense (French, Rotterdam, 1775; German, Philadelphia, 1776; Copenhagen, 1796), argued that separation from England and the establishment of a republic was the only sensible course to pursue. This was almost the earliest published tract to urge such a policy, and it lent impetus to the Declaration of Independence six months later. A translation of 1777 was by Wilhelm von Dohm, who was unaware of the earlier Philadelphia translation and who omitted the harsh attacks upon the king. The next translation was by Christoph Daniel Ebeling of Hamburg, one of the best authorities in Germany on American affairs. The translation was unexpurgated, hence the choice of Copenhagen as the place of publication. The work won the praise of Schubart, and even Helfrich Peter Sturz, despite his fondness for England, admitted that *Common Sense*, like the Declaration of Independence, was well written and that the arguments were strong but that they would soon be nullified by the cannons of General Howe.[17] Ebeling's enthusiasm cooled gradually with the approach of the French Revolution, and he took strong exception to Paine's later anonymous work, *The Age of Reason*. Ebeling could only surmise the authorship of *Common Sense:* "Franklin mag es sein, oder doch eher noch [Samuel] Adams; denn dies ist nicht der Stil des gesetzteren und gewiss nicht heftigen Franklin."[18] Paine's work *The American Crisis* beginning "These are times that try men's souls" appeared in 1776-1777. Ebeling published résumés and excerpts of the essay in his *Amerikanische Bibliothek*, 1777.

Georg Forster had looked forward to Edmund Burke's treatise on the French Revolution, only to be distressed at Burke's conversion to conservatism. Forster correspondingly expressed his gratification at the appearance of Thomas Paine's *The Rights of Man, Being an Answer to Mr. Burke's Attack on the French Revolution*, 1791. Forster added however: "Sie ist aber so democratisch, dass ich sie wegen meiner Verhältnisse nicht übersetzen kann." He therefore assigned the task to Mme. Forkel, later Frau Liebeskind. She was the author of several novels and one of the most prolific and successful translators of English fiction, but hardly competent to translate Paine's political work.[19] Forster arranged for the publication of the translation of *The Rights of Man* and wrote an introduction to it. To avoid censorship, it was published in Copenhagen, 1793.

To the followers of Burke belonged chiefly two Hanoverian civil officers, August Wilhelm Rehberg and Ernst Brandes, and in Prussia Friedrich von Gentz. Von Gentz began his political career as a liberal, but concluded it as a collaborator with Metternich. Rehberg reviewed Burke's work in the *Allgemeine Literatur-Zeitung* and Brandes in the *Göttingische Gelehrte Anzeiger*, and von Gentz translated Burke's *Reflections*. Forster's introduction to Mme. Forkel's translation of *The Rights of Man* is directed especially at Rehberg.[20]

Among the supporters of Paine against Burke, besides Forster and Ebeling, were Carl Friedrich Cramer (who lost his position as a professor at Kiel because of his revolutionary ideas), Johann Wilhelm von Archenholz, the editor of *Minerva* and of the *Brittische Annalen*, J. J. Eschenberg, who reviewed current

English literature for the *Annalen*, and the Freiherr von Knigge. The Viennese Leopold Alois von Hoffmann wrote: "Alle deutschen Demokratengeister sind der Widerhall des amerikanischen Schwärmers Paine und der ganzen deutschen Aufklärungspropaganda."

Forster visited Paine in Paris where he was living in the circle of Mary Wollstonecraft and Helen Williams. Forster wrote to his wife, May 17, 1793:

> An Thomas Paine habe ich nicht viel gefunden; er ist besser in seinen Schriften zu geniessen. Das Launige und Egoistische mancher Engländer hat er in hohem Grade. Sein ganzes Gesicht ist voll purpurner Knöpfe, die ihn sehr hässlich machen. Sonst hat er geistreiche Züge und ein feuriges Auge.[21]

Archenholz's journals were strong supporters of Paine. In the *Minerva* of 1793 and in the *Brittische Annalen* were published detailed accounts of Paine's career, and for the *Annalen* Eschenberg wrote an attack upon a "schmähsüchtige" Paine biography by George Chalmer.[22]

The last phase of Paine's journalistic career is represented chiefly by his deistic tract, *The Age of Reason*, 1794 (German, by H. C. Albrecht, Hamburg 1794-1795). The essay was the subject of much comment, for the most part unfavorable, in Germany and America. For a time after that Thomas Paine was little discussed but he came into prominence again at the time of the German uprisings.

Before the publication of his drama *Thomas Paine*, Georg Büchner had shown some interest in the man. There are echoes of Paine in the *Hessische Landboten*, and in Büchner's club "Die Gesellschaft der Menschenrechte," founded by Büchner and his associates, 1834, there are traces of a direct influence of Paine's ideas. Paine came into still greater prominence during the uprising of 1848. A new translation of *The Rights of Man* appeared in Leipzig in 1851. For this edition the fugitive Friedrich Hecker, then living near St. Louis, Missouri, wrote an enthusiastic preface.

28

[1] *C. F. D. Schubarts Gesammelte Schriften*, VIII, 17; VIII, 115.

[2] Herder, *Werke*, XVI, 126 f.

[3] *Loc. cit.*, Oct. 1775, p. 89.

[4] August von Platen-Hallermünde, *Sämtliche Werke*, ed. Koch und Petzet, Leipzig, Hesse (n.d.), II, 23 f.

[5] von Hofe [50] 64.

[6] Friedrich von Schlegel, *Sämtliche Werke*, ed. 2, Wien, 1946, XI, 362 f.; XI, 167.

[7] von Hofe [50] 64.

[8] *Ibid.*, 65.

[9] Kahn [60].

[10] Kahn [61] [62].

[11] Herder, *Werke*, XVII, 76 ff.

[12] *Ibid.*, XVIII, 9, ff.

[13] *Ibid.*, XVII, 10 ff; XVIII, 503 ff., 538 ff.

[14] Victory [52] 82.

[15] *Ibid.*, 106.

[16] Georg Forster, *Sämtliche Schriften*, Leipzig, 1843, VI (3), 204, 208.

[17] *Deutsches Museum*, Feb., 1777; p. 187. See also *Allgemeine deutsche Bibliothek*, Anhang IV, p. 2305.

[18] Arnold, [64] 367.

[19] *Ibid.*, 371.

[20] *Ibid.*, 372 f.

[21] Forster, *Schriften*, IV, 25 f.

[22] *Loc. cit.*, IX (1796), 251.

PART II

FROM POLITICAL TO LITERARY INDEPENDENCE

III. VARIOUS GERMAN VIEWS OF AMERICA

In the twenties and thirties of the nineteenth century, Germans were well supplied with descriptive books about the new land. Over fifty such works appeared in Germany. It will suffice to mention the contributions of Gall, Duden, Körner, Zschokke, and the Duke Bernhard of Saxe-Weimar.

Ludwig Gall's work appeared in 1822 under the title *Meine Auswanderung nach den Vereinigten Staaten in Nord Amerika im Frühjahr, 1819.* For him America was a land in which every prospect pleased but only man was vile. He described the Americans as sordid, dishonest seekers of wealth, amidst intriguing political parties and a corrupt press. The wars of 1776-1784 and of 1812-1814 were strictly mercantile enterprises. A man's social standing in the community depended on the amount of wealth he possessed. Many immigrants, he said, were homesick and would like to return.

The most controversial account of the time was Gottfried Duden's *Bericht einer Reise nach den westlichen Staaten Nordamerikas und eines mehrjährigen Aufenthalts am Missouri (1824-1827) oder Das Leben im Innern der Vereinigten Staaten und dessen Bedeutung für die häusliche und politische Lage der Europäer,* 1829. An appendix to the work offered information and advice to German peasants intending to emigrate to America. It was regarded as an authoritative work and was widely read. It was prevailingly favorable to American life and sometimes was almost lyrical regarding the beauties of American landscape. Duden contrasted the freedom of the settler with the restricted social and economic conditions in his fatherland. A new history has begun in America, he said, a history of liberty and of great ideas. There is religious liberty in America, but it has not led to religious indifference. Beggars are unknown, and higher education of the masses is on a par with education in Germany. Whoever seeks work and success in America will find them. Duden's work did much to speed the flow of immigration to America, and many who came with exalted hopes were disillusioned.

This situation led to a response, written by a German-American diplomat, Gustav Körner, who came to the United States in 1833. The next year he published *Beleuchtung des Duden'schen Berichtes über die westlichen Staaten*, in which he regretted the disastrous effect of Duden's treatise. Disillusionment became so widespread that Duden was compelled to take notice of it. In 1837 he published a treatise *Die nordamerikanische Demokratie und das von Tocquevillesche Werk darüber als Zeichen des Zustandes der theoretischen Politik*, and to this he added as an appendix a "Selbstanklage wegen seines amerikanischen Reiseberichtes zur Warnung vor fernerem leichtsinnigem Auswandern." Duden regretted the unfortunate influence of his work, but asserted he had been misunderstood. Moreover, he maintained, the prevailing attacks on American life and institutions were equally unguarded in their emphasis.

An entirely different picture of America was presented by Heinrich Zschokke, who had left Germany in 1795 to become a citizen of Zürich. America was a lifelong interest to him, although he never crossed the sea. He read all the available literature on America in German, English, and French. As a further basis for his work he interviewed a Swiss traveler, Suchard von Neuenburg, and in 1827 there appeared a work entitled *Mein Besuch Amerikas im Sommer 1824. Ein Flug durch die Vereinsstaaten Maryland, Pennsylvanien, New York zum Niagarafall, und durch die Staaten Ohio, Indiana, Kentucky und Virgi-*

nien zurück, signed S.v.N.. Zschokke's hand in the matter was readily recognized from the style. Among other favorable comments, the book noted that there was spread through all classes in American cities a certain moral independence, a sense for decency and nobleness, which had neither been drilled into the people nor imitated from others but had its origin in the consciousness of right and in respect for other people's convictions. Zschokke prophesied that America, in another quarter century, would become a mighty power, able to defy Europe and to influence the Old World more than to be influenced by it.[1]

The travel journeys of Duke Bernhard of Saxe-Weimar were edited by Luden in 1828 and published under the title *Reise Sr. Hoheit des Herzogs Bernhard von Sachsen-Weimar-Eisenach durch Nordamerika in den Jahren 1825 und 1826.* The duke's expedition was projected for scientific purposes, which it fulfilled in good measure, but his diaries are also rich in social observations. His high position at home opened up to him acquaintanceships with distinguished citizens not accessible to most of the other German travelers, but he became acquainted with other social levels as well. He was quite at home with the Herrenhuters and Mennonites in Pennsylvania. He was invited to a state dinner at the White House and was deeply impressed by President John Quincy Adams. He praised the United States as a happy and prosperous country. Duke Bernhard's picture of the United States was one of the most favorable of its kind. It pleased the public and was promptly translated into English in the year of its appearance. Duke Bernhard traveled in good part as a state guest, and too sharp a criticism of national faults would have been undiplomatic, yet as a whole it would appear that his admiration was sincere. It was, of course, one of the American books that Goethe read with greatest interest.

De Tocqueville's *De la Démocratie en Amérique*[2] was based on the author's observations of American life and institutions. It was objective and was one of the most highly regarded treatises on the subject. Democracy was a notable success in

32

America, he wrote, but the success was not due for the most part to the democratic institutions, but rather to the fortunate conditions under which they originated. America was a land that had no fear of invasion and required no expensive standing army. It was a land of homogeneous middle-class citizens accustomed to local self-government, a land of opportunity, and a land having no fear of a restless proletariat. It marked a new beginning, unencumbered with the traditions of feudalism.

De Tocqueville assumed that the trend of history in Europe would lead eventually to democracy, but that the course of the development would not be as easy as it had been in America. What had been accomplished in America could not be simply taken over by Europe with its persistent heritage of feudalism and its division of aristocratic and proletarian population.

Of the journalists of "Das Junge Deutschland," Ludwig Börne almost alone was enthusiastic concerning America. "Asia," he said, "was the cradle of the human race; Europe saw the joy, the vigor, and the exuberance of the youth of mankind. In America the fullness and wisdom of the manly age are developing."[3]

In his earlier years, Heinrich Heine looked hopefully toward America. "Aristocratic England," he said (1828), is no longer the last refuge of freedom:

> Freie Geister haben jetzt im Notfall einen noch besseren Zufluchts-ort: würde auch ganz Europa ein einziger Kerker, so gäbe es jetzt noch immer ein anderes Loch zum Entschlüpfen, das ist America.[4]

But in 1830 he spoke of America as of "diesem ungeheuren Freiheitsgefängnis... wo der widerwärtigste aller Tyrannen, der Pöbel, seine rohe Herrschaft ausübt,"[5] and in 1832 he referred to the "amerikanische Lebensmonotonie, Farblosigkeit und Spiessbürgerei."[6]

More thoroughgoing are Karl Gutzkow's discussions of American life and institutions. To his liberal mind not America but

33

England was the model for political emulation. He wrote in 1837:

Geben wir auf England acht! Es lässt von seinen Eroberungen im Bereich politischer Aufklärung nichts mehr fahren. Diese ächte Verschmelzung von Freiheit und Gesetz, vom Menschenurrecht und politischem Vorrecht, soll, wie sie sich in England finden, den Lauf um die Welt machen.[7]

Gutzkow devoted more than one essay to the question: What could the United States contribute to European welfare? His answer was: "nothing." He regarded America as a strictly materialistic land. Americans have a way of appraising the monetary value of everything in heaven and on earth. With all their merits – practical activity, intellectual disposition, temperance, self-control – Americans still lack political organization and culture. What good to the Americans is their small quota of taxation! They have a republic, a government without splendor, an administration which has to bow to its citizens, a history without memories, a people without a nation, a country which no one can claim as his homeland.[8]

When, in the year 1848, a group of statesmen gathered in the Paulskirche in Frankfurt to devise a more perfect union for Germany, it was their undisputed assumption that the governmental goal was not to be the unified state of France nor the constitutional monarchy of England but the American state with its checks and balances and its division of powers between the state governments and the central government. The constitutional provisions of the United States were well known to the representatives at Frankfurt. Copies of it were at the desks and were passed from hand to hand. Five of the delegates had spent much time in the United States and nearly all, perhaps all, were familiar with the extensive literature on American institutions.[9]

Among the works most frequently referred to was de Tocqueville's before-mentioned *De la Démocratie en Amérique*, for this work pointed out the difficulties in the transplantation of a constitution from a land of its growth to an unaccustomed soil. The debates of the Paulskirche turned on the question as to what compromises must reluctantly be made to adapt the American pattern to German conditions. Should the universal right to vote be assured in Germany, despite the rule of the dominant middle class in America and the existence of the massive proletariat in Germany? Should religion and state be separated? Should equal representation of states prevail in the upper house, giving Prussia and Bavaria only equal representation with every duodecimo dukedom or principality? Again, should the central government have the power to raise taxes, establish a standing army, and declare war – all of which would tend to make of Germany a "Bundesstaat" rather than a "Staatenbund?" Such questions as these were debated with the constitution of the United States always regarded as a norm. Decisions wise and unwise were made and the result has properly been called a "literarisches Machwerk." It was followed by suppression of liberal tendencies in Germany and a new and larger flight of German political liberals to Switzerland, England, and France, but in greatest number to the United States.

By the year 1860 the United States had felt the impact of several waves of German immigration. Before 1817 hunger had driven some 20,000 refugees to America. Thereafter the United States census reported:

```
1821-1830 . . . . . . . . 6,761
1831-1840 . . . . . . 152,454
1841-1850 . . . . . . 434,626
1851-1860 . . . . . . 951,667
```

The total was exceeded no doubt only by the Irish, who, however, settled chiefly in New England and New York, the Germans rather in Pennsylvania and southwards to Florida, then westward through Illinois, Missouri, Arkansas, and Texas.

The German immigrants and their descendants did not present a united front. The earliest, chiefly arriving before 1800, were religious dissenters – Moravians, pacifists, and other sectarians. Some, like the Mennonites, refrained on principle from political engagement. Such groups were to be found in Pennsylvania, Maryland, South Carolina, Missouri, and Texas. The question was once debated in the Pennsylvania provincial legislature as to what should be the official language. English won over German by a majority of a single vote.

The religious group formed the first wave of immigration, the hunger-driven groups the second, and the German uprisings of the thirties and forties the third and fourth influxes. The later groups, particularly the forty-eighters, were largely made up of imaginative liberal idealists. In the richly endowed but materialistic minded America they wished to found a new Germany based on old German "Geist." To this they would assimilate by example all America, and with this as a spring-board elevate all of old Germany and old Europe. Certain non-Germanic Americans looked askance on such a project, and the situation led to election riots in some German settlements between the Germans and groups of Americans often led by the Know Nothing Party. On one occasion in Louisville, Kentucky, German voters were driven from the polls with sticks and stones. Nor could the newly arrived Germans count on the support which they fully expected of the earlier arrived fellow countrymen, for many of these had by now adjusted themselves to American conditions and had no desire to bestir themselves. This conflict of interests became openly acknowledged, and there arose two definite German parties "die Grauen" and "die Grünen"; the "Zweiunddreissiger" were called "Die Grauen" and the "Acht-undvierziger" "die Grünen." In another way, however, the German liberals were eventually effective. To them is to be accorded a fair share of the success in saving Illinois and Missouri for the Union. Carl Schurz was rewarded with the ambassadorship to Spain, which he later resigned to become a general in the Union army.

Another distinguished German revolutionist who participated in American politics was Reinhold Solger, 1817-1866. He became involved in the frustrated German revolution and fled to Switzerland. In 1852, he left Zürich for England and the following year he came to America. In 1856 he stumped for Fremont and in 1860 for Lincoln. He was by that time a highly regarded scholar and had delivered lectures at the Lowell Institute of Harvard University. Lincoln appointed him assistant registrar of the treasury in 1863. Solger was a rather prolific writer of political works and of poetry. He was also the author of an interesting novel of American life, to be described presently.

Thus, as the century wore on, German immigrants became more and more involved in American affairs, and consequently the Germans in the homeland looked upon America with increasing interest. Their views were expressed chiefly by four groups of German writers, the novelists, the poets, the literary historians, and the journalists.

Early in the century several novels emanating from the German romantic group dealt with the subject of emigration to America. In a novel by Sophia Mereau Brentano, *Das Blüthenalter der Empfindung*, the chief characters decide to emigrate to America, for "Amerika freut sich des Genius der Menschheit."[10] In the novel *Die Familie Seldorf*, 1795, by Therese Huber, the widow of Georg Forster, Seldorf fights for the colonies and then, like Lothario in *Wilhelm Meister*, returns to Germany.

Friedrich Schlegel's wife Dorothea wrote a novel *Florentine*, 1801, in which the title hero expresses a desire to side with the Americans and observe the birth of a sovereign republican state. It is well known that August Wilhelm Schlegel and Madame de Staël were laying plans for emigrating together to America in 1795, when the project was thwarted by Madame de Staël's misadventure in Switzerland.[11]

Another emigrant to America was the errant son of Sophie La Roche. He tarried for a time in 1794 on the shore of Lake

Oneida in New York state. His wife Elzy wrote interesting letters to Sophie about a French refugee family living on an island in the lake. This provided the background and the characters for one of the last novels of Sophie La Roche, *Erscheinungen am See Oneida*, 1798.[12] The author had finally freed herself from the influence of Richardson. The mood of this novel was rather that of Bernardin de St. Pierre's *Paul et Virginie*.

The novel of Reinhold Solger was called *Anton in Amerika. Seitenstück zu Freytags "Soll und Haben": Aus dem deutschamerikanischen Leben*, 1862. Anton Wohlfahrt senior is treated with light irony. By dint of honest labor, subservience to authority, and avoidance of Jews and aristocrats, he has risen from humble circumstances to well-being and has married the correct and somewhat uninteresting boss's daughter. His son Anton, however, is of a careless and roving disposition. His wanderings take him to New York, Niagara Falls, the White Mountains, and Chicago – all places with which Solger himself was familiar. The novel introduces fair pictures of many American types, Yankees, Irishmen, Negroes, and German-Americans with some of their corrupted language: "Er ist süss auf die Lady," "Ich will mich einen Spruch setzen" ("I'll sit down a spell"). The *Belletristisches Journal* offered a prize for the best German-American novel, and the three judges were unanimous in declaring Solger's novel the winner. Josef Nadler in his history of German literature called Solger's work the best German-American novel.

Therese Albertine Luise von Jacob (acronymic pen name Talvj) was of Danish birth and was a gifted and many sided woman. Goethe admired her translations of Serbian folk songs. She lived from 1828 to 1864 in New York. In 1851 she wrote a novel called *The Exiles*. In the next year she published it again under the title *Die Auswanderer*. In the introduction she indicated that she chiefly wished to describe the parts of the country which she had seen and the different types of people. She includes Methodists and Cavaliers, rich philanthropists, and farmers. The descriptions and character sketches are held

38

together by a plot slightly reminiscent of Longfellow's *Evangeline*. To mention all the German novelists who made use of the American setting without ever having seen the New World would carry us too far. The list would include such names as Spielhagen, *Deutsche Pioniere*, 1879, a *Hermann und Dorothea* story in an American setting; Stifter, *Kondor*, 1840; Zschokke, *Die Gründung Marylands*, 1820; and *Die Prinzessin von Wolfenbüttel*, 1804; Auerbach, *Das Landhaus am Rhein*,[13] 1869; and Fontane, *Quitt*, 1840, with the scene laid in a Mennonite colony in Arkansas.[14]

With an abundance of full but often contradictory descriptions of the new land, and with novels of slightly varying fidelity to the realities, Germans were able to derive a rather fair idea of land and people. As a corrective to misleading generalities there was information by letters, for by the middle of the century there were few German households without relatives, friends, or acquaintances in America.

On the subject of America, its type of freedom and its materialism, the German poets were of the same divided opinions as the novelists. As early as 1816 August von Platen seriously considered emigrating to America, "Land der Pracht/ Wo der Freiheit stolzes Leben zwischen Palmen auferwacht,"[15] and land of the future: "Denn nach Westen flieht die Weltgeschichte."[16] But shortly afterward he determined to stay at home to serve his fatherland, and referred to his earlier intent as an

> Erhitzter Wahn der Jugend,
> Der das Glück von fern verheisst.[17]

Adalbert von Chamisso, as a scientist, accompanied Captain Otto von Kotzebue aboard the *Rurik*, 1815-1818. Arriving in California, he learned to know the flora and fauna of the region and also became acquainted with the natives, for whom he came to have sympathy and respect. As early as 1820 and as late as 1823 he considered the possibility of emigrating to America.

39

One of his most touching poems is his "Rede des alten Kriegers Bunte-Schlange im Rate der Creek Indianer."

The best known victim of disillusionment over America was Nikolaus Lenau. A romanticist by temperament, but suffering from the restrictions of the Metternich regime in Austria, he thought of emigration to America in his student years, 1827-1830. His picture of America was derived from the abundant descriptions of the time, but chiefly from the enthusiastic Duden. In a poem "Abschied," 1832, an emigrating Portuguese greets the new land:

> Du neue Welt, du freie Welt,
> An deren blütenreichem Strand
> Die Flut der Tyrannei zerschellt:
> Ich grüsse dich, mein Vaterland.[18]

In the "Maskenball," 1832, Lenau calls American forests "heilige Waldverliesse" and "der Freiheit Paradiese, wo noch kein Tyrann sich Throne schlug."[19]

Lenau left for America in 1832, intending to stay about two months and then to return with new poetic inspiration: "Ich will meine Phantasie in die Schule, in die nordamerikanischen Urwälder schicken, den Niagara will ich rauschen hören und Niagaralieder singen,"[20] but as early as October 16th, eight days after his landing, he wrote to his friend Schurz that America has no wine and no nightingales and that the Americans are "himmelanstinkende Krämerseelen."[21]

He gave vent to his disillusionment in verses written shortly after his return:

> Es ist ein Land von träumerischem Trug,
> Auf das die Freiheit im Vorüberflug
> Bezaubernd ihren Schatten fallen lässt
> Und das ihn hält in tausend Bildern fest.[22]

At the same time the "Urwald," which Duden so eloquently described, is disappearing:

40

Wo sind die Blüten, die den Wald umschlangen?
Wo sind die Vögel, die so lustig sangen?
Längst sind die Blüten und die Vögel fort:
Nun ist der Wald verlassen und verdorrt.[23]

As the frontier is pressed forward, the Indians are driven ahead. Lenau expressed their misery in many sympathetic poems, among them "Die drei Indianer":

Fluch den Weissen! Ihren letzten Spuren,
Jeder Welle Fluch, worauf sie fuhren,
Die, einst Bettler, unsern Strand erklettert!
Fluch dem Windhauch, dienstbar ihrem Schiffe![24]

Lenau's fellow-countryman "Anastasius Grün" (i.e., Anton Alexander Graf von Auersperg) gave evidence of a more consistent and better balanced conception of America. Uncomfortable under the restrictions of the Metternich regime, from 1835 to 1838 he contemplated emigration to America. This led him to inform himself thoroughly about conditions in the New World, which he looked upon favorably though with certain reservations. In a poem "Cincinnatus" he pictures a Yankee sailor boy on the deck of the *Cincinnatus*, anchored near Naples, thinking of his homeland and greeting it:

Land! Land! O, meines Vaterlands Gestade!
Willkommen Baltimores schöner Strand;
Der mit den grünen Armen die Najade,
Das Meer, als seine süsse Braut umspannt.[25]

Later in the poem, America greets the incoming emigrants:

Willkommen Fremdling! Sprich, was tut dir not?
Verlangst du Brot? Sieh, meine Frucht ist Brot,
Und dürstet dich, trink meinen Palmenwein;
Ich will dir Acker, Quell und Weinberg sein.[26]

Anastasius Grün does full justice to the beauties of American

41

scenery. He is a poetic Duden, but he condemns the expulsion of the Indians from their homes, and the inhuman treatment of the Negroes.

Hoffmann von Fallersleben began with emigration poems of negative attitude. In "Die neue Welt," 1843, he declared:

> Die Freiheit ist dir nur ein Fetisch,
> Ein Sorgenstuhl und Schlendrian;
> Sag' an du Krämervolk am Teetisch,
> Was hast du für die Welt getan?[27]

But political tyranny in Germany changed his attitude almost immediately, and he began to sing the praise of American civil liberty:

> Freies Denken gilt,
> So wie freies Sprechen
> Nirgend, nirgend hier
> Für ein Staatsverbrechen.
> Hier macht kein Gendarm
> Jemals uns Bedrängnis,
> Und kein Bettelvogt
> Führt uns ins Gefängnis
> Hier am Mississippi.[28]

In 1842 an organization was founded called "Mainzer Adels-verein zum Schutze deutscher Einwanderer in Texas." The company found in Hoffmann von Fallersleben one of its most vocal supporters. From now on emigration poetry meant to him almost exclusively Texas poetry. The collection *Texanische Lieder*, 1846, included such poems as "Der Stern von Texas," "Ein Gaudeluperlied," "Wohlgemeinter Rat," "Ade Deutschland," "Yankee Dudle," "Aus Texas," "Der deutsche Hinterwäldler," "Nacht in der Prärie," and "Der Schutz von Bragos,"[29] The collection *Heimatklänge aus Texas* included "Der Fall von Bexar," "Sturmlied am San Jacinto," and "Der alte Sam."[30]

Hoffmann von Fallersleben shared the crusading zeal of the

German Texan colonists, who hoped to found there a Germany true to German ideals and so finally to rouse the Fatherland from its political torpor and also to overcome the materialism of the other American states. A crusading note prevails in his poems. Some could be set to music, some even to march time:

> Hin nach Texas, hin nach Texas,
> Wo der Stern im blauen Felde
> Eine neue Welt verkündet,
> Jedes Herz für Recht und Freiheit,
> Und für Wahrheit froh entzündet,
> Dahin sehnt mein Herz sich ganz.

To another beat one might sing:

> Ich sitz' auf dem Mustang, die Büchs' auf dem Knie,
> So trab' ich, so jag' ich, durch Wald und Prärie.

But the desire to fuse the old and the new Germany is ever in the background of the settlers' minds:

> Nein ich will dein nie vergessen,
> Nie, so lang mein Geist noch denkt,
> Denn du hast die Freiheitsliebe,
> Diesen schönsten Trieb der Triebe,
> Mir zuerst ins Herz gesenkt.
>
> Könnt' ich bald den Tag erleben,
> Wo du stehest vor mir da,
> Lächelnd in der Freiheit Glanze,
> Mit dem schönsten Eichenkranze
> Holde Maid Germania.

Among the many exotic poems of Ferdinand Freiligrath there are several devoted to America and especially to the American Indian. There were times, about 1835, among others, when Freiligrath considered going to America, but when an opportunity arose to join a colonizing group bound for Texas in 1844 he declined. Freiligrath wrote several poems about emigrants, among them "Die Auswanderer," 1832, and "Tod des Führers," 1845:

> Dorten lasst uns Hütten bauen,
> Wo die Freiheit hält das Lot.

But his enthusiasm for American freedom was dampened by the thought of the victimized Indians:

> Kahl und nüchtern jede Stätte!
> Wo Manittos hehrer Rauch
> Durch des Urwalds Dickicht wehte,
> Zieht der Hammerwerke Rauch
> Bietet Trotz, ihr Tätowierten,
> Eurer Feindin, der Kultur!
> Knüpft die Stirnhaut von skalpierten
> Weissen an des Gürtels Schnur.

Freiligrath's pictures of the American scene are as vivid as if he had seen them for himself:

> Sie dehnt sich aus von Meer zu Meere,
> Wer sie durchschnitten hat, den graust's.[31]

It is next in order to inquire what nineteenth-century German historians of literature had to say concerning the American products. Discussion of American literature found a place in four different frameworks:

1. In histories of world literature, where the treatment of American literature is naturally only cursory. Johannes Scheer's *Allgemeine Geschichte der Literatur* . . . 10th ed. 1851, is an example.

2. In general histories of English literature, in which more extensive comments on American authors find a place, for example in Scheer's *Geschichte der englischen Literatur*, 1854. Such works are numerous.

3. In histories of English literature which recognize American

44

literature specifically in their main title or in an "Anhang."

> KARL ELZE, *Englischer Liederschatz aus britischen und amerikanischen Dichtern des XIX. Jahrhunderts*, vierte, vermehrte und verbesserte Auflage, 1859.
> EDUARD ENGEL, *Geschichte der englischen Literatur...* mit einem Anhange: "Die anglo-amerikanische Literatur," 1883.
> ADOLF MAGER, *Geschichte der englischen Literatur...* Mit einem Anhange: "Die amerikanische Literatur," 1893.
> E. R. SCHMIDT, *Abriss der englischen und amerikanischen Literatur*, 1893.
> F. J. BIERBAUM, *History of the English Language and Literature... including the American Literature*, third revised and enlarged edition, 1895.

4. The following works indicate by their titles that American literature is their chief concern and, with varying reservations, attribute to it an autochthonous existence:

> LUDWIG HERRIG, *Handbuch der nordamerikanischen National-Literatur*, 1854.
> K. BRUNNEMANN, *Geschichte der nordamerikanischen Literatur*, 1866.
> ADOLF STRODTMANN, *Amerikanische Anthologie*, 1870.
> ERNST OTTO HOPP. *Unter dem Sternenbanner. Streifzüge in das Leben und die Literatur der Amerikaner*, 1877.
> RUDOLF DOEHN, *Aus dem amerikanischen Dichterwald. Literarhistorische Skizzen*, 1881.
> KARL KNORTZ, *Geschichte der nordamerikanischen Literatur*, 1891.
> E. P. EVANS, *Beiträge zur amerikanischen Literatur- und Kulturgeschichte*, 1898.
> KARL FEDERN, *Essays zur amerikanischen Literatur*, 1899.[32]

One of the earliest German historians of English literature to call for comment here was Johannes Scheer with his *Geschichte der englischen Literatur*, 1854. Johannes Scheer (also Scherr) was a disappointed liberal. As a participant in the German uprising of '48, he had to take flight to Switzerland. It was natural that his views should be colored by his experiences and that he was led into a species of racism. His *Geschichte der englischen Literatur* is misleadingly named. He distinguished between races prone to fall victims to tyranny and to the race which maintains the ideal of "freie Selbstbestimmung," and this was the Germanic race, to which belonged not only the Germans and the English but also the Scandinavians. Although America might owe much else to England, the important line of connection was that it was a stalwart upholder of the Germanic ideal, and this led Scheer to echo a prophecy that had been uttered a century before: Should Europe fall a total victim to tyranny and should even England fail to support the ideal of freedom, there was still hope for self-government, and America should be the land of its rebirth and final victory. Scheer is one of the few to inject the idea of race into the subject under discussion.

Ludwig Herrig's *Handbuch der nordamerikanischen Literatur* of the same year was, as its title indicates, a work of reference rather than a formal history. Of interest is Karl Elze's review of the work in his journal *Atlantis*, II (1855), 657 ff., in which he prophesies a glorious development of American literature, although at the time of writing he admits that there have been few truly great American works.

K. Brunnemann's *Geschichte der nordamerikanischen Literatur*, 1866, the earliest professed history of the subject, was well spoken of by all the critics. Brunnemann had obviously read the works he evaluated. The title of his work need not imply that he believes an American literature already exists, but he sees a growing tendency of its writers to free themselves from colonial bondage. To this view he is helped by his broad inclusiveness. He takes within his purview not only belletristic works but also histories, state papers, and political orations. Many of these have a strong anti-English tendency, and he finds a sturdy independence in them which augurs well for a separate American literature in the future.

Fairly early the question arose as to whether the American

people could ever have a literature of its own. The prognostications were generally unfavorable. It was pointed out that the American people had no past, hence no heroic epic, and no courtly epic. Without a past there was little hope for a future. Furthermore history has shown that monarchical rule was most propitious for letters and the other arts. The striving citizen of America, after an exhausting day of labor or business, had free time only for his duties as a citizen, and if he read anything it would be the political news in the evening paper. Others argued that American life was realistic and unimaginative and that no poetry could develop out of it. Then there was the frequently recurring race idea. America was a nation, but Americans were not a people. They were made up of a fusion of early settlers with succeeding waves of immigration from various European lands. Only Herrig seems to have recognized that this confrontation of different mores had useful possibilities for the dramatist.

One characteristic of a people, some philosophers maintained, was the possession of a distinctive language, and such thinkers believed in the possibility of an American fusion of languages in the course of centuries. A variation of this was the ideal of Hopp, who looked forward to the time when the German language should crowd out the Anglo-Saxon. Meanwhile the English language and literary standards ruled. Irving was regarded as the successor of the English moral essayists, and Cooper was dubbed the American Walter Scott.

Although Karl Knortz (1841-1918) was an American citizen, lived most of his life in America, taught in several public schools, and edited German-American newspapers, he is to be regarded as a German writer. He wrote in the German language, published his works in Germany, and addressed himself to a German public. His *Geschichte der nordamerikanischen Literatur*, 1891, was the most misleading that had yet appeared. It is in two volumes, but many pages are wasted. For example, he tells us that "Home Sweet Home" was a poor poem, and then devotes sixteen pages to the life of John Howard Payne. It is an exasperating book to read, for he lays down for himself a plan for the disposition of his material, and then crosses it with some other arrangement. To be sure, American literary history with its many cross currents is prone to such inconsistencies, but Knortz seems to have made little effort to mitigate them. At times the reader has the feeling that Knortz has combined earlier literary essays with little attempt at fusion and without being aware of the resultant contradictions.

Knortz's work falls into the category of cultural history and only incidentally of aesthetics. He treats with great enthusiasm dull periods and dull books which throw light upon American life, and welcomes purposeful works, such as *Uncle Tom's Cabin*, which are intended to affect public life. Whittier, Bryant, and Lowell stand high in his regard as antislavery crusaders. Bryant was also a fighter for states rights and free trade, and was the editor of the liberal *New York Nation*. Lowell's poems have merit as a chronicle of public life. Knortz's "Weltanschauung" gives unity to all his criticisms. His philosophy is deterministic atheism. He has to condemn certain periods of American literature and many revered writers because of their underlying presupposition that there is a God, a future life, and that man possesses freedom of the will. Because of such time-worn heritages a rational literature, he says, has not developed, but with the appearance of Whitman American literature has begun at last a period of rationality.

With Darwin, Knortz believed that heredity and environment, not human will, determines what man is. With Karl Marx, he believed that economic conditions determined history, including literary development, and that there could be no flowering of the arts until a comfortable life provided leisure for it. Hence at times he speaks indulgently of the American pursuit of the almighty dollar. Knortz valued reason above imagination, positive ideas higher than intrinsic beauty, and to theological, philosophical, historical, and political treatises he accorded a more important role than to simply belletristic works.

But it was not enough that these substantial values should be recognized. Literature had also the mission to storm the entrenched bulwarks of Christian superstition. Hence Knortz pays particular homage to such men as Franklin, Thomas Paine, Oliver Wendell Holmes, and Thoreau, while Longfellow and Emerson found no favor with him. On the whole he found in American literature little to his taste until, toward the end of his life, Walt Whitman appeared on the scene. He regarded Whitman as the saviour of American democracy and himself as his chief prophet. (*Walt Whitman, der Dichter der Demokratie*, 1899; *Walt Whitman und seine Nachahmer*, 1911).

Knortz's work was reviewed and sharply censured by Alexander Baumgartner, S. J., who was an active participant in the German "Kulturkampf."[33] As a Catholic he believed in a holy church universal, and hence in a literature transcending national lines and having its unity in Christendom. He interpreted Knortz's history as a proclamation of secession from this ideal community and as a return to barbarism. Walt Whitman was the literary spokesman of this negation. If his message were generally accepted, literary history would lose its continuity.

In Baumgartner's estimate Longfellow was indisputably the greatest American poet. Although not a Catholic, Longfellow was productively receptive to the stores of Christian European literature. Longfellow represented romanticism at its American best. Baumgartner was also a defender of Poe, despite Poe's obvious aberrations, but in view of the quality of *Evangeline*, *Hiawatha*, and *The Golden Legend*, he held it to be ridiculous to proclaim Poe as the greatest American poet.

A third critic and historian, who treated literature in a nation-transcending frame, was Julian Schmidt (1818-1886). To his mind the important conflict of the time was between subjective idealism, mysticism, romanticism, on the one hand, and materialism on the other. This formulation was in near accord with those of Baumgartner and Knortz, but Schmidt took his stand between the two. He was a political and religious liberal and an admirer of Schleiermacher, Theodore Parker, and William Ellery Channing. He was opposed to the mysticism of the second part of *Faust* and of Longfellow's *The Golden Legend*. Chapter II of his *Übersicht der englischen Literatur im neunzehnten Jahrhundert* is called "The Great Poets," chapter III, in strong contrast, "The Spiritualistic Poets," under which heading he lists Carlyle, Shelley, the "Lake Poets" and also Longfellow, Poe, and Emerson. Here we note that American-born poets are listed without distinction as English poets, but these again are by the context subordinated to the European conflict between romanticism and materialism. Against the "überspannte" mysticism and "subjektive Idealismus" of the romanticists, Julian Schmidt advocated realism, but not the crass pessimistic realism of the young German and young English writers, but the "gesunden Realismus" of English literature as represented by Fielding, Goldsmith, and Dickens.

If now we turn from the historians to the journalists of the mid-century we find that they too are interested in the question of the existence of an independent American literature. Five of the journals thus concerned are:

> *Die Grenzboten*, edited by Julian Schmidt and Gustav Freytag,
> *Unterhaltungen am häuslichen Herd*, edited by Karl Gutzkow,
> *Magazin für die Literatur des Auslands*, edited by Josef Lehmann,
> *Blätter für literarische Unterhaltung*, edited by Hermann Marggraff,
> *Deutsches Museum*, edited by Robert Prutz.

On one fact there was almost unanimous agreement: there existed no independent national literature in America. American literature stood, to be sure, under the sway of English literature in general, but quite particularly under the influence of English men of letters and philosophers, who, in turn, had been affected by German literature and thought. This was the view of critics in the *Grenzboten*, in the *Magazin für die Literatur des Auslands* and the *Deutsches Museum*.[34] An exception here was Hermann

Marggraff in the *Blätter für literarische Unterhaltung*. He saw in America "Ansätze zu einer wirklich originellen Literatur":

> Trügt unser Blick nicht, so werden künftige Zeiten jenseits des Oceans eine Literatur entwickeln sehen, welche die Vorzüge der deutschen und der englischen Literatur verschmelzen und die Einseitigkeit der einen wie der anderen vermeiden wird.[35]

About twenty years later, moreover, another critic, or perhaps this same one, saw this prophecy fulfilled:

> Die Amerikaner haben auf einem ganz eigenen Boden in ganz eigener Luft und in einem ganz eigenen Geist geschichtlicher Entwicklung ein ganz eigenes Leben und somit auch eine ganz eigene Literatur. Obgleich sie noch immer wesentlich mit Leben und Literatur Englands und Deutschlands zusammenhängen und englische wie deutsche Geisteswerke immer frisch bei ihnen sich einbürgern, haben sie doch längst auf eigene Weise denken und dichten gelernt.[36]

The intellectual leaders of the German revolution of the 30's and of 1848 constituted a group called "Das Junge Deutschland." After their political failures they tried to express themselves in literature, particularly in the novel. They believed in literature with a mission, and against a literature of outmoded romanticism they offered bleak pictures of realism with a bold assertion of the rights of individuals in opposition to an oppressive social order.

Owing to his opposition to "Das Junge Deutschland" Julian Schmidt became a leading controversial figure at the mid-century. He opposed the entry of literature into the metaphysical realm, the invention of characters with superhuman ambitions – "Faustic" characters – and the flight into the Middle Ages. He said: "Den Geist der alten Zeiten zu schildern... ist eine würdige Aufgabe, aber im Geist der alten Zeiten zu dichten ist unnatürlich und romantisch." Walter Scott, in contrast to the German romanticists, always wrote from the standpoint of his own time, which Schmidt held to be the correct attitude. The

"Faustic" tendencies continued in European literature throughout the first half of the century. Such tendencies Schmidt termed "subjective idealism," and to it he opposed "künstlerischen Idealismus," which should be evident even in realistic works:

> Der Realismus der Poesie wird dann zu erfreulichen Kunstwerken führen, wenn er in der Wirklichkeit zugleich die positive Seite aufsucht, wenn er mit Freude am Leben verknüpft ist, wie früher bei Fielding, Goldsmith, später bei Walter Scott und teilweise auch noch bei Dickens.[37]

In the contemporary English novelists, especially in Walter Scott and Charles Dickens, Schmidt sought an antidote to the poisonous literature of the Germans of his time, but unfortunately several of the contemporary English authors suffered the same maladies of German origin as the Germans of the time.

Parallel to "Das Junge Deutschland," Schmidt distinguished a group of authors whom he called "Das Junge England," and a chief characteristic of them was "subjective idealism." This quality was found in Germany in Schiller, Goethe, Fichte, and Schelling; in France in Mme. de Staël and other followers of Rousseau; in England in Shelley and Byron, Bulwer Lytton, Thackeray, and Carlyle. "Subjective idealism" led to disillusionment, "Blasiertheit," and pessimism, while "Freude am Leben" and optimism were essential to "künstlerischem Idealismus," as Schmidt defined it.

In his *Übersicht der englischen Literatur im neunzehnten Jahrhundert*, 1856, Schmidt accorded to Wordsworth two pages, to Keats three and a half lines, to Shelley twenty-four pages. In Schmidt's opinion Shelley and Carlyle were chiefly responsible for the "Young English" school of writers, "die mit der Tradition der älteren Literatur vollständig bricht und sich der metaphysischen Richtung der deutschen Poesie anschliesst."[38] Shelley was, he said, the channel through which the "Faustic" tendencies of German literature gained entrance into English letters. Among the followers of Shelley were Keats, Maturin, Godwin, Mary Godwin Shelley, Philip Bailey, Robert Browning, Elizabeth Barrett Browning, and Tennyson. Next after Shelley in importance was Carlyle, who served as a connecting link between the revolutionary ideas of the Shelley school and the literature of social unrest 1850-1860. He was also an important link between Goethe and Emerson, and he introduced into the English language a ponderous imitation of German style at its worst.

With few exceptions, Schmidt's discussions of American authors are motivated by the purpose of supporting his thesis of "Idealismus." He did not believe in the existence of an independent American literature:

> Gerade die bedeutendsten Schriftsteller, z.B. Washington Irving, gehören in ihrer Form, wie in ihrem Inhalt ganz zu England. Die Versuche Coopers, nationale Stoffe zu gewinnen, haben keine bedeutenden Nachfolger hervorgerufen, und die junge romantische Schule, die jetzt in der Poesie sich immer mehr ausbreitet, beruht ganz auf Reminiszenzen der jung-englischen und der deutschen Literatur.

The works of Longfellow, Bryant, Poe, Dana, and Halleck, he adds, "sind durchaus nicht aus dem nationalen Leben hervorgegangen. Wir hören in ihnen Byron, Shelley, die Schule der Seen, Goethe, und andere deutsche Dichter heraus."[39]

The American authors who are made the subjects of special essays by Schmidt are Cooper, Longfellow, Margaret Fuller, Hawthorne, and Emerson. The latter three Schmidt characterizes as belonging to a school "die durch den Philosophen Waldo Emerson mit Carlyle in Verbindung steht, und sich in letzter Instanz auf Shelley zurückführen lässt." The aim of the school, he says, is, "die eingeschränkte Sittlichkeit und den geistlosen Materialismus, die bisher in der neuen Welt geherrscht haben, durch Einführung der transcendentalen, spiritualistischen Denkweise des jungen Europas zu brechen."[40] Schmidt regards Margaret Fuller, rather than Emerson, as the leader or prophetess of the New England Transcendentalists. He compares her with Mme. de Staël "in ihrer äusseren Stellung," with Rahel Varnhagen von Ense "in ihrem geistigen Wesen" and with George Sand's Lelia "in ihrem halb-männlichen, herrschsüchtigen Geist."[41]

Schmidt regarded Longfellow as the most notable American poet, although he found in the works of Bryant a more national content than in Longfellow's, but even in Bryant's work the influence of German lyrical poetry was undeniable. Longfellow's first works, "*Die Stimmen der Nacht* und 'Der Glockenturm von Brügge,'" he found, "zeichnen sich durch eine kontemplative Stimmung aus. Ihrem wesentlichen Charakter nach gehören sie in 'die Schule der Seen,' nur dass sich schon Shelley's Einfluss geltend macht. Die lyrischen Gedichte erinnern am meisten an die deutsche Ballade."[42]

Naturally Schmidt's view of *The Golden Legend* is unfavorable:

> [Longfellow ist] in's unübersehbare Transzendente übergetreten. Es ist dieses angeblich dramatische Gedicht einer von den vielen unglücklichen Versuchen, die Goethe's *Faust* in der neuen Literatur hervorgerufen hat.[43]

Schmidt assigned to *Evangeline* the highest rank among all American poems, recognizing at the same time German influences in its form, as well as in the form of *Hiawatha*.[44] He noted the appearance of translations of Longfellow's poems into German, for he said: "Die Gedichte sind teilweise wert, übersetzt zu werden; mehr als die der gleichzeitigen Dichter aus der Schule Shelleys."[45] "Völlig befriedigt hat uns mit Ausnahme der *Evangeline* kein einziges von seinen grösseren Werken." *Hyperion*, he noted, is a work, "welches den massenhaften Eindruck der deutschen Literatur versinnlicht."

To Edgar Allan Poe Schmidt concedes a certain measure of plastic talent and a highly developed sense of melody, but found the effect of his poems, "seltsam, im Ganzen hässlich und unheimlich."[46] Regarding *Eureka* he said:

Man sieht, dass die Naturphilosophie auch in Amerika Anklang findet, dass Schopenhauer auch dort seine Geistesverwandten herauserkennen wird, und dass wir Deutsche aufhören, das Privilegium der Metaphysik zu haben.[47]

In his *Übersicht der englischen Literatur*, Schmidt recorded that Poe's works "übertreffen bei weitem die 'Lake School' in der Erfindung von Geschichten ohne Pointen, die dabei an Fratzenhaftigkeit noch weit über unsern Hoffmann hinausgehen." Shelley and Carlyle, however, he says, have exerted the greatest influence upon Poe.[48]

Of all the Shelley-Carlyle school in America, Schmidt said, Nathaniel Hawthorne should be best appreciated in Germany. *The House of Seven Gables* and the *Blithedale Romance* he regarded as his best novels. "Seine Romane und Erzählungen verraten ein Talent, welches ihn zu der ersten Reihe erheben würde, wenn seine Natur so gesund wäre, wie sie lebhaft ist."[49] Schmidt preferred literature "die das Sonnenlicht verträgt," but, he conceded, "auch die Krankheit führt zuweilen zu Phänomenen, die für ein empfängliches Gemüt reizender sind als die Gesundheit selbst."[50] Such an admission on Schmidt's part is quite exceptional, but

The *Blithedale Romance* ist von allen Romanen des geistvollen Dichters am meisten geignet, uns in das innere Leben der jungen amerikanischen Dichterschule einzuführen, die man in vielen Beziehungen unsern Romantikern an die Seite stellen kann.[51]

In this connection Schmidt sums up his thesis: "Seltsamerweise ist es nicht die englische Dichtung und Philosophie, auf welche das strebsame Jungamerika hinblickt, sondern die deutsche," and he adds: "Daran sind keineswegs die deutschen Einwanderer schuld, deren Ansehen viel zu gering ist, um auf die herrschenden Anglo-Amerikaner einen Einfluss auszuüben."

Since the appearance of Julian Schmidt's *Übersicht der englischen Literatur im neunzehnten Jahrhundert*, 1859, the process of differentiating English and American literature has gone on apace.

Brunnemann, "zweite Auflage," 1868, and Karl Knortz, 1891, were next to devote their histories exclusively to American literature, but meanwhile there had appeared Eduard Engel's *Geschichte der englischen Literatur,... Mit einem Anhange: Die anglo-amerikanische Literatur*, 1883. In the course of his discussion Engel noted that, although the United States had not yet produced any work which would promise to remain, American literature doubtless wins in the competition, if compared with contemporary English literature, and Scheer in his *Illustrierte Geschichte der Weltliteratur* (10th ed., 1899), wrote that it seemed as if in America a fresher, more vigorous and more vital spirit was active in literary life than in England.

A thoroughly scholarly history of American literature came from the pen of Ewald Flügel, a professor of German literature and philology at Stanford University, under the title *Geschichte der nordamerikanischen Literatur*, 1906-07. Flügel's work appeared as part III, pp. 423-451, in Richard Wülker's *Geschichte der englischen Literatur* 2nd ed., 1907. It was withdrawn from the later editions in the conviction that American literature was a theme apart, requiring a separate treatment – a belief that soon began to find new adherents.

Shortly after the end of the First World War appeared the much-read work of Oswald Spengler *Der Untergang des Abendlandes*, 1921-1922. Spengler, like Nietzsche, made a sharp distinction between "Zivilisation" and "Kultur." Technical and materialistic affluence, "Zivilisation," such as prevailed in America foreshadowed the decline of "Kultur." The Baltic Count Hermann Keyserling found additional causes for the poverty of American culture – Puritanism, Prohibition, and the overrating of the importance of children. East and West were far apart, and should they ever meet it would be because Europe had Europeanized America. Spengler and Keyserling were among the last publicists to reiterate the long-time, almost stereotyped view of a soulless America.

Differentiation of English and American literature proceeded apace. Leon Kellner's *Geschichte der nordamerikanischen Literatur* I, II, 1923, 2nd ed., 1927, is devoted to a single topic. Walther Fischer's history is entitled *Die englische Literatur der Vereinigten Staaten von Amerika*, 1929. The title is open to possible misinterpretation. By "englische Literatur" is meant literature in the English language. Fischer is a strong believer in the separate identity of American literature. The same holds true for Werner P. Friederich, whose *Werden und Wachsen der USA in 300 Jahren* (Bern, 1939) endeavors "der unhistorischen Betrachtungsweise der meisten Amerikabücher etwas entgegenzuarbeiten... und ein Verständnis für das geistige Werden... des amerikanischen Volkes zu erwecken." To this end, Friederich includes chapters on "Der Vater der amerikanischen Literatur: Washington Irving; Ein amerikanischer Gottsucher: Herman Melville; Die amerikanische Kurzgeschichte: Edgar Allan Poe; Ein Erbe des Puritanismus: Nathaniel Hawthorne; Der romantische Nationaldichter: Henry Wadsworth Longfellow; Der realistische Nationaldichter: Walt Whitman" – up to Mark Twain, Jack London, Eugene O'Neill, and Sinclair Lewis. Henry Lüdeke in his *Geschichte der amerikanischen Literatur* has shown how American literature has likewise outgrown much of its English heritage as a result of American history and American conditions of life.

Contrary to the prevailing tendency, Walther Schirmer in his *Geschichte der englischen und amerikanischen Literatur von den Anfängen bis zur Gegenwart* attempted to treat the two literatures as one, but was constantly plagued by the recalcitrant presupposition. To the several sections devoted to English literature he appended a few paragraphs on American literature, the connection in many instances being little more than chronological, or again he treated American literature and English literature in the same paragraph or the same passage. In a review of this work, Walther Fischer complained that the reader is driven to too many "Geschwindflügen über den Atlantik," in order to follow the author.[52]

The Anglo-American tie will always remain close, we may hope, based as it is on a common heritage and a common language, but even the language tie is becoming looser. The American language is no longer regarded as contaminated English, but as a "gleich-berechtigte" variant. Of the scores of works translated yearly into German, several bear on the title page the rubric "aus dem Amerikanischen." "Amerikakunde" is regarded as a separate "Fach" in German universities. Sigmund Skard counted a hundred and sixty-nine courses in "Amerikakunde" in twenty-three German universities between 1919 and 1933.[52] The *Zeit-schrift für Anglistik und Amerikanistik* recognizes by its title two fields of research, while the *Jahrbuch für Amerikastudien* devotes itself to the one.

[1] Weber [83] 111.

[2] *Op. cit.*, 1835.

[3] Ludwig Börne, *Gesammelte Schriften*, Hamburg, 1862, VII, 101 f.

[4] Heinrich Heine, *Sämtliche Werke*, ed. Elster, Leipzig, [1887-1890], III, 279.

[5] *Ibid.*, V 38.

[6] *Ibid.*, VII, 44.

[7] Karl Gutzkow, *Bulwer Lyttons Zeitgenossen*, 26. unveränderte Auflage, Pforzheim, 1842, 413 f.

[8] Karl Gutzkow, *Gesammelte Werke*, Jena, 1872-1878, X, 35.

[9] Franz [78], 272-295.

[10] von Hofe [39].

[11] von Hofe [49].

[12] Lange [45].

[13] See below, p. 101.

[14] Correll [85].

[15] Platens *Sämtliche Werke*, ed. Koch and Petzet, Leipzig. n.d., II, 62.

[16] *Ibid.*, II, 23 f.

[17] *Ibid.*, II, 62 f.

[18] Nikolaus Lenau, *Werke*, ed. Koch, Berlin [n.d.] I, 95.

[19] *Ibid.*, I, 115.

[20] Anton X. Schurz, *Lenaus Leben*, Stuttgart und Augsburg, 1855. I, 158.

[21] *Ibid.*, 199.

[22] Lenau, *Werke*, I, 237.

23 *Ibid.*, I, 237 f.

24 *Ibid.*, I, 187.

25 Anastasius Grün, *Werke*, ed. Castle, Berlin, 1900, I, 228.

26 *Ibid.*, I, 246.

27 Heinrich Hoffmann von Fallersleben, *Deutsche Lieder aus der Schweiz*, Zürich und Winterthur, 1843, I, 175 f.

28 In his *Gesammelte Werke*, Berlin, 1871, IV, 346.

29 *Ibid.*, V, 3-16

30 *Ibid.*, V, 327.

31 See also Learned [55].

32 Johanna Siedler, *History of English Literature* ... 10th ed., 1911; pp. 163-164. Karl Brunnemann, *Geschichte der nordamerikanischen Literatur*, 2nd ed., 1863, p. 1 ff. Other references in Locher [6] and [65].

33 Baumgartner was the author of a *Geschichte der Weltliteratur*. A supplementary volume was entitled *Untersuchungen und Urteile zu den Literaturen verschiedener Völker. Gesammelte Aufsätze.* The essays on American literature in this volume were all written between 1890 and 1895. Locher [65] 56.

34 *Grenzboten*, 1854 I, 79; MFLA, 1856, 470; BLU, 1852, 426-428; *Deutsches Museum*, 1854 I, 364-365.

35 BLU, 1857, p. 739.

36 MFLA, April 1876, p. 288.

37 *Grenzboten*, 1851 III, 333; 1856 IV, 474.

38 *Ibid.*, 1852, II, 376.

39 *Ibid.*, 1854, I, 79.

40 *Ibid.*, 1852, II, 425.

41 *Ibid.*, 1852, II, 270.

42 *Ibid.*, 1852, II, 265.

43 *Ibid.*, 1852, II, 267.

44 *Ibid.*, 1856, II, 135.

45 *Ibid.*, 1856, IV, 440.

46 *Ibid.*, 1856, IV, 139.

47 *Ibid.*, 1856, II, 143.

48 *Op. cit.*, 122 f.

49 *Grenzboten*, 1852 II, 429 f.

50 *Ibid.*, 431.

51 *Ibid.*, 1855, IV, 290.

52 JAS I (1956), 208.

The Germans were able to gain a blurred image of American poetry through the misted glass of translation. American poems were included in over a score of anthologies during the nineteenth century, some of which were devoted exclusively to American poetry.[1] Among the best of these were Friedrich Spielhagen's *Amerikanische Gedichte*, 1859, and Adolf Strodtmann's *Amerikanische Anthologie*, 1870. Ferdinand Freiligrath was one of the best translators. American poems are included in his *Neue Gedichte*, 1877. Karl Knortz published *Amerikanische Gedichte der Neuzeit*, 1883, *Lieder aus der Fremde*, 1887, and *Poetischer Hausschatz der Nordamerikaner*, n.d. Knortz was one of the first to call attention to Walt Whitman. Ernst Otto Hopp's *Unter dem Sternenbanner*, 1883, contained "patriotic poems," most of them not included in other collections. Other poems were included in anthologies of wider scope, such as Johannes Scheer's *Bildersaal der Weltliteratur*, zweite Auflage, 1885.

William Cullen Bryant was one of the earliest American poets to attract the attention of German translators, and "The Winds," translated by Freiligrath in 1844, was probably the first to be honored. Alexander Neidhart's *Bryants Gedichte*, 1855, included all of Bryant's poems written before that date. Adolf Laun's authorized translation of 1863 is better but selective. Bryant expressed his satisfaction with the work. Better still are certain translations in anthologies – Spielhagen (6), Elze (11), and

Strodtmann (3). All three tried their skill on *Thanatopsis*, and seven others did so with less success. Knortz included in his anthology translations of thirty-six of Bryant's poems. They have been rated by Roehm as "mittelmässig."

Only the poems of Longfellow and of Poe were translated in their entirety. It has been estimated that Longfellow's poems made up about fifty percent of all German translations of American poetry during the nineteenth century. Simon, 1883, was the first in the field with a complete translation of Longfellow's poems, but Neidhardt had preceded him, 1856, with selections based chiefly on *Voices of the Night*. Better than these are the *Balladen und Lieder* of A. R. Nielo, 1857. This collection is little known, as no second edition followed. Longfellow is represented in nearly all the anthologies of the century but best by Spielhagen (10), Strodtmann (6), and Freiligrath (6). Roehm asserts: "An dichterischer Wirkung stehen beide [Spielhagen und Freiligrath] auf der Höhe der deutschen Übersetzungskunst."

Hiawatha has attracted at least nine translators, among them Adolf Böttger, 1856, Freiligrath, 1857, and Knortz, 1872. Roehm regards Knortz's translation as one of the worst. He finds merits in Böttger's and he regards Freiligrath's translation as "die Glanzleistung auf dem ganzen amerikanisch-deutschen Übersetzungsgebiet." *Evangeline* was translated thirteen times between 1850 and 1900. It seems agreed that the translation by Gasda, 1863, is the best, but it has long disappeared from print. Nearly approaching it in merit, however, is a translation by Otto Hauser, 1908. Of *The Courtship of Miles Standish*, there have been four translations, of which J. Mannfeld's, 1867, is unquestionably the best. The translation of *The Golden Legend* by the Freifrau von Hohenhausen has found particular favor. Roehm writes: "Das genaue Nachempfinden und die echt dichterische Gestaltung, die man hier empfindet, erheben diese Übertragung zu den Leistungen allerhöchsten Ranges."

It would be interesting to know what impression the American poems made upon the inarticulate element of the reading public.

Its views could only be expressed by its purchases. One fact is obvious: the poems of Longfellow in translation were the ones most likely to pass into later editions. A chief merit of Longfellow was that he broadened a prevailing orientation toward English models into a relationship to European literature as a whole, and not the least to German literature. That may have been one reason, though only one, for the German preference for Longfellow. More important is the unanswerable question: how did these American poems, abundant, good, even though not great, and certainly not materialistic, modify the prevailing view that America was a land of exclusively materialistic values? Another characteristic often imputed to America was Puritanism. The poems offered, notably Longfellow's, had an inclination toward moral preachments, but of a generally ethical rather than a puritanical cast.

Despite efforts by Knortz, Freiligrath, and Strodtmann, representative translations of Walt Whitman did not appear until the twentieth century and shall be mentioned later.[2] Bayard Taylor was more fortunate in his time, in part, perhaps, because his role as an American-German mediator was appreciated. Taylor was well pleased to have as his translator the competent Karl Bleibtreu, who translated eighty poems in 1879. Among the other translators were Knortz, eighteen poems, Strodtmann, seven poems, and Spielhagen six. For the most part these surpassed Bleibtreu's offerings.

John Greenleaf Whittier was represented by translations of *Snowbound*, "Maud Miller," and "Barbara Fritchie," but not by his anti-slavery poems. James Russell Lowell expressed more satisfaction with Laun's version of *The Vision of Sir Launfal* than it deserved. The poems of Bret Harte appealed to the anthologists – Freiligrath, eleven poems, Knortz nine, and Prinzhorn three. Of Ralph Waldo Emerson's poems two were included in Knortz's collection and seven well translated in Spielhagen's anthology. Emerson's belated fame still rested chiefly on his essays. Knortz included ten poems of Oliver Wendell Holmes in his collections. Joaquin Miller, Thomas Bailey Aldrich, and Richard Henry Stoddard were known chiefly through the agency of the anthologies. Hopp's *Poetischer Hausschatz der Nordamerikaner* included poems by John Howard Payne, William Gilmore Simms, Francis Scott Key, Philip Freneau, Eugene Field, Edwin Markham, and poems of many others who might else have been overlooked.

In 1883 Eduard Engel declared that Longfellow was not a great poet, that he lacked originality, and that his greatness would have to be sought in his translations.[3] Locher sets this as a definite date for the turn of the tide. After Engel's pronouncement several critics, among them Stern, Bleibtreu, E. R. Schmidt, Mager, and Körting, found themselves in agreement with him.

A total re-evaluation had set in. Brunnemann said in 1866 that Longfellow's popularity was due to his ability to express feelings familiar to everyone in beautiful language. Knortz added in 1891 that Longfellow expressed general, stale, commonplace truths. Early critics found Longfellow's poetry and prose charming, simple, tender, highly moral, chaste, idealistic, optimistic, humane, surpassing that of his contemporaries in elegance of style. Bleibtreu called Longfellow's poems the pretentious bad verse of a moralist, and held that moral didacticism was an unbearable Yankee trait. Schönbach said that Longfellow's purity prevented him from describing passions realistically but all the critics allow him the merit of being an extraordinarily successful translator of German verse.

The curve of Longfellow's popularity in Germany corresponds closely to that in his homeland, and in Europe and America he rather suddenly had to yield the first place to Edgar Allan Poe. It is obvious, however, that until about 1880 the German critics regarded Longfellow as the greatest American poet. This was the opinion of Siedler, Herrig, Büchner, Graesse, Pauli, Ahn, Gesenius, Karpeles, Leixner, Feyerabend, and Baumgartner. Graesse ventured to prophesy that Longfellow was one of the few poets who will be remembered after centuries.[4] The Germans were pleased to see their own culture reflected in America – to point out that *Hermann und Dorothea* gave a suggestion to *Evangeline* and *Der arme Heinrich* to *The Golden Legend*, but this relation, to their minds, did not detract from Longfellow's originality. A rare example of sheer imitation was "The Building of the Ship," following closely the structure of Schiller's "Glocke." *Hiawatha*, on the other hand, was commended for its originality and for its exclusively American subject matter and treatment.

That Longfellow felt the lure of romanticism was one of the traits that early commended him to the Germans, but later lost him the favor of such critics as Julian Schmidt and Karl Knortz. For Alexander Baumgartner and his Catholic following it was a positive element.

The works of five American poets appeared in collections under the authors' names: Longfellow in nine collections, followed by Whitman (4), Poe (3), Bryant (2), and Bayard Taylor (1). The relative popularity of Taylor is somewhat greater than these numbers supplied by Roehm would indicate. There were three additional translations by Taylor's friend, Charles Theodor Eben, and three by John Straubenmüller. German journals in the United States, such as *Die New York Staatszeitung, Der Beobachter am Hudson,* and *Der deutsche Pionier* were open to German translations of Taylor's poems. A still larger number of translations appeared in newspapers in Germany. Taylor came into personal relationship with several of his translators – Bleibtreu, Strodtmann, Spielhagen, and Freiligrath. "The Bedouin Song" attracted four translators. "The Song of the Camp" was the basis of the best of Karl Vollheim's translations. The personal popularity of Bayard Taylor and the recognition of his services as an American advocate of German literature did much to stimulate the German interest in his poems.[5]

In the year 1842 appeared Rufus Griswold's volume *Poets and Poetry of America*. This was a revelation even to the better informed German critics. Hermann Marggraff wrote in the *Blätter für literarische Unterhaltung*, Dec. 14, 1844:

> Wer sich gewöhnt hat, Amerika nur als Land der Eisenbahnen und
> Maschinen zu betrachten, der wird sich dem uns vorliegenden
> grossen und schön ausgestatteten Band voll Poesie gegenüber des
> Staunens nicht erwehren können und mit Zweifel und Bedenken an
> die nähere Prüfung seines Inhalts gehen.

Quite unforseeably, Edgar Allan Poe appeared on the horizon with poems, tales, and critical essays which German literary historians could never have predicted from the pen of an American. In America Poe was an outsider. He belonged to the Gothic European romanticism as represented in England by the ballads of Wordsworth and Coleridge and by the works of "Monk" Lewis, Ann Radcliffe, and Horace Walpole; in Germany by Novalis, Fouqué, Achim von Arnim, Annette von Droste-Hülshoff, Tieck in his early years, and above all by E. T. A. Hoffmann. There is every reason to believe that Poe read the tales of the German romanticists in translation or in the original. His reading knowledge of the German language is sufficiently attested. Poe was well aware that he was open to the charge of heavy borrowings from the German terror school, especially from E. T. A. Hoffmann. To such an insinuation Poe wrote: "If in many of my productions terror has been the thesis, I maintain that terror is not of Germany but of the soul."

The facts and fictions of Poe's life were well known to the Germans who added some lurid myths of their own. From Griswold's work they could learn of Poe's accusation of plagiarism against Longfellow. Better information regarding Poe's life began to modify or contradict Griswold's prejudiced account. Among the defenders of Poe were John Ingram, Edmund Clarence Stedman, and J. H. Harrison in their editions of Poe's works, 1891, 1895, and 1902.

Of all American authors Poe was one of the most frequently translated into German, but the list of translations presents some peculiar features. First, more than nine tenths of the entries announce translations of his tales chiefly in collected or selected form. In the second place, most of the translations appeared tardily, and, finally, volumes of verse are rare, and the critical essays appear almost not at all. This suggests that Poe had two types of reading public: the one made up of specialists in English literature, together with such others as could read English without effort, and then a broader public which was enthralled by his weird tales of horror.

Edgar Allan Poes sämtliche Gedichte in the translation of Theodor Etzel did not appear until 1909, but good translations of separate poems had been published earlier. Poe's poems offered tempting tasks to the translator, as well as formidable difficulties. The German language lacks abundant masculine rhymes, and the German assonances do not correspond to the English. Without equivalences here the art and artifice of Poe's poems are lost. One may agree with the German critics that sometimes artifice takes the place of art, as in "The Bells," but Poe is rarely led into this banality. Spielhagen made good selections for translation and succeeded remarkably with "Annabel Lee," "To Helen," and especially with "To One in Paradise."

> Ach, alles warst du mir, mein Lieb,
> Mein Lieb, so hold und rein,
> Ein Eiland in der See, mein Lieb,
> Ein Brunnen und ein Schrein
> Umkränzt mit Blumen ohne Zahl
> Und alle Blumen mein.

Almost as good is his adaptation of "Annabel Lee":

> Ich war ein Kind und sie war ein Kind
> In diesem Reich an der See:
> Doch wie sie mich liebte, und wie ich geliebt
> Die reizende Annabel Lay,
> Das sagen nicht Worte – es weinten vor Neid
> Die Engel in himmlischer Höh.

"The Raven" was the most challenging goal for the translator. The two earliest German versions appeared in 1853; they were followed by at least seventeen further attempts, as follows:

ELISE VON HOHENHAUSEN, MFLA, no. 70, in 1853.
ALEXANDER NEIDHARDT, ASNS, XIII (1853), 241 ff.
LOUISE VON PLOENNIES, MFLA, no. 131, in 1857.
C. F. EBEN in *Four American Poems*, Philadelphia, 1864.
A. STRODTMANN, in *Amerikanische Anthologie*, Hildburghausen, 1870.
NIKOLAUS MÜLLER, New York, 1874.
EDUARD MAUTNER, *Neues Wiener Theater*, XXXV, Wien, 1874.
BETTY JACOBSEN in MFLA, No. 9, in the year 1880.
"The Raven" in Five texts: English, German, Hungarian, French, and Latin, New York, 1885.
HEDWIG LACHMANN, *Ausgewählte Gedichte von E. A. Poe*, Berlin, 1891.
A. BAUMGARTNER, *Stimmen aus Maria-Laach*, 1892.
A. STRODTMANN in Scheer's *Bildersaal der Literatur*, III, 1898.
JULIUS BRUCK in Knortz, *Poetischer Hausschatz der Nord-Amerikaner*, Leipzig, 1902.
EMIL HÄUSSER, Prog. Mannheim, 1906.
PAUL SCHAFENACKER, Prog. Mannheim, 1906.
THEODOR ETZEL in *Kunstwart*, 1909.
K. MERLING in *Edgar Allen Poe's gesammelte Werke*, VI, München and Leipzig, n.d. [1922].
OTTO BABLER, *Edgar Allan Poe, "Der Rabe", aus dem Amerikanischen*, Olmütz, 1931.
INNOZENZ GRAEFE, pp. 353 f. in *Die schönsten Gedichte der Welt*, Wien, 1936.

This does not mean that "The Raven" was regarded as Poe's best poem. In fact it was regarded by some as the most artificial apart from "The Bells." Nor did it escape the notice of the critics that Poe could create ethereal as well as sinister, lowering atmospheres. No fault of any kind was to be found in "To Helen" and "To One in Paradise."

In addition to the Poe poems included in the collected editions edited by Moeller-Bruck, 1910-1904, and Etzel, 1909, there were scattered translations by the Graf von Schack, by Bleibtreu, Knortz, Baumgartner, Spielhagen, Jacobson, Engel, Möllenhoff, and several others during the time 1853-1910.[6] Moreover the two volume Tauchnitz edition of the American original went through many editions.

Also Poe's critical works were known to his colleagues in Germany. Most frequently discussed was his *Poetic Principle*, 1850. The value of all literary types, Poe said, is to be measured by their capacity "to excite by elevating the soul," but such an exaltation is transient and must not be interrupted; hence a poem must be short. A short poem, Poe maintained, is the highest form of "literary art."

Poe's *Philosophy of Composition*, 1846, has been a controversial essay. In it Poe reduced to a formula the process of composing "The Raven." Many readers were skeptical, believing that the poem was the outgrowth of a weak and weary mood rather than of a well thought out process. They regarded the essay as a "bewusste Irreführung des Lesers," or as a "Verkennen des wahren schöpferischen Vorgangs." Recent criticism has taken a different view. Max Bense said: "Poe's *Philosophy of Composition* mag als Schaffungsprotokoll fragwürdig sein;... als Programm, ist sie überzeugend, und als solches hat sie in die Zukunft gewirkt," and Hans Egon Holthusen called it a "Stiftungsurkunde" for, he said, "die Dichterfamilie der Poe-Tradition arbeitet bewusst" and needs not rely on "göttliche Eingebung." Holthusen called Poe's poem, "The Raven," "eines der einflussreichsten der Weltliteratur"[7]; Poe sought to hold his readers in shuddering thrall as long as the reading lasted. The most thoughtful German critic of Poe's literary theories was Friedrich Spielhagen, who broadened Poe's view of the beautiful and foreboding to include elevations of the soul that endure beyond the time of reading. "Das Anmutige, Liebliche, Zierliche" belong also, he said, to the realm of high poetry.

Büchner, Breitinger, Strodtmann, Baumgartner, Doehm, Knortz, Bierbaum, and several other German critics show that they have read many of Poe's literary essays. Bierbaum regarded Poe's criticism as unfair. Doehm said that Poe's character was reflected in his criticism. Baumgartner agreed in general with the *Poetic Principle* but found it lacked "den rechten religiösen Halt."[8] It is in this connection that he said it was "geradezu lächerlich" to regard Poe as a greater poet than Longfellow.

Spielhagen commented on Poe's analysis of "The Raven" in the *Philosophy of Composition* and wrote two essays on the Poe-Longfellow controversy, "Edgar Poe gegen Longfellow" and "Longfellows Balladen." He was sympathetic toward Poe's personal shortcomings, regarding him as one of the "problematischen Naturen."

Spielhagen was interested in Poe's theory of the short story. Poe's definition of the short story is not greatly different from Goethe's definition of the Novelle: "Was ist die Novelle anders als eine sich ereignete unerhörte Begebenheit?" Poe regarded the short story as a form of literature outranked only by the short poem. He regarded Hawthorne as one of the best creators of this form. Like the short poem, the story must have brevity and pace. Development of a character serves only to delay and distract. A prose composition may be longer than a poetic one since it permits of more rapid reading, but brevity is still essential. It has been asserted that Spielhagen made some practical application of this theory in his fictional work. This contention is difficult to support, for Spielhagen's narratives are too digressive to fall in with Poe's demands. A comparison here is of some interest. The average length of a Spielhagen story is one hundred fifty-one pages, of Poe's *Tales of Mystery and Imagination* thirteen pages.[9] In one instance, however, Spielhagen made an effort toward brevity. His narrative *Mesmerismus* resembles in title Poe's *Mesmeric Revelation*, and in content Poe's *Assignation*.

On the recurrence of Poe's hundredth birthday in 1909 we are informed that "Gedächtnis-Artikel" appeared in every important German journal from "Memel bis Bern, von Kiel bis Graz."[10] The *Literarisches Echo* listed twenty-nine of these. Many of the German critics agreed with Eduard Engel that Poe,

69

if not one of the greatest world poets, was at least the greatest American poet, thus placing him above the long-honored Long-fellow. Should one venture to speak of the influence of Poe's poetry, the discussion would perforce be limited to the turn of the century. Baudelaire experienced a compelling enthusiasm on reading Poe's works. He translated several of Poe's tales into French, produced his own *Fleurs du Mal*, and wrote a *Vie de Poe* which Hanns Heinz Ewers, a confessed follower of Poe, translated into German. Ewers also wrote for *Die Dichtung*, Bd. 42, 1905, an appreciation of Poe and dedicated it to a fellow-admirer of Poe, Gustav Meyrick. For Ewers Poe was "der erste moderne Mensch,... ein Pionier der Kultur in dem Neuland des Unbe-wussten," a poet who recognized in the fullest sense the "par-nassische Kunstprinzip." Poe's influence operated in Europe rather than in America. Through Baudelaire, Mallarmé became interested in Poe and translated his lyrics into prose poetry. The poets of the "décadence" welcomed Poe, among them Villiers de l'Isle Adam and Barbey d'Aurevilly. Those who believe in art strictly for art's sake and the neoromanticists in general share in the type of poetry which Poe practiced and defended in theory; in England, Dante Gabriel Rossetti, Arthur Swinburne, Oscar Wilde, in Germany chiefly Stefan George and his circle.

The impact of the poetry of Poe is still effective. In his essay "The Unity of European Culture," T.S. Eliot referred to the indebtedness of himself, of Yeats, and of Rainer Maria Rilke to the French poets from Baudelaire to Valéry, but added that this French movement owed a good deal to Edgar Allan Poe. In recent times, however, interest in Poe's poetry has become secondary to interest in his prose narratives, which shall be discussed later.

Walt Whitman's reception in Germany needs to be viewed against a background of social re-orientation in North America and in Europe. Economic materialism was strong in the United

States and it coincided with the commerical upswing in Germany beginning with the "Gründerjahre" and the Bismarck era. It also coincided with the philosophic materialism of Darwin, Marx, Engels, Feuerbach, von Helmholz, Liebig, Haeckel, Nietzsche, and Strauss. At the same time a counteracting idealistic trend was less conspicuously at work. Carlyle was stimulated to enthusiastic expression by his acquaintance with the works of Schiller and Goethe, and he communicated his enthusiasm to Emerson. Through Carlyle and Emerson, and to some extent directly, Whitman was touched with Weimar's idealism. His non-partisan ministrations during the Civil War inspired in him a feeling of human brotherhood, and this coincided with the idealistic element in the upswing of the social democratic trend in Germany. Germany responded to Whitman's outpouring earlier than the United States, and set the example for a reconsideration there, but as late as 1875 Johannes Scheer, in his *Allgemeine Geschichte der Literatur*, disposed of Whitman with the sentence: "Walt Whitman, in welchem... die eine Hälfte seiner Landsleute einen grossen Dichter, die andere einen grossen Narren sieht." In a footnote Scheer continued:

> Whitman scheint der Meinung zu sein, die Verachtung von Gesetz, Regel und Form sei die richtige Voraussetzung von echter Poesie. Seine *Leaves of Grass* und seine *Drum Taps*... sind in hinterwälderischen Streckversen geschrieben, welche häufig ganz rhythmuslos einherstürmen oder einhertorkeln.[11]

Theologically the views of Whitman, like those of Emerson, were compatible with the prevailing trend away from the belief in an anthropomorphic god.

Before the year 1919 the history of Whitman's acceptance in Germany was an account of non-understandings and misunderstandings. Ferdinand Freiligrath was the first to translate a selection of Whitman's poems into German. He had become acquainted with these poems during his exile in England in 1868. William Rossetti, the brother of Dante Gabriel, had published a

Whitman anthology, in which the Civil War poems, *Drum-Taps*, constituted one group. Freiligrath called attention to these poems in the *Augsburger Allgemeine Zeitung*, 1868, and published them with introductory remarks which chiefly paraphrased Rossetti's preface.[12] Freiligrath was well aware of Whitman's metrical innovation and admired it. The verses were as the surge of ocean waves; they reminded him of Ossian's metrical prose, of Carlyle's oracular periods, and of passages from the Bible. The throbs of Whitman's verses he felt would make the metrics and rhymes of traditional poetry seem puerile, but Freiligrath was unable to produce a good metrical substitute for Whitman's rhythms. It could hardly be expected that the congenial translator of Longfellow should have equal success with Whitman.

The next translator of Whitman's poetry was Freiligrath's friend, Adolf Strodtmann. His *Amerikanische Anthologie der Gegenwart*, 1870, with eight Poe selections, provided a more representative collection than Freiligrath's, but he was no more successful than his predecessor in reproducing Whitman's metrical effects, and like Freiligrath he sometimes misinterpreted his meanings. In his anthology *Unter dem Sternenbanner* Ernst Otto Hoppe, 1877, translated, or rather paraphrased, "O Captain! My Captain!" and "When Lilacs Last in the Dooryard Bloomed."

With the sanction of Whitman, the Irish critic T. W. Rolleston and the long-time German resident in America, Karl Knortz, published their translations jointly in Zürich under the title *Grashalme*, 1889. In the introduction Knortz wrote: "Die Sprache der Übersetzung wird den meisten Lesern holprig, steif und unedel vorkommen; mit den Originalen sieht es in dieser Hinsicht noch viel schlimmer aus." This statement is hardly true. The Rolleston-Knortz translation is neither in prose nor poetry, and the constructions are not consistently either German or English.

Passing over scattered translations of the remainder of the century we should note Schölermann's *Grashalme in Auswahl* and Karl Federn's *Grashalme, eine Auswahl*, both of 1904.

Schölermann was duly criticized for embellishing two of Whitman's poems with rhymes. Federn's translations were, in many instances, more poetic than those of his predecessors. By his edition of Whitman's *Prosaschriften*, 1905, Professor O. E. Lessing of the University of Illinois extended the knowledge of Whitman. Lessing's translation of "When Lilacs Last in the Dooryard Bloomed" has been recognized as "sprachlich... wie auch stilistisch dem Original in nichts nachstehend."[13] At about the same time Lessing wrote an essay defending Whitman against what he believed to be a misinterpretation of Whitman's gospel of friendship, but in 1905 Eduard Bertz, one of Whitman's earliest appreciators, published in the *Jahrbuch für sexuelle Zwischenstufen* an article entitled "Walt Whitman, ein Charakterbild"[14] and followed it with a volume called *Der Yankee Heiland*. Bertz's revelations led to a reorientation on the part of O. E. Lessing and many other admirers of Whitman. The assertion of Whitman's reputation for an all-human love was restricted by the discovery that it had no dignified place for women. In an essay of 1910, O. E. Lessing recanted much that he had said in previous essays.[15]

Bertz's *Der Yankee Heiland* established an important fact. In a chapter called "Whitman und Nietzsche" he was the first to point out that the much discussed coincidence of the views of the two went back to a common source in Novalis, transmitted to Whitman through Carlyle.

Johannes Schlaf published a selection of Whitman's poems in the Reclam edition, 1907. Critics soon discovered that he had taken over whole strophes from his predecessors, while at the same time disparaging their accomplishment. Earlier, in 1904, he had written a monograph on Whitman for *Die Dichtung*, vol. XVIII. Schlaf posed as a chief authority on Whitman. In his *Whitman-Mysterien*, 1907, Bertz exposed Schlaf as an incompetent, who had read less than fifteen percent of Whitman's writings, and those chiefly in translation. Bertz doubted that Schlaf was able to read English.

New translations of Whitman's poems continued to appear. Franz Blei published a small collection in 1914 under the title *Hymnen für die Erde*. Beginning in 1915, *Die sozialistischen Monatshefte* printed about sixty of Whitman's poems in translations by Max Hayek, Max Hochdorf, Hermann Curth, and August Brückner, notable more for their democratic enthusiasm than for their accuracy and artistic merit. About the same time Gustav Landauer issued several translations under the title *Walt Whitman, Krieg, zehn Gedichte*, 1915.

These and other translations were rendered obsolete by the translation of Hans Reisiger, 1919-1921, on which he had been quietly working since 1900. The German critics hailed his achievement. Hermann Stahr said: "Reisigers Übersetzung wirkt wie das Original, wirklich so, als habe der grosse Amerikaner nicht in englischer sondern in deutscher Sprache gedichtet."[16] *The Kunstwart* exclaimed: "Walt Whitman ist entdeckt. Ein deutscher Dichter hat ihn entdeckt. Gespürt, geahnt, gerühmt, auf ihre Art übersetzt haben ihn schon viele. Doch Hans Reisiger hat ihn entdeckt und erobert."[17]

Nearly all publications of Whitman's works in Germany were linked with critical estimates of the poet, mirroring the ebb and flow of German social and political thought more accurately than they portray Whitman's message. Rolleston and Knortz, from 1880 to 1889, proclaimed Whitman as "Der Dichter der Demokratie." Eduard Bertz said much the same in 1889. Widmann in 1889 compared him with Jacob Boehme and Angelus Silesius.[18] In 1896, Johannes Schlaf compared him with Nietzsche, in 1910 rather with Jesus of Nazareth,[19] in agreement with the Bostonian, R. M. Bucke, who had published Whitman's war letters in 1898. Such comparisons were by no means stopped by the revelations of Bertz, 1905, mentioned above. From 1914 on Whitman was much celebrated as "Der Sänger des Krieges" especially by the Social Democrats, who counted him as one of themselves: "Wenn wir Sozialismus mit Gemeinschaft übersetzen und Demokratie mit Freiheit, so ist er der beste und wahrhafteste Sozialdemokrat

The reference is to the collection *Auf Erden*, 1904/1905. Paquet added however:

> Der freie Rhythmus, der Prosa-Vers, hatte mich schon beschäftigt, ehe ich eine Zeile von Whitman kannte. Von allen diesen formalen künstlerischen Dingen abgesehen, ist für mich Whitman der ganz grosse Freund und Bruder des amerikanischen Menschen.

The relationship of Arno Holz to Walt Whitman has been recorded by Holz himself. Independently of Whitman he had developed his theory of poetry as expounded in his *Revolution der Lyrik*, 1899. He read Freiligrath's translations and received no impression whatever from them. But in 1889 he read the selections of Rolleston and Knortz and reported:

> Und jetzt erst wirkte Walt Whitman selbst auf mich. Er wirkte so ungeheuer, dass ich sofort fühlte: Der Mann deckt sich so vollkommen mit seiner Art; was mit ihr zu erreichen war, ist durch ihn so erreicht worden, dass es purer Wahnwitz wäre, an diesen Weg auch nur einen Schritt zu verlieren. Damit war für mich als Künstler Walt Whitman erledigt.[29]

Holz's admiration for Whitman as "Mensch" was unbounded. He lent his copy of Whitman's poems to his friends, among them Gerhart Hauptmann, who found them "unverdaulich" and his optimism "pathologisch" and also to Schlaf, whose enthusiasm resulted in mere imitation. Holz was convinced that rhyme and traditional metrics no longer had a place in modern poetry. New rhythms must take their place, but he felt that Whitman had not solved the problem. He regarded the influence on his friend Johann Schlaf as deleterious. In the poem "Dingsda," Holz found no trace of Whitman's influence, but in the poem "Frühling," which appeared shortly afterward, 1893, it is there in full force. Holz said: "Diese Dichtung schätze ich ausserordentlich, aber sie ist nicht mehr Schlaf, sondern Schlaf minus Whitman. Plus lässt sich in diesem Fall nicht sagen."[30] He correctly saw that Schlaf's merit was in the field of "Kleinmalerei" and not adapted to the cosmic range of Whitman's poetry. Thomas Mann's discovery of Walt Whitman, through the translations of Reisiger, was a decisive revelation to him. In the *Frankfurter Zeitung* he wrote an open letter to Reisiger, saying

> Für mich persönlich, der ich innerlich um die Idee der Humanität seit Jahr und Tag mit der mir eigenen Langsamkeit bemüht bin,... ist dies Werk ein wahres Gottesgeschenk, denn ich sehe wohl, dass, was Whitman "Demokratie" nennt, nichts anderes ist, als was wir altmodischer "Humanität" nennen; wie ich auch sehe, dass es mit Goethe allein denn doch nicht getan wird, sondern dass ein Schuss Whitman dazu gehört, um das Gefühl der neuen Humanität zu gewinnen.[31]

In his notable address "Von deutscher Republik," 1923, Thomas Mann retraces his way from Goethean humanism through Novalis to a humanism with a "Schuss" of Whitman democracy.[32] Then came his determination to become a self-appointed cultural ambassador, to explain America to the Germans, and Germany to the Americans. In so doing he became interested in the planned economy of the welfare state and thought of Joseph as an earlier "provider." In view of its subject-matter, the several Americanisms in the Joseph Legends are appropriate.[33]

In one passage the indebtedness of Thomas Mann to Walt Whitman is distinctly concrete. Whitman wrote a poem "I Sing the Body Electric" (a portion of the poem *Children of Adam*), in which he insisted that body and soul were one, that body *was* soul, and that body, love, and death were inseparable. In the poem "Scented Heritage of My Breast" Whitman wrote, as translated by Reisiger and quoted by Mann in his essay *Von deutscher Republik:*

> So gib mir deinen Ton, O Tod, dass ich danach stimme,
> gib mir dich selbst, denn ich sehe, dass du mir vor allen gehörst
> und dass ihr untrennbar verschlungen seid, Tod und Liebe.

In German translation, "The Song of Myself" begins with the assertion: "Wenn irgend etwas heilig ist, so ist der menschliche Körper heilig," and then proceeds to name one after another about a hundred anatomical portions. The chapter "Walpurgisnacht" in the *Zauberberg* records an interview between Hans Castorp and Clawdia Chauchat. The conversation is chiefly in French. After trivialities are over, Castorp begins "Oh, l'amour, tu sais,... Le corps, l'amour, la mort, ces trois ne font qu'un" and then, in a page-long paragraph, he proceeds to name different parts of the body, but with a modicum of restraint. Of Whitman's hundred specifications, about thirty remain.[34]

Of the later American poets Carl Sandburg seems closest to Whitman. His verse forms are reminiscent of Whitman's and he is as closely oriented to Chicago and the Illinois of Abraham Lincoln as Whitman to New York and the Civil War.

At about 1900 a new trend in poetry became evident. The new poets learned to make use of all available resources – assonance, meter, verse, alliteration, rhyme and repetition, whatever supported the mood of the moment. The movement owed much to the French *vers libre*. The polyphonic form was employed among others by Amy Lowell, Vachel Lindsay, Ezra Pound and the Imagists.

American anthologies have appeared, several of them devoted to translations of individual American poets in about this sequence: Masters, Dickinson, Faulkner, Doolittle, Frost, William C. Williams. It may be that these poems in translation made little impression on the German public as a whole, but they were appreciated by the critics. F. Schönemann [516] admired especially the work of Edwin Arlington Robinson. To his essay on Robinson Schönemann appended a translation of "Richard Cory" by Toni Harten-Hoenke (Mrs. Schönemann).

---

[1] The following evaluations are by Roehm [2].
[2] See above, p. 70.
[3] Locher [65] 239.

[4] *Ibid.*, 245.
[5] Krumpelmann [240] 180-182.
[6] Kühnelt [231] 197.
[7] Max Bense, *Literaturmetaphysik*, Stuttgart, 1950, 26-29; 68-71, 88-91; Hans Egon Holthusen, *Das lyrische Kunstwerk*, Berlin, 1951, p. 962.
[8] Locher [65] 269 f.
[9] Mitchell [234] vs. Cobb [233].
[10] Kühnelt [231] 197 f.
[11] *Op. cit.*, 5 ed., 1575, II 115.
[12] *Loc. cit.*, May 10, 1868; Freiligrath, *Gesammelte Dichtungen*, IV, 75 f.
[13] Law-Robertson [526] 20, 22.
[14] *Loc. cit.*, VII (1), 1905.
[15] Lessing [518].
[16] *Vossische Zeitung*, Nov. 17, 1919; Law-Robertson [526] 30.
[17] *Loc. cit.*, XXXVI, Feb. 1923. In 1947 appeared two further collections of translations, one by Elisabeth and Walther Küchler and one by Max Geilinger.
[18] MFLA, XXXVIII (1889), 584.
[19] Law-Robertson [526] 41, 46.
[20] A. Siemsen in *Freie Jugend*, I (1), 1919; Law-Robertson [526] 71.
[21] H. Eulenberg, *Erscheinungen*, 1923.
[22] Jacobson [524].
[23] Neue Freie Presse, Wien, 28. III. 1918.
[24] *Zeitschrift für neusprachlichen Unterricht;* At the same time Schönemann called attention to Whitman's poems translated by Toni Harten-Hoenke [i.e. Frau Schönemann] in her collection *Amerikanische Lyrik*, 1935.
[25] Schumann [528]
[26] Schumann [529].
[27] Law-Robertson [526] 69.
[28] *Ibid.*, 46, 27.
[29] Arno Holz, *Werke*, Berlin, 1924, X, 301.
[30] *Ibid.*, 302.
[31] *Loc. cit.*, April 16, 1922.
[32] *Op. cit.*, in Thomas Mann's *Bemühungen*. Berlin, 1925, 166.
[33] Suhl [294].
[34] Hunt [540].

From the above it can be seen that before 1820 the Germans were aware of many American works of worthy content and couched in suitable style, but nearly all of them of political tendency. Few works of belletristic intent were translated. One of the few was Charles Brockden Brown's *Ormond or the Secret Witness*, 1790 (German, 1802), another was *The Adventures of Alonzo* by Mr. Digges of Warburton, "a native of Maryland," 1775 (German, 1787),[1] but long after political independence was gained America remained colonial in respect to literature, and Sidney Smith was well justified in asking in the *Edinburgh Review*, January, 1820: "Who reads an American book?"[2]

The appearance of Irving and Cooper provided a prompt answer to this disparaging question. On closer examination, the mild reputation of Irving preceded the popularity of Cooper by a few months. The London *Literary Gazette* reprinted some portions of the *Sketch Book* in 1819, which were promptly translated by the *Morgenblatt für gebildete Stände*, and Jeffrey's praise of Irving in the *Edinburgh Review*, August 1820, was also noted in the *Morgenblatt* and other less known journals. The German journals accepted the English view that Irving belonged to the school of Addison, Goldsmith, and Mackenzie.

A French translation of *Bracebridge Hall*, 1822, was widely read in Germany, and Irving found himself favorably known in Dresden on his arrival there in that year. Irving's friends stated that he had a good command of the German language at the time. This was an opinion which Irving himself shared. The account of his stay in Germany is a story of missed opportunities to talk with men of letters of high importance. His leading translator and advocate in Germany was Heinrich Spirer of the Royal Library in Berlin, and his best friend and adviser was the archeologist Böttiger in Dresden.[3]

The much read French journal, *Le Globe*, published in 1825 a survey of American literature, which commented on Irving's excellent literary style; but two years later it took exception to his preference for pictures of English life and his neglect of the American scene. For this reason it favored Cooper over Irving. Goethe's poem "Amerika, du hast es besser" signifies agreement with this judgment. We know, however, that before this time Goethe had read "The Legend of Sleepy Hollow" with pleasure.[4]

The appearance of such a work as *Bracebridge Hall* by an American caused astonishment in Europe, Willibald Alexis regarded it as proof that the poetic spirit is inborn and can gain victory over untoward conditions.[5] The British journal *The Athenaeum* published an appreciation of Irving's work, which the *Blätter für literarische Unterhaltung* translated and quoted with approval.

> Den Irving'schen Skizzen ist . . . ein fast unbeschreiblicher Reiz eigen. Der Inhalt läuft oft fast auf nichts aus, aber die Kunst der humoristischen holländischen Genremalerei bis ins Kleinste mit dem sorgfältigsten Pinsel und im klassischsten Sprachkolorit geführt, besitzt auf literarischem Gebiet wol keiner in solchem Grad wie Washington Irving.[6]

The German journals reviewed Irving's accounts of the exploration in Western America as they appeared, but despite *A Tour of the Prairies*, *Astoria*, and the *Adventures of Captain Bonneville*, Irving did not become a typical American author in the opinion of the critics, but rather a genteel expatriate. The reviewer of *Astoria* stressed the fact that Irving's grace was more than a veneer. "Irving has freed himself from the vulgar trends of his fatherland through the acquisition of a high intellectual culture; the national in him has become ennobled."[7]

The *Life and Voyages of Christopher Columbus* was called a "historisches Kunstwerk" and its sequel, *The Voyages of the Companions of Columbus* was favorably reviewed, but Willibald Alexis was unable to commend Irving's Spanish histories. *The Chronicle of the Conquest of Granada* was interesting reading, but poor history.[8] *Alhambra* was written with grace and charm, but is lacking in substantial content. Alexis insisted that he was and remained a genre painter, as exemplified by his best works, *The Sketch Book* and *Bracebridge Hall*.

One of the earliest German writers to voice his approval of Irving was Heinrich Heine. Like Irving before him, he used as a guide-book Gottschall's *Taschenbuch für Reisende in den Harz* for his trip in 1824. Of his *Harzreise* Heine wrote: "Das Hübsche-ste, was ich unterdessen schrieb, ist die Beschreibung einer Harz-reise, die ich vorigen Herbst gemacht, eine Mischung von Natur-schilderung, Witz, Poesie und Washington Irving'scher Be-obachtung."[9] Heine's *Harzreise* could vie with *The Sketch Book* and *Bracebridge Hall* in every respect excepting unfailing good humor.

Wilhelm Hauff took amiss his own countrymen's disparage-ment of German writers. The popular expression ever and again was: "Es ist doch nicht so schön als Walter Scott und Cooper und nicht so tief und witzig als Washington Irving." Translations and reprints were in such demand and production that he could say, "es ist, als ob Scott und Irving in Frankfurt oder Leipzig lebten."[10] Nevertheless Hauff was one of the heaviest borrowers of characters and incidents from Irving. The *Phantasien im Bremer Ratskeller, Jud Süss*, and *Das kalte Herz* borrow from "Rip van Winkle" and "The Legend of Sleepy Hollow." *The Inn at Terracine* provides a framework for travelers' tales just as does *Das Wirtshaus im Spessart*. "The Devil and Tom Walker" suggests a similar confrontation in *Das kalte Herz*. Other stories of Irving, "The Belated Travelers" and "The Painter's Adventure," gave further suggestions to Hauff. "The Mysterious Stranger" is a predecessor of "Der Man im Monde."[11]

Fritz Reuter was a chary borrower from Washington Irving. It is quite certain that his *Urgeschicht von Mekelnborg* was written as a parody of a "Chronik" by D. Franck rather than as an imitation of *Knickerbocker's History of New York*, which may have been used incidentally – but the *Abenteuer des Entspektor Bräsig* has one incident modeled upon an episode in *Knickerbocker's History*. One can compare the newspaper advertisements for the recovery of Onkel Levi with the similar search for Knickerbocker.[12]

Wilhelm Raabe was an admiring reader of contemporary English fiction. He read the works of Dickens and of Thackeray, but also of Washington Irving, "dessen milder und gemütvoller Humor," as his biographer says, "dem deutschen und Raabe'-schen eigentlich näher steht als der oft scharfe und grobdrähtige der englischen Satiriker."[13] There are references and situations in *Die Kinder von Finkenrode*, in *Abu Telfan*, and in *Die Leute aus dem Walde* which affirm his mindfulness of "Rip van Winkle" and of *Bracebridge Hall*. Raabe's *Der Student von Wittenberg* and Irving's *The Student of Salamanca* both deal with the theme of love threatened by intolerance.[14]

Annette von Droste-Hülshoff wrote to a friend of her earnest intention, "ein ellenlanges Buch im Geschmacke von *Bracebridgehall* auf Westfalen angewendet zu schreiben."[15] The theme was highly suitable, since in many respects the features of life in her own Westphalia resembled those in rural England. *Bracebridge Hall* describes the lower aristocracy, the gentry, the tenants with their superstitions, and the servants on an English estate as viewed through the eyes of a guest. *Bei uns zu Lande auf dem Lande* follows the same pattern, and the persons seen in the Westphalian house correspond in status with those in Bracebridge Hall. They were even to be introduced in much the same sequence. The book remained uncompleted, partly because the portraiture was so exact that it might have given offense, and partly for another reason: "Die Manier Washington Irvings und einiger französischer Genremaler hatte doch mehr auf mich influiert als ich mir bewusst war, und keine Manier hält vor."[16]

Charles Sealfield's *Lebensbilder aus der westlichen Hemisphäre,* 1835, contains many sketches of American life in the manner of Irving. His *Cajütenbuch,* 1847, owes much to *Bracebridge Hall* and to *Astoria,* as well as to works by other American authors. *Christophoros Bärenhäuter in Amerikaland* treats of German and Irish settlers in America with much of the gentle humor of *Knickerbocker's History of New York.*

Irving's *Sketch Book* is one of the most widely known works of American literature in Germany. In English language-instruction it has about the same "selbstverständlich" initial position which Storm's *Immensee,* of like "genteel tradition," long held in American schools. Thus the German youth had before it an example of the best American English as defined by Noah Webster.

The novels of James Fenimore Cooper appeared in German translation a few months later than the sketches of Washington Irving, but they had from the outset a wider appeal to the Europeans. *The Pioneers* and *The Spy* were translated into German in 1824, and other works followed closely. Cooper did not invent his formula, but wrote under the spell of Chateaubriand's *René* with its romantic conception of the unspoiled savage and the beauty of life close to nature's heart. From his own observation Cooper was also able to add realistic touches to the prevailing concept of the noble Indian and to describe the nature of the contact of red man and white man.

Cooper's success in Germany began with his first novels, and he maintained his popularity for a century in only slightly diminishing degree. Every year from 1824 to 1914 Germans brought forth new editions of his works in German translation or in the English original.[17] The works were of unequal merit and unequal popularity. A critic noted in 1834:

85

So oft Cooper die Wälder und die Meere schildert, kann ihm niemand zur Seite gesetzt werden. Niemals hat ein Schriftsteller die Naturszene mit so grosser Kraft, mit so viel Glück und Wahrheit dargestellt... Alles ist Handlung, Charakter, Poesie. Er ist unvergleichlich, wenn er die Sprache der Indianer und wenn er das Leben in der Wüste beschreibt.[18]

German critics were still wont, rightly or wrongly, to regard American literature as a branch of the English. As they connected Irving's *Sketch Book* with Addison's and Goldsmith's journals, so they now frequently assumed that Cooper was a follower of Walter Scott. But one critic declared:

Er Walterscottisiert nicht; urtümlich und frei betritt er das von seinem Vorbilde neugebahnte Gebiet; copiert nicht seine Manier und Darstellungsweise; sein Geistiges nur hat er in sich aufgenommen und dieses Geistige tritt in selbständiger Kraft aus ihm hervor.[19]

One of the early readers of Cooper's novels was Goethe, who saw the reports of Hüttner to Karl August and the notices in the French reviews. *Le Globe* called Goethe's attention to Cooper in 1826. By the end of the year Goethe had read all the novels so far translated – *The Pioneers, The Last of the Mohicans, The Spy* and *The Pilot*. Here ad *The Prairie* the following year, and in 1828 *The Red Rover*. On the 30th of September 1826, Goethe recorded the reading of *The Pioneers* and added some "Betrachtungen über den Roman überhaupt." On October 1st, he noted in his diary: "Den Cooperschen Roman zum zweiten Mal angefangen... Auch das Kunstreiche daran näher betrachtet, geordnet und fortgesetzt." The 15th and 16th of October were divided between reading *The Last of the Mohicans* and work on the *Novelle*, the 24th of October between the reading of *The Spy* and work on the "Schema zum Manne von fünfzig Jahren." The next summer the readings were resumed, e.g., June 24, 1827: "*Die Wanderjahre* bedacht. Den ersten Teil des Romans [*The Prairie*] ausgelesen."[20] June 26: "Las den Cooper'schen Roman bis gegen das Ende und bewunderte den reichen Stoff und dessen Behandlung. Nicht leicht sind Werke mit so grossem Bewusstsein und solcher Consequenz durchgeführt wie die Cooper'schen Romane."[21]

In an essay entitled "Stoff und Gehalt zur Bearbeitung vorgeschlagen" (1827) Goethe sketched a concrete outline for any ambitious young author:

> Die Hauptfigur, der protestantische Geistliche, der, selbst auswanderungslustig, die Auswandernden an's Meer und dann hinüber führt und oft an Moses in den Wüsten erinnern würde, müsste eine Art von Doktor Primrose sein, der mit so viel Verstand als gutem Willen, mit so viel Bildung als Thätigkeit bei allem, was er unternimmt und fördert, doch immer nicht weiss, was er thut, von seiner "ruling passion" fortgetrieben, dasjenige, was er sich vorsetzte, durchzuführen genötigt wird, und erst am Ende zu Atmen kommt, wenn zu gränzenlosem Unverstand und unübersehbarem Unheil sich zuletzt noch ein ganz leidliches Dasein hervorthut.

But Goethe warned: "Der Bearbeitende müsste den Stolz haben, mit Cooper zu wetteifern, und deshalb die klarste Einsicht in jene überseeischen Gegenstände zu gewinnen suchen."[22]

Many years earlier, about the year 1797, Goethe was occupied with a narrative tentatively to be called "Eine Löwen- und Tigergeschichte" or "Die Jagd." He let the plan rest for a time until the reading of *The Pioneers* stimulated him to take up the theme again and to complete it under the title *Novelle*. It has been pointed out that there is a close resemblance between Goethe's work and Cooper's not only in the landscape background and the grouping of characters, but also in their manner of speaking.[23]

In *Wilhelm Meisters Wanderjahre* Lothario returns to Europe with the conviction: "Hier oder nirgends ist Amerika," but later he plans to lead a group of chosen followers to America. His experiences would need to be related in a novel to be called *Wilhelm Meisters Meisterjahre*, which the octogenarian Goethe seems to have contemplated, but not too hopefully. In such a novel he would have needed the courage at times to vie with Cooper, but for this he was equipped, as few other Germans of his time, with acquaintance of America's physical characteristics and of American conditions of life. Goethe's reports on the progress of *Wilhelm Meister* are combined with the reading of Cooper's novels, as the *Tages- und Jahreshefte* for the years 1826-1827 show.

At various times in his life Goethe contemplated, perhaps not very seriously, emigration to America. The earliest occasion was at the time of his involvement with Lili Schönemann, as already related.[24] To Sulpiz Boisserée, Goethe once wondered "was möchte daraus geworden sein, wenn ich mit wenigen Freunden vor dreissig Jahren nach Amerika gegangen wäre."[25] To Cogswell he remarked in 1819: "Wären wir zwanzig Jahre jünger, so segelten wir noch nach Amerika,"[26] but to Eckerman in 1827: "Ich danke dem Himmel, dass ich jetzt in dieser durchaus gemachten Zeit nicht jung bin. Ich würde nicht zu bleiben wissen. Ja selbst wenn ich nach Amerika flüchten wollte, ich käme zu spät, denn auch dort wäre es schon zu helle."[27] Goethe also had a clear vision of the future development of America. As early as 1827 he foresaw the crossing of the North American continent, the establishment of cities on the Pacific coast, and the thrust of the canal through the Isthmus of Panama.[28]

Cooper's novels came into Germany's view at a rather favorable time. The German novelists could offer but little competition. The chief rival for favor was Walter Scott, and next in importance were historical novels after the manner of Scott, such as Tieck's *Der Aufruhr in den Cevennen*, 1826, *Der wiederkehrende griechische Kaiser*, 1830, and *Der Hexen-Sabbath*, 1832, Willibald Alexis' *Walladmor*, 1823, and his succeeding novels, and Hauff's *Lichtenstein*, 1825. Of these, Hauff's novel was the most popular. In his *Studie*, written in 1826, Hauff refers to the popularity of Walter Scott and "die beiden Amerikaner." It has been observed that there is a close resemblance between the figure of Hauff's

Pfeiffer von Hardt and that of Harvey Birch in Cooper's *Spy*, 1822 (German, 1824), and that the two characters play a similar role.[29] There is also the situation, favored by Cooper, of friendship and love between men and women on opposite sides of the struggle, and the rescuing and succoring of opponents by the heroes. Walter Scott was probably the most widely read novelist of the twenties and it was natural, though not wholly justifiable, to dub the historical novelist Cooper, "the American Walter Scott."

There were of course differences of opinion regarding the merits of Cooper's novels. Nearly all the critics regarded as Cooper's chief success the pictures of the American landscape, some calling them romantic, others realistic. It was agreed at home and abroad that *The Pilot* was the truest to reality of Cooper's novels, for he was an experienced sailor and when he left the land for the sea he was on firm footing. It was also agreed that Cooper's chief merit was that he laid the scene of his early novels in America. His later European novels were either disregarded or condemned. His pictures of the American Indian were much admired and were at first generally regarded as accurate. Later the quality of his ethnology was called into question, but Eduard Engel in 1883 agreed with Cooper that it is the privilege of the novelist to idealize his heroes.[30] There are several generally admitted faults in Cooper's work. A certain political intolerance, for example a hostility to England, detracts from his admirable love of liberty. His women characters lack liveliness; they are self-sacrificing, courageous, steadfast, free from passion, colorless, and scarcely distinguishable one from another. Cooper's writing is careless, sometimes faulty in syntax. His works are loose in composition, but interest is held by the swift action and the effectual use of suspense. The most popular of his works in Germany have been *The Last of the Mohicans, The Spy*, and *The Pilot*.[31] Cooper still holds his place as the most translated American novelist or narrator followed by Edgar Allan Poe, Mark Twain, Upton Sinclair, Jack London, Pearl Buck, Bret Harte, Washington Irving, and Zane Grey.[32]

Cooper's novels are still in great demand in Germany, but by a changed public. In the earliest years the novels were read in good part for their informative value. The Germans of the time, often with the thought of emigration in their minds, appreciated social studies of American life. This interest, in course of time, became less lively, but, beginning about 1865, his works became boys' books. Between 1862 and 1900 two thirds out of one hundred editions of his novels were edited chiefly for the use of the youth and even of younger children. In the field of the sea and exotic novel the works of Mayne Reid vied with Cooper's, then came Karl May, who offered his readers thrilling adventures on lands and seas he had never seen. There has existed in Germany a far flung Karl May society, but no corresponding Cooper club has made itself known.

Soon after the publication of Cooper's earliest works, German authors began producing numerous pioneer novels bearing in various degrees traces of Cooper's influence. Among these may be mentioned Karl Postl (pen name Charles Sealsfield), Strubberg, Möllhausen, Gerstäcker, Ruppius, and Johannes Scheer. Of these the most important was Sealsfield.

Karl Postl (1793-1861) was an Austrian monk, who, tiring of his bonds, took refuge in Switzerland, where he wrote a book attacking Metternich, and was compelled again to flee (1822). The next eight years he spent in America, which he revisited in 1837, 1850, and 1853-1858. As early as 1857 Sealsfield was extolling American institutions, and as late as 1862, while resident in Germany, he was referring to America as his country, and he prescribed to be written on his tombstone "Charles Sealsfield, Bürger von Nordamerika."

Sealsfield claimed to be as realistic as the recently invented photography. He asserted that he had visited Louisiana three times and Mexico once. This last claim is not sufficiently verified. His first-hand knowledge of America has often been doubted, for his Negroes are caricatures, his Indians idealizations, and his

90

pictures of American life and character too roseate to be plausible. But despite recent challenges, it would appear that his observations were often accurate.[33] For his plots, and quite particularly for his local color, he drew upon Cooper, Irving, and certain lessknown Americans of the time. Sealsfield once asserted that not Cooper but Walter Scott gave direction to his novels. In an exchange of letters with Cooper, he differentiated his methods in some particulars from those of his rival.[34]

Cooper's novels did not meet entirely with Sealsfield's favor. *The Pilot*, he said, was best, for Cooper had had experience on the sea, but his feminine characters were uninteresting, his Indians were too sophisticated, his knowledge of them was second hand, and Natty Bumppo, the trapper, was too loquacious. Cooper, he said, undertook to describe a trapper without ever having known one. Much the same might be said of Sealsfield, his heroines and his Indians.

Sealsfield's first novel, *Tokeah or the White Rose*, written in English, 1828, after he had been in America six years, might be taken as an attempt to vie with Cooper. The revision and continuation, *Der Legitime und die Republikaner*, 1833, like most of his later works, was written in German and showed that he had intentions more ambitious than Cooper's. He thought of novels after the manner of Mme. de Staël's *Corinne ou l'Italie*, not slightly retrospective novels such as Scott's and Cooper's, but with a nation rather than an individual as a chief center of interest - novels dealing with the whole past and present panorama, and suggesting the developments of the future.

For Sealsfield's novels, personal observation was the chief source, although from time to time he did not scorn to draw upon other authors. His Nathan Strong, the Squatter, in *Lebensbilder aus zwei Hemisphären*, 1834-1837, has some characteristics in common with Natty Bumppo, and Sealsfield also borrowed from less well known American novelists and travelers. Some of these have been identified, others not; for example, one critic regarded Irving's *Astoria* as the source of an episode in *Das*

Cajütenbuch, a second found the source in the anonymous *A Journey to Texas,* while a third ventured the suggestion that Postl himself was the author of the *Journey.*[35]

A particular interest attaches to Sealsfield's language. Not only in reporting conversation but in narrative and description his sentences are full of American words and American constructions. Sealsfield adopted his style deliberately. He maintained that primitive German had allowed itself to be corrupted first with Latin, then with French forms, while English, however much infused with words of French origin, remained fundamentally Anglo-Saxon-Danish-Germanic. His own German, he said, was more Germanic than "latinisiertes gelehrtes Deutsch."[36] Sealsfield's proposed language reform has frequently been examined and with varying severity, condemned,[37] but need not concern us here, since no later German novelist has adopted his manner.

About the middle of the century a new group of novelists appeared who, like Cooper and Sealsfield, treated of Indians, settlers, and trappers. Strubberg was a frontiersman and colonizing agent, Möllhausen a scientist and explorer, Gerstäcker was, as need arose, a jack of all trades but chiefly a traveler, Scheer was a literary historian, and Ruppius a musician. Strubberg wrote over sixty volumes of novels, Möllhausen and Gerstäcker each over one hundred and fifty, and Ruppius over twenty.[38] Scheer deserves mention on account of one admirable novel.[39]

Friedrich Armand Strubberg (1806-1889) was compelled to leave Germany on account of a duel. He spent several years in America. From 1846 to 1854 he served in a German settlement in Texas and was familiar with frontier life. He had direct knowledge of Indians, their manner of life, and their characteristics. Some of his sketches are drastically realistic, but to introduce romance into his novels he also invented some Indians of the Chateaubriand-Cooper type. Like Cooper and like Sealsfield in his novel *Tokeah*, Strubberg showed his sympathy with the dying race (*Ralph Norwood*, 1860).[40]

Baldwin Möllhausen (1825-1905) participated in several explorations in America, first with Duke Paul of Württemberg to the Rocky Mountains, 1850, then as a topographer in a government expedition conducted by Lieutenant Whipple to find the nearest route for a railroad to the Pacific, 1853, and yet again as an assistant to Lieutenant Ives, explorer of the Colorado River, 1857. Möllhausen knew the broad span of the American territory as no other German of the time. He could describe the rougher elements of life on the frontier, but could not restrain his romanticism. His artistic sense led him sometimes to prefer idealized pictures of the Indians. His exotic novels of America are among the best of his time. He too wrote feelingly of the dying races (*Wildes Blut*, 1856; *Die Söldlinge*, 1892).[41]

Friedrich Wilhelm Christian Gerstäcker (1816-1872) fled from a dreary future as a businessman in Germany and came to America in 1837, remaining until 1843. He tarried at various times in New York, Cincinnati, St. Louis, and New Orleans, eking out a meagre existence with often menial occupations and sometimes depending on the charity of acquaintances. His life in the cities was least tolerable; he was happiest as a hunter and seller of pelts in Arkansas. On his return to Germany he recounted his adventures in *Streif- und Querzüge durch die Vereinigten Staaten von Amerika*, 1844, in order to let prospective emigrants profit from his experiences. He warned against roseate hopes of an easy life and quickly gained riches. America was only for emigrants ready to endure hardships. In Gerstäcker's scale of values, the frontiersman held the highest place, and far below him were the grubby German city dwellers and the sharp and dishonest Yankees. He had opportunity to see at close hand the despoiled Indian and could picture him realistically; but he sometimes also introduced the idealized Cooper Indian for romantic effect. In later travels to the New World he visited Mexico, South America, and the South Seas. He mingled travel descriptions with narratives, and was one of the most popular representatives of the exotic novel. It has recently been pointed out that he made use of the town of Combs in the Ozarks as the setting for his *Germelshausen*,[42] the Gerstäcker novel best known in America.

Otto Ruppius (1819-1864), a journalist in Berlin, in 1848 was condemned to imprisonment on account of an article published in his paper. He fled to America, gained a small fortune as a musician, lost it in a fire in 1853, and then began a successful literary career, the best-known products of which are *Der Pedlar*, 1857, and *Das Vermächtnis des Pedlars*, 1859. When an amnesty was declared in Prussia, he returned to his fatherland in 1861. From this time on until his death in 1864 he produced novels on American life in rapid succession. He professed little knowledge of the Indian or of frontier life, but he had studied well and almost too sympathetically the German settler, who invariably appears as a paragon of virtue and industry and stands in marked contrast to the dishonest Yankee exploiter. His works did much to perpetuate the pattern for German novels about America. Ruppius wrote only one "Wild West" novel, *Der Prärieteufel*, 1861, and in this he was the most dependent on Cooper.[43]

Johannes Scheer (1817-1886), author of the well known *Allgemeine Geschichte der Weltliteratur*, 1851 (eleventh edition, 1926), was a liberal representative for Württemberg at the time of the Revolution of 1848. In 1849 he fled to Switzerland and became a professor at Zürich. He wrote many novels, one of which was *Die Pilger der Wildnis*, 1853. Like Cooper's *The Wept of Wishton-Wish*, this novel has as its background King Philip's War. Scheer's novel, however, has an entirely different interest – the struggle for religious independence. Roger Williams is a character in the novel. Other important characters, real or fictitious, are Miles Standish and the trapper Grote Willem.

Almost indispensable in the romantic pioneer novel are the trapper and the noble Indian, and the trappers are often but slight variations of Natty Bumppo with the same characteristic

94

pose, leaning on their long rifles. This is true of Grote Willem in Scheer's *Die Pilger der Wildnis* and of Nathan Strong, "der Squattor Regulator," in Sealsfield's novel of that name, 1837. Such a figure is also old Gregor in Stifter's *Hochwald* (1842): "Der alte Jäger stand auf seine Büchse nach vorn gelehnt, wie ein Standbild und keine Fiber an ihm verriet, was in ihm vorgehen könnte." Cooper and Stifter are alike in their reverence for the silent forest. One critic has said that it was Cooper's example which loosed Stifter's tongue, and concludes: "Durch Coopers Eingreifen ist aus einem mittelmässigen Maler ein hervorragender Dichter geworden."[44]

As time went on, the noble Indian became more and more a questionable figure. Fanny Lewald and the Gräfin Ida Hahn-Hahn began their literary careers as rival adherents of "Das Junge Deutschland," but the countess became ever more aristocratic. Fanny Lewald was moved to parody her as Diogena in a novel of the same name, 1847. Diogena is a late descendant of Diogenes, and she undertakes a mission to find a real man. Her wanderings bring her to America, but the search is long: "Man muss jetzt in Amerika lange reisen," she says, "ehe man Wilden begegnet. Die Welt ist terribel civiliziert, nirgends mehr ein Zug lieblicher Sauvagerie." Finally she finds a chief of unspoiled grandeur. Pausing only to pick up her lorgnette and "sal volatile" she follows him on his march silently, for the Indians do not tolerate chatter. She then enters his tent, addresses him in his Delaware language and offers to be his wife, but when he discovers that she can neither cook nor fetch him pails of water, he sends the disillusioned Diogena away. "Mir schauderte vor dieser unbezwingbaren Rohheit," she exclaims, "O! wo blieben meine Hoffnungen? Was fand ich in dieser horriblen Realität von den Idealen Coopers?"[45]

However much they differed in other respects, the writers of pioneer life were alike in their regrets over the tragedy of the dying race. Both Scheer and Sealsfield quote Thomas Jefferson: "Ich zittere für mein Volk, wenn ich der Ungerechtigkeiten gedenke, deren es sich gegen die Ureinwohner schuldig gemacht hat." The noble, despoiled American Indian was an object which aroused the indignation of the poets. Best known of the many poems on the subject are Schiller's "Nadowessiers Totenlied," Seume's "Der Wilde," Lenau's "Der Indianerzug" and "Die drei Indianer," and Freiligrath's "Audubon."

Among the hopeful novels of the time, *Die Europamüden,* 1838, of Ernst Adolf Willkomm is particularly representative. A group of citizens are gathered together at Köln. The group includes a clergyman, a scholar, a merchant, a monk, and a Jew. The author presents pictures or caricatures of all. They inveigh against the dull restrictions of effete Europe and the unhealthy state of politics, religion, and social life hampering all good progress. The leader of the group, Sigismund, may well have derived his vision of America from the accounts of Sealsfield and Zschokke. He would infuse German "Gemüt" and German "Glaubenskräftigkeit" into American life. A new race would arise with German blood and German perseverance, and this new race would then return to revitalize Germany. An American, Burton, joins the group. He has been in Germany two years and has discovered that the Germans in their homeland lack the vigor and enthusiasm of the citizens of the States. The group is contemplating emigration. Burton manly, unaffected, cheerful, honest, and impressive represents the best of the American pioneers. He gives them encouragement and good advice: only if the emigrants are ready to work and to endure hardships can they hope for success. They should seek their fortunes not in the already well-settled valleys of the Hudson, Delaware, Susquehanna, and Connecticut, but rather in the untouched expanses of Tennessee, Ohio, Indiana, and Illinois. Burton is uncultured in the European sense, and to his compatriots he admits the fact, but the faults and vices of "Unkultur" are fraught with more hope of progress than the feeble "Überkultur" of Europe. At the end of the novel the bolder members of the group embark for America and Willkomm promises to continue his account of their adventures if sufficiently urged by his friends. No second part appeared.

Nathaniel Hawthorne fared well with the German critics and literary historians who regularly placed him in the list of the five greatest American literary figures (Neukirch, 1853; Breitinger, 1868; Ahn, 1869; Federn, 1894; Bube, 1899; Schönbach, 1900). Bierbaum, quoting Lowell for support, called him the greatest imaginative writer since Shakespeare and said that *The Scarlet Letter* was by far the best American novel. Schönbach said Hawthorne was one of the great personalities of world literature, greater than Poe. Johanna Bube, in 1899, called him the greatest American novelist.[46] Elise von Hohenhausen asserted that through his *Scarlet Letter* and *House of Seven Gables*, he had outdistanced his English rivals and predecessors.[47]

The flow of translations has hardly been commensurate with the critical esteem. The chief works of Hawthorne were promptly translated into German: *The Scarlet Letter*, 1850, in 1851; *The House of Seven Gables*, 1851, in 1852; *The Blithedale Romance*, 1852, in 1852; and these novels also appeared in Hawthorne's *Sämtliche Werke*, 1851-1852. Next appeared a translation of *The Marble Faun*, 1860, in 1862, under the title, *Miriam oder Graf und Künstlerin*. After that there was a perceptible slackening of German versions for a time, until the year 1923 produced a new collection translated by Franz Blei. Separate translations of *The Scarlet Letter* had appeared in 1853. Then, after a pause, fifteen separate translations came out between 1897 and 1957. The separate translation of *The House of Seven Gables* in 1851 was followed after a long pause by versions of 1925, 1928, 1947, 1954. *Blithedale*, 1852 and 1870, was finally likewise translated by Franz Blei *(Ein tragischer Sommer)* in 1925. *The Marble Faun* was never retranslated separately. Because of its lack of New England background it probably interested German critics and readers less than Hawthorne's other novels.

It is not easy to account for the seeming lack of interest in

Hawthorne in the latter decades of the nineteenth century, as evinced by the paucity of translations between 1856 and 1912. Thereafter Hawthorne's novels and tales profited by the increase of interest in "Amerikakunde."

As might have been expected, the German literary critics were prone to compare and contrast the works of Hawthorne and of Poe, for both were story tellers who tried to describe supra-realistic situations in a realistic manner. Poe was admittedly the stronger narrator. His tales aroused horror and suspense, while Hawthorne's provoked at most an uncanny feeling. Poe's imagination was also more fecund, but in the description of characters it was Hawthorne who excelled. Poe's background was a weird universe of his own invention, while Hawthorne's was New England's past and present, treated realistically and unsparingly. This was a chief positive element, the lack of which led to the mentioned apathy toward *The Marble Faun*.

The German explorers of America had abundant opportunity to observe the American Negro, to judge his qualities, and to note his status in the various centers of the South. As most of the travelers were liberals, objecting to the restraints in their home-land, one might expect them to protest the hardships imposed on the Negroes. This they did sometimes, with certain reservations. Sealsfield, for example, said that those who favored the abolition of slavery ought first to learn what the slaves were like. The German travelers were able to base their conclusions on observations ranging from Virginia to Louisiana and thence to the Southwest.

The most thoughtful and serious observer of American slavery was Friedrich Armand Strubberg. During the years 1858 and 1859 he published six works dealing more or less incidentally with the subject, and in 1862 appeared a three-volume work entitled *Sklaverei in Amerika oder Schwarzes Blut*, consisting of 1) *Die Quadrone*, 2) *Die Mulattin*, and 3) *Die Negerin*. These are three separate fictional works, each based on some situation of

Southern life. Strubberg was captivated by the charm of a "Quadrone" he had observed, "mit ungewöhnlichen körperlichen Reizen, mit allen geistigen Fähigkeiten auf's reichste begabt, meist frei und unabhängig, zum grössten Teil wohlhabend,"[48] but with no tolerable future in store for this type of woman. To marry a black man, she would consider the worst humiliation. The other choice was to live unmarried with a white man. There she might be treated with consideration and, if she had a daughter, the daughter might be accepted by the household and could even sit at the table with the family if no guests were present, but if the master ran into financial difficulties, he could sell his offspring into slavery.

In the slave auctions families were often broken up. The slave trader was usually a New Englander, for no proper Southern gentleman would soil his honor by such a business. Strubberg noted also that segregation was practiced within the Negro community. When the mulattos went to the Negro church they sat in a balcony reserved for them. The slave trader, the unprovident owner of a cherished slave, and the tragic victim were well fixed types, and it is not necessary to suppose that Strubberg in 1862 borrowed from *Uncle Tom's Cabin* exclusively. The antislavery advocates of the 50's had brought out a mass of supporting evidence for their cause.

In his *Mississippibilder*, 1847, Friedrich Gerstäcker included two narratives, *Die Sklavin* and *Der Pflanzer*. In *Die Sklavin* he tells of a supposedly free quadroon of white complexion who is revealed to have Negro blood. His happy life is ended and he becomes the victim of persecution. *Der Pflanzer* has as its hero a Negro named Hannibal, who risks his life to save his master's. Gerstäcker also takes note of legal injustices: ten or more Negroes might observe an atrocity on the part of a white man, but the white man would go free, for no Negro was permitted to give testimony against a white man.

Gerstäcker's sharpest anger is vented against the sale of

Negroes without regard to the preservation of families. He advocates the immediate abolition of slavery, and as early as 1844 he predicted that slavery would one day be the cause of the separation of the South from the North.[49]

Thus it may be seen that even before 1852 German readers were well informed about the evils of slavery, but there was no great emotional response before the appearance of Harriet Beecher Stowe's *Uncle Tom's Cabin or Life among the Lowly*, April, 1852. It is reported that 3000 copies were sold on the first day after publication, that 120 editions were published in the United States during the following twelve months, and that eighteen editions were brought out in England during the same time. An English publisher estimated the sale of copies in England and in the colonies at 1,500,000. It was translated into at least twenty-one languages before 1910, and in most of these languages there were multiple editions. Of German editions there were fifty-eight or more. The best was probably that of Adolf Strodtmann, intended especially for the German-American public. There were those who doubted the veracity of the author's pictures. This led the author to publish *A Key to Uncle Tom's Cabin*, 1853, wherein she indicated her sources. Of this work 90,000 copies were promptly sold, many of them in the southern states. There were four translations of the *Key* into German. The author also wrote a children's version called *A Peep into Uncle Tom's Cabin*, 1853, and an adaptation for the stage, *The Christian Slave*, 1855. These versions were translated into German, and there were similar adaptations by Germans as well.[50]

For decades *Uncle Tom's Cabin* was a popular fixture of the American theater, and it remained on the German-American stage until 1879. In Germany there were five distinct dramatizations of the play, with 39 "Aufführungen" during the season 1853-1854. Better works of Harriet Beecher Stowe were translated into German – *The Minister's Wooing*, *The Pearl of Orr's Island*, and *Oldtown Folks*[51] – but none of these made a strong impression in Germany.

The new editions and the various adaptations of *Uncle Tom's Cabin* were constantly reviewed, in Germany often at great length. The consensus was that the plot lacked unity and the style was often imperfect, but that the author had achieved her purpose to arouse the sympathy of the reader.

Uncle Tom's Cabin in various ways suggested themes for German novelists: Auerbach's novel *Das Landhaus am Rhein* tells of a certain "Streber," Herr Sonnenkamp of German birth, who has made a fortune as a slave merchant and now, concealing his past, attempts to be accepted by the aristocratic circle near the "Landhaus" which he occupies. He is on the point of succeeding when one of his previous Negro victims happens on the scene, displays his whiplashed back, and reveals Sonnenkamp's merciless past. The citizens of the neighborhood surround Sonnenkamp's house and compel him to leave his estate.

It was sometimes asserted at that time that the condition of the Negro slave was more tolerable than that of the wage slaves in Europe. Friedrich Wilhelm Hackländer's novel *Europäisches Sklavenleben*, 1854, presented pictures of the poverty-stricken economic slaves, but the aristocrats and the wealthy feel that they too are slaves of their environment:

> Alle sind Sklaven, alle haben keinen freien Willen, auch die nicht, welche stolz auf uns herabblicken; und je höher sie stehen, desto herber fühlen sie ihre Sklaverei.

Hackländer wrote the book in answer to a call by several reviewers: "Es sollte einmal einer eine europäische *Uncle Tom's Hütte* über das weisse Elend schreiben." By many references and situations, Hackländer tries to emphasize rather than conceal his close relationship to Mrs. Stowe's novel.

Of the numerous other writers who followed in the footsteps of Harriet Beecher Stowe, one may be singled out because of the author's declaration of purpose. Bernhard Hesslein wrote two novels, *Abraham Lincoln* and *Jefferson Davis*. The latter is intended as a continuation of *Uncle Tom's Cabin*. In a note at the beginning of the work Hesslein states:

> Die Verfasserin von *Onkel Tom* gestand, dass ihr berühmtes Werk nur eine unvollständige Schilderung der Sklaverei enthalte, und zwar deshalb, weil diese in vielen ihrer Wirkungen mit solchen Schrecknissen verbunden sei, dass ihre Enthüllungen sich für die Zwecke der Kunst nicht eignen. Der Verfasser dieses Werkes aber glaubt, jede Rücksicht, welche das Entsetzliche nicht in seiner ganzen Schändlichkeit erscheinen lässt, bei Seite legen zu müssen.

Ralph Waldo Emerson did not become well known in Germany until near the end of his literary career. The Swedish woman of letters, Frederike Bremer, visited him in Concord in 1854-1855 and published *Die Heimat in der neuen Welt, Ein Tagebuch in Briefen, aus dem Dänischen.* This contained in German translation excerpts from works by Emerson and also an interesting account of a visit with him, together with an appreciative character sketch. Shortly thereafter, 1856, an English edition of *Representative Men* was included in Durr's *Collection of Standard American Authors*, and Hermann Grimm translated into German its essays on Shakespeare and on Goethe. A correspondence began between Emerson and Grimm, and with Grimm's wife, Gisela von Arnim. This correspondence continued at long intervals for fifteen years. It was published in 1903.[52] Grimm made systematic efforts to interest his acquaintances in Emerson, but found no response or unfavorable responses. One friend asked: "Was brauchen wir einen Amerikaner wie Emerson, da wir doch Goethe haben?"

This was a reasonable reply on the part of a Weimar-oriented critic, but Weimar idealism was yielded to worldly realism, and the optimistic idea of human perfectibility to pessimism and materialism. The Bismark era brought power to Prussia and the associated states. It was also the time of Germany's commercial growth, and of materialistic philosophers.

Emerson's Unitarianism was a point of contact with the German iconoclasts, but only an incidental one. Emerson was a pantheist and did not believe in a personal God. He believed in a "Weltseele," an "Oberseele," of which man's soul was a part. As words are but symbols of not fully expressible thoughts, so the visible and tangible elements of nature are but hints of an inscrutable, all-encompassing total nature. The harmony of man with divine nature was the basis of Emerson's ethical philosophy. Such ideas seemed to the leading materialistic German thinkers of the time to be remnants of a supposedly outlived mysticism, and thus Emerson's message could not be delivered until it found a more favorable atmosphere toward the end of the century.

Among the Germans who took note of Emerson, by far the most important was Friedrich Nietzsche. One critic said, perhaps too unguardedly, that the relationship of Emerson and Nietzsche was "das einzige grossgreifbare Beispiel einer echten Begegnung zwischen Deutschland und Amerika."[53] Charles Andler, in *Les Précurseurs de Nietzsche*, 1921, was the first to call attention to the close kinship, which since that time has been fully documented.

The points of contact between Emerson and Nietzsche are numerous. One critic has summed them up succinctly:

> Beide verwerfen das System und lieben einen bilderreichen Stil. Sie haben den Gedanken des Sich-Wandelns. Beide stellen die Bedeutung grosser Männer der Masse gegenüber heraus, kämpfen gegen die Macht des Historismus und sind stark individualistisch. Sie haben beide die Idee vom Übermenschen. Beide reden vom Zerbrechen der alten Gesetzestafeln, von dem Willen zur Macht und vom heroischen Menschen. In ihren erkenntnistheoretischen Anschauungen haben sie biologische Elemente. Beide haben die Idee von der "Fröhlichen Wissenschaft". Gemeinsam ist beiden die Kritik am historischen Christentum. Emerson ist der Prediger des inneren Lebens, Nietzsche rang um vertieftes wahres Leben.[54]

The evidences of Nietzsche's relationship to Emerson are various.

They include two essays written in Pforta and not intended for publication: "Fatum und Geschichte" and "Willensfreiheit und Fatum." These were animadversions occasioned by the reading of Emerson's *The Conduct of Life,* more precisely by the first essay in that collection, entitled "Fate." There also exists a commonplace book with many quotations from Emerson's essays, and Nietzsche's hand copy of the *Essays* with many underlinings and marginal notes, which have recently been evaluated and interpreted. There are also many direct references to Emerson in Nietzsche's collected works, and finally we have the illuminating correspondence between Nietzsche and his friends, chiefly with Karl von Gersdorff.

It was sometime during his last school years at Pforta that Nietzsche happened upon a volume of Emerson's *Essays* and began entering in his notebooks quotations from it with comments thereon. In 1863 he noted Emerson as his "meistgelesener" author. He purchased Emerson's works as fast as they appeared, made marginal notes in them, and carried them in his briefcase on his journeys. He called him "den reichsten Amerikaner" and dedicated to him his *Fröhliche Wissenschaft,* 1882, with the words of Emerson: "Dem Dichter und Weisen sind alle Dinge befreundet und geweiht, alle Erlebnisse nützlich, alle Tage heilig, alle Menschen göttlich."

In his boyhood Nietzsche had written pious poems within an orthodox framework, assuming a personal God and a personal saviour. An immediate and permanent result of his Emerson readings was that he joined Emerson in the negation. It was in 1864 that Nietzsche wrote to his friend Karl von Gersdorff advising him to read Emerson's *Essays.* Gersdorff did so and forthwith became a lifelong disciple of Emerson. The Nietzsche-Gersdorff correspondence continued with only one interruption (1877-1883) until the failure of Nietzsche's powers. Though Nietzsche's own letters are not available, much may be inferred from Gersdorff's replies.

Even before the interruption, Gersdorff may have noticed that Nietzsche was beginning to take a more critical view of Emerson. Gersdorff wrote to him from Hannover, April 19, 1876: "Hier liegt in einem Schaufenster R.W.Emerson's *Neue Esasys,* übersetzt von Julian Schmidt, also das Allerneueste unseres herrlichen Freundes, dessen *Führung des Lebens* ich hierher nahm und auf der Reise mir vorhielt, um mich daran zu stärken." To this Nietzsche replied: "Der neue Emerson ist etwas alt geworden. Kommt es Dir nicht auch so vor? Die früheren Essays sind viel reicher, jetzt widerholt er sich."[55]

About the year 1883 Nietzsche became aware that his philosophy was diametrically opposed to that of Emerson. Emerson's ethics have their basis in a metaphysical and humanistic view of life, Nietzsche's in a worldly conception. Emerson's philosophy was optimistic, Nietzsche's pessimistic. There was a Grecian background to the philosophy of both, but Emerson accepted the humanistic, christianized Hellenism of Weimar. Nietzsche set in its place the unrestrained Dionysian heathenism of the early Greek civilization. He felt that it was his mission to destroy the foundations of the prevailing ethical code and to nominate as the present–day heroes the believers that "Macht ist Recht," the "Herrenmenschen, jenseits von Gut und Böse."

Nietzsche's views held sway throughout the remainder of the century, but toward its end an opposition asserted itself, which reached its highest plateau at the centennial of Emerson's birth, 1903. Between 1894 and 1907 there were eighteen German translations of works of Emerson. In 1903, there appeared in German journals more than thirty discussions of his philosophy. The dominance of the materialistic and naturalistic philosophy was being challenged. The metaphysical, Christian sanctions for the traditional moral code had lost their power, but the code itself was found to be good. In Germany, in England, and also in America ethical culture societies were founded. The founder of the Ethical Culture Society in America was Felix Adler. His chief work was translated into German in 1895. Nearly all of these

105

numerous ethical societies in America, England, and Germany had their own journals, and these journals had frequent occasion to call upon the memory of Emerson. Presumably the most widely effective work of the time in this field was Friedrich Lienhard's *Wege nach Weimar*, 1905-1908, which had over ten thousand readers. Emerson's words and works were mentioned frequently in nearly all its volumes, for Lienhard treated Emerson almost as a living and corresponding member of his group. At about the same time, 1899-1903, Karl Federn interested himself in Emerson and made at least seven contributions to the subject, and Alexander von Gleichen-Russwurm supported him with four articles between 1904-1907. Interest seems to have ebbed thereafter for a time, but more recently it has come to flow again. Here may be mentioned Paul Sakmann with several contributions between 1927 and 1932, followed by Julius Simon's *Ralph Waldo Emerson in Deutschland, 1851-1932*, Berlin, 1937, our chief authority on this subject, and by an essay on Emerson and Nietzsche in the *Jahrbuch für Amerikastudien* for 1958.[56]

Of Emerson's works, *Representative Men* seems to have interested the Germans most particularly. Partly in view of Emerson's early friendship with Carlyle, *Representative Men* is often mentioned in connection with Carlyle's *Heroes and Hero Worship*. Though the two works treat of a like subject, it is clear that Emerson's conclusions are not based on Nietzsche's or Carlyle's. His representative men are not "Herrenmenschen" possessed by a "Wille zur Macht" for its own sake. Nietzsche's turning away from Emerson about the year 1882 left Carlyle's status with Nietzsche unchanged.

Some Germans were inclined to take issue with Emerson's classification of Goethe as the representative "writer." This may be in part because the term "Schriftsteller" in German conveys slightly less prestige than the word "writer" in English. The honor of representing poetry had to be reserved for Shakespeare.

Emerson's style in his essays was conditioned by the fact that they had for the most part an origin as lectures. Emerson's rhetoric was a matter of interest to the Germans. His use of the short sentence, and of a sequence of such, was a novelty to them. Hermann Grimm admittedly imitated it, and others imitated Emerson or Grimm. Any influence of such a trend can hardly have done injury to German writers.

Opinions varied in Germany in regard to the form of Emerson's essays. Leo Berg wrote:

> Nur sind sie eigentlich keine Essays, d.h. keine geschlossenen Abhandlungen über bestimmte Gegenstände oder Fragen... Emerson vielmehr gibt nur eine Reihe prachtvoller, häufig gänzlich loser Einzelbemerkungen zu einer Frage... Es wäre nützlicher, wenn er seine Aufzeichnungen niemals zu Essays zusammengestellt hätte.[57]

Alexander von Gleichen-Russwurm, on the other hand, wrote:

> Sie sind gleich den Essays Montaignes, ein glänzendes Vorbild für jene Art künstlerischen Schaffens, die aus dem Quellenstudium von Fachgelehrten emporgewachsen, ihren Stoff nicht ergründen, sondern nur von verschiedenen Seiten beleuchten will... Emersons Eigenart gab dem Essay die Form, deren sich die Jugend als klassisches Vorbild von nun an bediente, nicht nur in Amerika, auch in Deutschland, in England und bei nordischen Völkern.[58]

Emerson's poems, on the other hand, are little known in Germany. Friedrich Spielhagen included seven of them in his anthology, *Amerikanische Gedichte*, 1859. It was noted that Emerson cared little for meter and rhyme. His poems were characterized as "starkgedanklich, philosophisch." The symbolic element was appreciated chiefly by A. von Gleichen-Russwurm.

Of the Transcendentalist group and its associates William Ellery Channing enjoyed a high esteem in England and in Germany. A critic in *Frazer's Magazine* regarded his style as the cause of his reputation as "America's best writer." The German translator of Channing's essay "The Church," 1841 (German, 1846), called him the "Zierde der Schriftsteller Nord-Amerikas" and said that his reputation as "America's best writer" was due to his style, the pictorial quality of his language, the brevity of his sentences, the simplicity in the development of his thoughts, and the richness of his similes and metaphors. Another German critic called Channing the most famous writer and most successful Christian speaker in the United States.

It has been stated that Channing was fluent in German, and even that he visited Germany. Neither statement is true.[59] To Lucy Aiken he wrote: "I am no reader of German," and it has recently been surmised that he never read a German treatise all through in the language of the original. But nearly all the German works within his field of interest were available in English translation in book form, and the rest were supplied by manuscript translations, passed from hand to hand, and discussed at meetings of his group.

It is not to be inferred that Channing was influenced by German works he read. He stated that he read these works with enthusiasm because of the substantiation they gave to ideas that he had already conceived. He was familiar with works of Herder, Goethe, Schiller, Kant, Fichte, and Schelling. Of all these, he was most in consonance with Herder, and with good grounds he has been called the "Herder of New England Transcendentalism."[60] Of Herder's ideas the one which appealed to him most strongly was that of the upward progress of humanity through the self–cultivation of the individual. Herder was thinking here chiefly of the educated classes, while Channing addressed himself rather to the middle class and the working class.

Several of Channing's works were translated into German, among them his essay *The Elevation of the Laboring Class*, written in 1840 and *Self–Culture*, 1838, bearing the subtitle *The Thinking Middle Class*. This essay was made known in Germany by Berthold Auerbach through a treatise under the title *Der gebildete Bürger – Buch für den denkenden Mittelstand*. Auerbach began work on this essay early in 1842 and published it the following year. In a letter to Friedrich Spielhagen written four hours before his death, Auerbach asked Spielhagen not to include this essay in his completed works because it was not sufficiently original. He calls it a "Bearbeitung einer Abhandlung von Channing über Selbstbildung." It is, in fact, a "Bearbeitung" rather than a translation. Auerbach is led to make adaptations to fit German conditions. He also inserts ideas of his own. The "Bearbeitung" is much longer than the original and the style is different, more pedagogic and condescending, and also more sentimental.

These same characteristics are present in Auerbach's *Village Tales*, the earliest of which were written at the time he began his "Bearbeitung"; and the message of self-improvement is also ever present in the tales. Auerbach's *Dorfgeschichten* were soon translated into English and were for a time apparently the most popular of German works in America. Thus we notice a reciprocal movement from America to Germany and then from Germany to America.

American and German literatures were brought closer together by the consistent efforts of Bayard Taylor. As originally planned, Germany was hardly included in his first European trip, but it turned out otherwise. He stayed in Heidelberg from September 1844 to the end of the year, devoting himself to the gaining of a good working command of the German language. Before the end of his life he visited Germany seventeen times and spent at least a total of seventy months there. Unlike Washington Irving, Taylor seized every opportunity to converse with German men of letters. On a visit to Frankfurt, in no other quality than that of a young traveling American, he was politely received by Mendelssohn. Among his German acquaintances were Alexander von Humboldt, Ferdinand Freiligrath, Friedrich Gerstäcker, Adolf Strodtmann, Ludwig Uhland, Karl Bleibtreu, Berthold Auerbach, Friedrich Spielhagen, Friedrich Rückert, Fritz Reuter, Gustav Freytag, and Karl Gutzkow.

Taylor is best remembered today as the translator of *Faust*, but he also translated poems and passages from Walther von der Vogelweide, Wolfram von Eschenbach, and Hartman von Aue; and from Goethe, Schiller, Freiligrath, Rückert, Uhland, Heine, Schenkendorf, Arndt, Echendorff and Claudius. In his Appendix IV, Krumpelmann has attempted "a catalogue of Taylor's metrical translations from the German." There are 86 entries, in all.[62]

Translations of Taylor's poetry into German have been discussed elsewhere in this survey. His prose works were also liberally translated into German, including all four of his novels. *Hannah Thurston*, 1863 (German, 1864), *John Godfrey's Fortunes*, 1860 (German, 1865),[63] *The Story of Kennett*, 1866 (German, 1867), *Joseph and His Friend*, 1870 (German, 1887), and several works of travel and criticism. Krumpelmann [240], Appendix VI, lists thirteen prose works in all in book form.

Taylor's translation of Goethe's *Faust* appeared in 1871. Krumpelmann, more enthusiastic than most American critics, calls it "the most excellent English translation of the most philosophical poem of modern times."[64] The question at issue here is what the Germans thought of it. Lina Baumann's *Englische Übersetzungen von Goethe's Faust*, 1908, speaks well of Taylor's translation. Juliana Haskell's *Bayard Taylor's Translation of Goethe's "Faust,"* 1908, finds chiefly inadequacies. In a review of this study Richard M. Meyer concludes: "Sie wird B. T. nicht gerecht."[65] On the whole it would appear not only that the translation was favorably received in Germany at the time of its publication, but also that it is still in favor. Krumpelmann found no German criticism of the translation that was preponderantly unfavorable. Among the favorers of the translation was G. von Loeper, who referred to Taylor's "nicht genug zu rühmenden Faust Übertragung."[66] Presumably this work served best of all to gain him the favor of the German public.

At Gotha, December 12, 1872, Taylor delivered a lecture on *Amerikanische Dichter und Dichtkunst* and in Weimar a year later. Taylor's last project was a biography of Goethe. To that end he wished for means to stay in Germany. President Rutherford B. Hayes appointed him ambassador to Germany and said to him: "I want you to stay until your *Life of Goethe* is finished, and not allow your official duties to prevent you from working upon it. You must come back to us with the work accomplished."[67] Taylor died December, 1878, before the work was fairly begun. The "Leichenrede" was spoken by Berthold Auerbach, who called himself Taylor's earliest friend in the Old World. He described him as a representative of his people among a foreign people, "No, not among a foreign people, but one of ourselves." Taylor, he said, was a disciple of universal literature in the Goethean sense, high above all bounds of nationality.[68]

Of any "influence" of Taylor the poet, historian, and critic on German literature there is nothing to be said. His role was strictly that of a mediator working in two directions. He was influential in Germany only in so far as through his personality, his friendship with Germans, and his writings, he led the Germans to a greater appreciation of American literature.

For the greater part of the century Germans continued to derive their pictures of American life chiefly from the novels of Cooper and of German adventurers, travelers, and émigrés, but in the early '70's Bret Harte and Mark Twain opened up vistas into California and Nevada. Their earliest works appeared almost simultaneously. Bret Harte's *Tales of the Argonauts*, 1870-1875, were translated and published, 1873-1875. A collection of *Kalifornische Novellen* appeared in 1873, and of *Kalifornische Erzählungen* in 1876. Meanwhile there had appeared Mark Twain's *Jim Smiley's berühmter Springfrosch und dergleichen wunderliche Käuze mehr; im Silberlande Nevada*, 1874. This was followed by German translations of *The Innocents Abroad*, 1869, in 1875, of *The Gilded Age* and of *The Adventures of Tom Sawyer*, both in 1876, and of *Sketches New and Old*, 1877.

Since both authors wrote about California and Nevada it was natural that the critics should make comparisons, and in these early years the comparisons redounded to the benefit of Bret Harte. In a lecture at the University of Graz, Anton Schönbach said that Bret Harte surpassed Mark Twain as a "Dichter." Mark Twain, on the other hand, he described as a journalist. Life and journalism were the formative influences on Mark Twain's style, but he lacked the training that a study of the classics might have given him.[69] Similarly Wilhelm Lange called Bret Harte a poet and referred to his "ergreifende und stimmungsvolle Seelengemälde und Naturbilder," while he classified Mark Twain as a humorist and good natured satirist.[70] Rudolf Doehn was of a like opinion.[71]

On the basis of evidence up to about 1877 these relative evaluations were justified. Bret Harte was from the first a master of form in the genre of the short story. Here he could stand comparison with de Maupassant and the best European masters, and his tales were suitable for anthologies of short stories. He was also a writer of smooth and popular verse. In Freiligrath's anthology he appeared with eleven poems, in Knortz's with nine, in Prinzhorn's with five, and in Elze's with three. Harte's one grave error was his venture into the field of the full length novel, and yet the mediocre three volume *Gabriel Conroy* seemed, in view of Harte's reputation, a tempting risk for German publishers. Translations appeared by Udo Brachvogel, Carl Theodor Eben, Otto Randolf, and Mary Eichler-Cullimore, all in 1876. Bret Harte developed little after his first successes. In 1875, the critics could not surmise that Mark Twain would later display many new facets of interest and be able to write with equal confidence of King Arthur's Court, of Joan of Arc, of Heaven, of Eden, and of Hadleyburg, and that he was destined to be regarded as a philosopher.

Translations of Mark Twain's tales appeared promptly. Between 1874 and 1890 there were published German versions of "The Jumping Frog," *Innocents Abroad, Tom Sawyer, The Prince and the Pauper, Life on the Mississippi, Huckleberry Finn,* "The Million Pound Bank Note," *The American Pretender* and

Puddenhead Wilson. Among the translators were Moritz Busch, Udo Brachvogel, Margarethe Jacobi, and Henny Koch.

During the same time the Tauchnitz English reprints of Mark Twain's works began to appear under the remarkable title: *Collection of British Authors.* Sixteen volumes of reprints were published between 1876 and 1900, and five more shortly thereafter. Although he was not legally bound to do so in the absence of any copyright protection of authors, Tauchnitz paid Mark Twain an honorarium for the use of his works. In 1936 Hemminghaus estimated the total sales of Mark Twain books in Germany to that date at over a million.[72] *Tom Sawyer* appears to have been the first favorite, followed by *Huckleberry Finn.*

German surveys of American literature in the last quarter of the century – Scheer, 6th. ed., 1875, Engel, 1883, Körting, 1888, Bierbaum, 1889, and Knortz, 1891 – devoted not much space to Mark Twain and probably did little to spread his reputation. Engel, to be sure, wrote some appreciative reviews of his novels.[73]

More effective, no doubt, was the introduction of Mark Twain's works into the schools. Emil Lobetanz abridged *The Prince and the Pauper* for school use in 1895, Gustav Krüger did the same for *The Adventures of Tom Sawyer* in 1900, and Max Friedrich Mann for *A Tramp Abroad* in 1903.

The classification as a humorist was detrimental to Mark Twain's literary reputation at home and abroad; at home he was at pains to disassociate himself from such professional humorists as Bill Nye and Petroleum Nasby; abroad, and particularly in Germany, this type of humor was strange. The humor favored there was of the Jean Paul-Sterne-Dickens kind which mingled smiles and sympathetic tears. Mark Twain's humor was free from sentimentality and often was as devastating as Swift's. Ewald Flügel, for one, wished that Twain had curbed the burlesque in *A Connecticut Yankee at King Arthur's Court.*[74]

It could be contended that German critics, earlier than American, gained a well rounded view of Mark Twain's stature as a philosopher and man of letters. As early as 1901, a Catholic critic, A. Wurm, attributed to him a "Weltanschauung," in default of which in Germany a writer is unlikely to be taken seriously. Mark Twain's view of life, Wurm said, was not Christian but it was modern, that is to say practical and ethical. The goal was to achieve a better life, chiefly a physically better life, for posterity. To this end the good citizen should overcome feelings of fear and hate and give his support to law, which should care for the protection of the individual and should right injustices. The self-discipline required of the individual to this edn, Mark Twain had learned through the chequered school of his experiences.[75]

Archibald Henderson, a personal friend of Mark Twain, contributed two essays to the *Deutsche Revue*. One was called "Mark Twain, wie er ist," the other bore the significant title "Mark Twain als Philosoph, Moralist und Soziologe."[76] Henderson recognized in Tom Sawyer the incurable romanticist – the summation of the influence of Walter Scott, which Mark Twain always deplored. Tom Sawyer never develops, but Huckleberry Finn, illiterate as he is, struggles with his conscience and comes to a realization of his ethical responsibilities.

Henderson devoted much attention to certain works of Mark Twain which had not yet been translated into German, and these were chiefly works of ethical significance: among them "The Man that Corrupted Hadleyburg," "In Defense of Harriet Shelley," "Personal Recollections of Joan of Arc," "Was it Heaven or Hell?", "Captain Stormfield's Visit to Heaven," "Concerning the Jews," and "Christian Science." F. Schönemann, who seems not to have known of Wurm, said:

Es ist das Verdienst Archibald Hendersons zuerst Mark Twain in ein anderes als das übliche Licht gerückt zu haben. Er gibt uns einen ersten Begriff von der geistigen Entwicklung Mark Twains: "a progressive development, a deepening and broadening of forces, a ripening of intellectual and spiritual powers from the beginning to the end of his career."[77]

114

For the academic year 1910-1911 Charles Alphonso Smith was invited to become Roosevelt Professor of American History and Institutions at Berlin University. He lectured in German on American literature, and his stimulating remarks on Mark Twain were published shortly thereafter.[78] The Missouri of Mark Twain's early years, he pointed out, was the outpost of pioneers, battle ground of free soil and slavery, and the highway of the rich and poor, of Yankees and Southerners, and of natives and foreigners. This formed the basis of Mark Twain's education. Smith also stressed the fact that humor was not the object of Mark Twain's endeavor, but only the vehicle for the expression of his convictions.

The publication of Mark Twain's letters in 1917, edited and arranged by Mark Twain's "official" biographer Albert Bigelow Paine, aroused less interest than might have been expected. The first important review, that by F. Schönemann, did not appear until 1923.[79] Schönemann was annoyed by Paine's eulogistic footnotes, and vexed at the literary executors for withholding letters they felt to be indiscreet.

Admirers of Mark Twain had looked forward to the publication of his *Autobiography* which, by his instruction, should not be published until his death. He died in 1910, and the *Autobiography*, edited by Albert Bigelow Paine, was not published until 1925. Mark Twain wished it to be a revelation "speaking from the grave and as frank and free and unembarrassed as a love letter." In a letter to Howells, March 14, 1904, he said that it was the function of a good autobiography "to roam up and down the years without any attempt at sequence of events or deadly accuracy of detail or date." In this mission Mark Twain succeeded. Even in a chequered life such as Mark Twain's there were dull passages, but in the *Autobiography* there are none. It is a book for the reader rather than for the literary historian. For the benefit of the German reader, Sil-Vara provided a résumé of the most significant passages in the work.[80]

Van Wyck Brooks' study, *The Ordeal of Mark Twain*, appeared in 1920 and was reviewed by F.Schönemann in his monograph *Mark Twain als literarische Persönlichkeit*, 1925. The chief feature of Brooks' essay was the frustration theory. It is true, Schönemann said, that Mark Twain was aware of a divided loyalty. He had a deep-seated admiration for the English-New Englandish literary tradition, but by instinct and experience he was a Westerner. Schönemann found Brooks too partisan and concluded: "Er kann Mark Twain nicht voll würdigen, eben weil er dessen Amerika unterschätzt, ja missachtet." Henry Lüdeke and Eduard Engel were in near agreement with Schönemann,[81] and to W.P.Friederich [7] Mark Twain remained "der ungezügelte und selbstgeschulte Genius des Westens... der sich vom Osten nie ganz unterkriegen liess, sondern so oder so immer sich selber blieb."

In his *Mark Twain als literarische Persönlichkeit*, F.Schönemann sufficiently refuted a once prevailing opinion that Mark Twain was little versed in literature. Mark Twain said of himself: "I like history, biography, travels, and science, and I detest novels, poetry, and theology." He knew well American history and English history of certain periods. Of the biographers, historians, and philosophers, he knew best Carlyle, Lecky, Pepys, Boswell, Suetonius, and Schopenhauer. Of the novelists he was most akin to Cervantes. He appreciated Malory, Swift's *Gulliver's Travels*, Bunyan's *Pilgrim's Progress*, Goldsmith's *Citizen of the World* and Dickens, in so far as he was a realist. The romanticism of Scott and Cooper was abhorrent to him. To Shakespeare he felt himself indebted for providing welcome subjects for debunking.

The publication of the *Mark Twain-Howells Letters*, 1960, was an event of major importance. It revealed Howells as an encourager rather than restrainer, and also a giver as well as a receiver of literary impulses. It definitely disposed of the charge that Howells exerted a "verweichlichenden" influence on Mark Twain. It also showed that Howells was more important for the development of realism than had been noted hitherto.

Mark Twain's popularity was enhanced by his visits and long time residence in Europe. In Switzerland and in Vienna he found literary friends and an appreciative public.

An often quoted dictum of Ernest Hemingway declares that all American literature stems from a single book called *Huckleberry Finn*. German critics could not quite subscribe to this. They are well aware of earlier beginnings, but they regard Mark Twain together with Walt Whitman as the strongest evidence of an independent American literature.

[1] Cf. *British Museum, Catalogue of British Books*.
[2] *Loc. cit.*, pp. 69 ff.
[3] Reichart [209] 346.
[4] Goethe, *Werke* IV (27) 197; IV (9) 143 f.
[5] BLU, Nov. 8, 1822.
[6] *Ibid.*, April 26, 1845.
[7] *Ibid.*, Feb. 28, 1837.
[8] *Ibid.*, July 12, 1830; Oct. 18, 1835.
[9] Reichart [210] 540 f.
[10] Hauff, *Werke*, Verlagshaus Bong, IV, 69 f.
[11] Plath [213].
[12] Keerl [217]; Sprenger [216].
[13] Wilhelm Fehse, *Wilhelm Raabe...*, Braunschweig, 1937, pp. 47, 103.
[14] Brandes [216].
[15] Reichart [210] 546.
[16] *Ibid.*, p. 552.
[17] Barba [182].
[18] MFLA, Feb. 28, 1834.
[19] BLU, Jan. 28, 1830.
[20] Goethe, *Werke*, III (10), 251 f.; III (11), 168-172.
[21] For dates see also Goethe, *Werke*, III (10) 1257; III (10), 264-266; III (11) 276.
[22] Goethe, *Werke*, I (41:2) 296.
[23] Wukadinović [146].
[24] See above, p. 13.
[25] Biedermann, *Gespräche*, II, 389.
[26] *Ibid.*, II, 337.
[27] Eckermann, *Gespräche*, 95, 281.

[28] *Ibid.*, p. 281.
[29] Brenner [187].
[30] Edw. Engel, *Geschichte der englischen Literatur*, 1883, p. 240.
[31] Barba [182].
[32] Mummendey [1].
[33] Bibliography [123] ff.
[34] Arndt [110].
[35] Arndt [148].
[36] M. Kerbetney, *Erinnerungen an Charles Sealsfield*, Brüssel.
[37] Bibliography [149]-[154].
[38] Barba [182].
[39] See above, p. 99.
[40] Barba [193].
[41] Barba [189].
[42] [92] ff.
[43] Graewert [121]; Schrader [122].
[44] Sauer [192].
[45] Barba [182].
[46] Locher [65] 288.
[47] MFLA. June 11, 1853.
[48] Woodson [154] 79.
[49] *Ibid.*, 169.
[50] Maclean [236].
[51] Mummendey [1].
[52] Holls [200].
[53] E. Baumgarten; cf. Hubbard [204] 1.
[54] Simon [107] 140.
[55] Hubbard [204] 12.
[56] JAS, I-II.
[57] Simon [107] 94.
[58] A. von Gleichen-Russwurm, *Emerson*, 1907; p. 4.
[59] H. A. Rattermann, "Dr. Karl Follen," AG, IV (1902), 1, but cf. Puknat [157] 196.
[60] Puknat [157] 201.
[61] Puknat [158] 975.
[62] For additions to Roehm [2] see Krumpelmann [241] 159 ff.
[63] Mummendey [1] overlooks this translation.
[64] Krumpelmann [241] 35.
[65] *Anzeiger für deutsches Alterthum* XXXIII (1909), 312-313.
[66] Krumpelman [241] 53.
[67] Krumpelmann [241] 135.

118

[68] *Ibid.*, p. 164.

[69] Published in *Gesammelte Aufsätze*, Graz, 1900.

[70] Preface to Lange's translation of Bret Harte's *Sketches*, 1865.

[71] Hemminghaus [171].

[72] *Ibid.*, p. 144.

[73] MFLA, Oct. 9, 1880, 575-579; Nov. 27, 1880, 684 f., May 6, 1882, 259-261.

[74] Hemminghaus [171] 23.

[75] A. Wurm, "Mark Twain als Mensch und Humorist," *Alte und Neue Welt*, XXXVIII (1903-1904) 718-720, 748-754.

[76] *Loc. cit.*, LXXIV (Nov. 1909) 195-205; XXXVI, Feb. 1911, 189-205.

[77] Schönemann [167].

[78] Smith, Charles Alphonso, *Die amerikanische Literatur*, Berlin, 1922.

[79] Schönemann, F., *ASNS*, CLXIV (1922-1928) 184-213.

[80] *Neue Freie Presse*, August 13, 1925.

[81] Schönemann [167, 169].

PART III

FROM LITERARY INDEPENDENCE TO LITERARY COMMONWEALTH

VI. THE NOVEL

By the year 1900 American literature, in the view of the Germans, had almost reached its maturity. It is true that it included no heroic and no courtly epic and was destined never to have them, nor was there, to the knowledge of the Germans, an American drama, but the time was well past when American literature could still be regarded as the American branch of English literature. Its affinities were rather with world literature in general and with German literature in particular.

At the turn of the century there was a notable increase of interest in American literature on the part of German critics. The long-slighted Hawthorne and Melville rose into prominence; Poe's complete works were translated into German, 1901-1904, and forthwith aroused the enthusiasm of Baudelaire in France, of Ewers in Germany, and of the Swinburne circle in England. Bret Harte and Mark Twain were among the most widely read authors in Germany, and Karl May had not yet fully captured Cooper's place in the realm of the exotic and venturesome. Largely through the efforts of Karl Federn, Emerson became known to a new German public, and there were belated translations of Thoreau's *Walden*, 1854 (German, 1897, 1903, 1905, 1922, 1945, 1949).

Of the various genres of literature it was the American novel that came first into prominence. As there was no copyright protection for works of literature, American novels were freely reprinted by European publishers or published, if thought desirable, in translation. Between 1871 and 1913 almost a thousand American novels or collections of American short stories were published in Germany with more than a score of German publishers as the purveyors, the Tauchnitz firm being perhaps more instrumental than all the others taken together. Between 1871 and 1913 it published the works of about sixty-seven American novelists.

The most freely plundered works were those of Mark Twain and Bret Harte. Vollmer's record of such publications [8][1] has total entries for the most read American authors as follows:

Mark Twain	117	Richard Henry Savage	26
Francis Bret Harte	109	Gertrude Atherton	20
Francis Hodgson Burnett	71	Louisa May Alcott	25
Anna Katherine Green	71	William Dean Howells	20
F. Marion Crawford	59	Edward Bellamy	20
Lew Wallace	38	Julian Hawthorne	19
John Habberton	27	Kate Douglas Wiggins	18
Henry James	27		

Here it is interesting to compare these statistics with others regarding the relative popularity of certain American authors in the Soviet Union, unfortunately not of the same period. In the years between 1917 and 1947 more than 264 American authors became known to Soviet readers. Jack London stands highest in the group with 7,640 editions of a thousand copies each. Mark Twain follows with 2,534 editions, Upton Sinclair with 2,292, and Bret Harte with 801. Other interesting standings were:

Theodore Dreiser	8th place	Sinclair Lewis	16th
John Steinbeck	9th	Henry Wadsworth Longfellow	17th
James Fenimore Cooper	10th	Pearl Buck	20th
Erskine Caldwell	14th	Ernest Hemingway	21st
Edgar Allan Poe	15th	John Dos Passos	22nd

In Germany there were school editions of works by Alcott and

121

Burnett, as well as reprints and translations. There were translations of Green, Wallace, Bellamy, Crawford, and Habberton
(*Helen's Babies*, etc.). James and Wiggins were available both in
the original and in translation, and there were chiefly reprints
of works by Savage, Atherton, and Howells. Vollmer's bibliography contains the names of eighty-seven American novelists.
There is abundance here, but a certain lack of vigor. Many of
these novels were written by women or written chiefly for women
readers.

During the nineteenth century American life and American
letters stood in a harmonious relationship to each other. As
G. A. Blank has recently pointed out:

> Irving, Cooper, Emerson und Hawthorne, Melville, Longfellow,
> Mark Twain, und Howells fühlten sich den Idealen der amerika-
> nischen Gesellschaft verbunden. Sie waren durchaus nicht blind für
> die schlechten Seiten amerikanischer Wirklichkeit und für die
> gefährlichen Tendenzen... Sie brachten laut ihre Besorgnis über
> den stärker werdenden Materialismus, über den selbstgerechten
> Nationalismus und über den kurzsichtigen Optimismus zum Aus-
> druck.[2]

The American readers took such criticism in good part and felt
that the men of letters were giving voice to the conscience of the
public. There were writers of the twentieth century who continued in the calm, benevolent tradition of the nineteenth.
Many of their works were "best sellers" written not for the critics,
but for the wide reading public. Hans Effelberger has noted how
large a share was produced by women novelists, such as Edith
Wharton, Willa Cather, Betty Smith, Lilian Smith, Margaret
Mitchell, Edna Ferber, and Pearl Buck.[3] Of these, Pearl Buck
found especial favor with the public, but she aroused little
interest on the part of the critics, one of whom referred to "Pearl
Buck mit ihren dichterisch schönen aber rassenpolitisch nicht
ganz unbedenklichen China-Romanen" – a judgment in which
very few American critics concur.[4]

Toward the end of this idyllic period, 1916, Schönemann drew up a bill of complaints against the American novel with its Puritanism, gentility, prudery, emphasis on wealth, and optimistic faith that hard work brings success. Well said, but even as he wrote, the smug literary picture of American life was being discredited. Puritanism and prudery of expression are certainly not characteristic of the American novel of today. Many American novels represent the search for affluence as the road to disillusionment, and the American woman in life and literature is no longer idealized as a passive household queen but regarded as a helper or a competitor in the world of affairs. The literary picture of American life was adapting itself to new realities, and Schönemann himself became one of the staunchest exponents of the novels of Sinclair Lewis and later, in 1936, of Willa Cather:

> Sie ist von erfrischender Weitherzigkeit in der Menschenbeurteilung und wahrhaft schöpferisch in ihrer Kritik, die meist viel fairer ist als die in den Schriften von Sinclair Lewis und Theodor Dreiser.[5]

But not all was harmony in American life and letters. Lincoln Steffens, Ida Tarbell, Jack London, Frank Norris, and other "muck-rakers" protested the ruthlessness of the monopolies and the capitalists. Novelists began to challenge the self-righteousness of the public. Conservatives rallied to the defense. Stephen Crane's *Maggie, A Girl of the Streets* looked long in vain for a publisher. The Boston "Watch and Ward Society" assumed the role of censorship. Dreiser's *Sister Carrie*, 1900, was printed and then withdrawn from publication. Hemingway, Faulkner, Dos Passos took part in World War I and returned wearied of such high-sounding phrases as "honor," "patriotism," "heroism." It was a period of "debunking." As late as 1944, De Voto in *The Literary Fallacy*, called Faulkner, Hemingway, Wolfe, O'Neill, Pound, Dos Passos, and Steinbeck intellectual traitors. Van Wyck Brooks, Lewis Mumford, Archibald MacLeish, and

Howard Mumford Jones were of like opinion. There was no encouraging atmosphere for the secessionists in America. They found themselves more at home in France during the time that Gertrude Stein called "The Lost Generation."

About the year 1920 there were signs that the schism in American letters was narrowing. Sinclair Lewis's *Main Street* and *Babbitt* were works not of revolt but of benignant persiflage of American mores and standards in the best tradition of the nineteenth-century novel. John Dos Passos moved from Communism to Socialism and thence drifted further to the right with a growing interest in literary form rather than in propaganda. Hemingway's nihilistic *Farewell to Arms*, 1926, was followed by the collectivistic *For Whom the Bell Tolls*, 1940. During the Second World War, the depression, and the Roosevelt era orthodox Marxists became fellow-travelers or merely liberal supporters of the New Deal. German critics were fairly well informed in regard to the new tendencies and could relate them to conditions in Germany, generally approving the drift toward Socialism.

Among the most effectual novelists of the early twentieth century were Jack London, Frank Norris, Theodore Dreiser, Upton Sinclair, and Sinclair Lewis. But before discussing them it is in order to take into account two American narrators who gained belated appreciation in Germany in the twentieth century, namely Edgar Allan Poe and Herman Melville.

Poe, to be sure, had received a due amount of admiration in Europe at the time of his first successes, but it should be noted that the discussions at that time had to do chiefly with his poetry and his theory of poetical composition, while the new Poe criticism of the 1900's was directed chiefly toward his narratives. The comments on Poe have taken two directions little shared by the Americans. One of these is the psychological explanation, represented by Karl F. van Vleuten in an essay "E. A. Poe," in *Die Zukunft*,[6] and by F. Probst, "E. A. Poe," in

Grenzfragen der Literatur und Medizin, Heft 8, München, 1921. Furthermore, a treatise by Marie Bonaparte was translated from the French under the title *Edgar Poe: eine psychoanalytische Studie* and published with an introduction by S. Freud, Wien, 1934. Also, an essay by Karin Michaelis was translated from the Danish, under the title "Edgar Poe im Lichte der Psychoanalyse," *Almanach der Psychoanalyse,* 1936, pp. 153-157.

The other direction which German criticism took was toward the symbolic interpretation of Poe's work. The symbols discovered had to do chiefly with the precariousness of human existence and the need to face dangers with courage. One of the earliest of these monitors was Rainer Maria Rilke. In his *Briefe an einen jungen Dichter* under date of August 12, 1904, he referred to the loneliness of man in the life of today and commended the encouragement to be found in the works of Poe and Kafka. Poets of lesser note such as Hanns Heinz Ewers and Karl Hans Strobl saw in Poe not a troubled spirit, but a prophet to be trusted.[7]

H. H. Ewers, the advocate of Poe, was also an instinctive follower of him in his creative work. He had always had a taste for the strange and unnatural, and in Poe's tales he found what he had been seeking.[8] Parallels to these tales can be found in his collections: *Das Grauen* and *Die Besessenen,* 1907 and 1908, and in *Nachtmahr: Seltene Geschichten,* 1922. In these tales he followed Poe's prescription of brevity, and like Poe he hinted symbolically at an unearthly hidden world of realities rendering void the apparent realities of human perceptions. This is the expressed theme of *Der Teufelsjäger oder der Zauberlehrling,* 1909, as also of Poe's narrative *Morella.* Ewers published a collection of strange tales under the title *Galerie der Phantasten,* which included works by himself and by his like-minded friend Karl Hans Strobl. Strobl was the author of a Poe biography and of a collection of tales called *Lemuria: Seltsame Geschichten.* "Der Kopf" in this collection follows closely the plot of *The Pit and the Pendulum,* at one point almost literally. "Das Grabmal auf

125

dem Père Lachaise" is, in like fashion, related to *The Fall of the House of Usher.* Other such parallels could be listed.

Alfred Kubin distinguished himself more as an illustrator of works of Poe's followers than as an imitator of Poe himself. He contributed illustrations to Ewers' collection, *Galerie der Phantasten,* and illustrated his own phantastic novel, *Die andere Seite,* 1909. This novel deals with the problem of a split personality, as do also Poe's *Berenice* and *William Wilson.* The victim in Kubin's *Die andere Seite* suffers, as does Poe's victim in *The Pit and the Pendulum,* from a horde of rats. It has been pointed out that at least ten lines toward the conclusion are a plagiarism, or at least a paraphrase from Poe. Another disciple of Poe was Gustav Meyrink, the author of *Der Golem,* 1915.

Kafka belongs in a sphere with Poe in so far as he treats of anxiety, fear, and loneliness as literary subjects, but Kafka's protagonists live in an enigmatic world, and rational attempts to cope with it lead only to frustration. Poe postulates a logical, mathematically calculable world, and his threatened human beings survive by submission to its laws.

In the recognition of this fact, Ernst Jünger appears to be the most competent exponent of Poe's view of humanity's struggle.[9] To Ernst Jünger, Poe's tale *The Descent into the Maelstrom* always seemed allegorical and prophetic.[10] The narrator of this misadventure is saved by a rational faith in a cask to which he clings while his more timorous brother, who grasps the ring-bolt, is sucked into the vortex. Jünger compares the "Ausweglosigkeit" of our time to such a maelstrom: "Die beste Schilderung des voll automatischen Zustandes enthält die Erzählung *Hinab in den Malstrom,*" and again: "Der Malstrom erscheint mir noch als eine besonders gelungene Diagnose und Prognose unserer Zeit. Ihre Tendenz ist auf die knappste Formel gebracht," and still again: "Im Malstrom Edgar Allan Poes besitzen wir eine der grossen Visionen, die unsere Katastrophe vorausschauten." Because of this prescience Jünger agreed with the Goncourts, who called Poe the first author of the twentieth century.

126

In *Eureka,* in *The Pit and the Pendulum,* and in *The Fall of the House of Usher* Poe treats of similar terrors. In his tale *Der Hippopotamus* Jünger creates a situation comparable to that in the Usher house, but the narrator escapes from destruction not by rational means alone, but also with some help from incantations – by white magic – hence called "magischer Realismus." "Bei grossen Gefahren wird das Rettende tiefer gesucht werden und zwar bei den Müttern, und in dieser Berührung wird Urkraft befreit. Ihr können die reinen Zeitmächte nicht standhalten."

In commenting on *Eureka,* Jünger says one should tempt the death wish, should stand before the cataract, maelstrom, or precipice and defy it and thus pass beyond the "Nullpunkt." "Zahllose leben heute," he said, "welche die Zentren des nihilistischen Vorgangs, die Tiefpunkte des Malstromes passiert haben," and his wife wrote him during the World War II bombardments: "Was dich betrifft, so fühle ich mit Gewissheit, dass Du unbeschadet dem grossen Malstrom entrinnen wirst; verliere das Vertrauen zu deiner eigentlichen Bestimmung nicht."

To the narratives of ratiocination belong also Poe's detective stories. Sherlock Holmes is a confessed follower of Poe in this field, and the later writers are chiefly followers of Poe or Conan Doyle. Detective fiction is abundant in Germany but with little literary pretention, and so needs not to be discussed here. Friedrich Dürrenmatt has expressly denied that he is a writer of crime fiction. Horst Oppel [14] observed that German readers seeking only entertainment tend to choose American rather than German light novels.

Herman Melville gained no due appreciation in America, Germany, or elsewhere until about 1925. His literary career began auspiciously with the publication of *Typee, a Peep at Polynesian Life,* 1846, and *Omoo, a Narrative of Adventures in the South Seas,* 1847. Both of these novels were translated into German in the year of their appearance, *Omoo* by Friedrich Gerstäcker, who forthwith set sail for the South Seas to gather like information

127

for his *Tahiti, Roman aus der Südsee,* 1856, [11] and other novels of travel and adventure. Tales of exotic life were in high favor at the time. Melville's next novel, *Redburn; His First Voyage,* 1849 (German, 1850), found less favor. During the next six years, he wrote *Mardi,* 1849, *White Jacket,* 1850, *Moby Dick,* 1851, *Israel Potter,* 1855, a short story "Bartleby," 1856, and in the same year, *Piazza Tales* containing "Encantadas" and "Benito Cereno." None of these works was translated into German in its time and they all found so little appreciation in America that Melville believed he had lost his public. During the remaining thirty-five years of his life he published no further novels.

Mardi was the first of a series of disappointments to the public which hoped for more *Typee* and *Omoo* romances. *Mardi* was a "Südsee-Allegorie" whose importance lay in the fact that it paved the way for *Moby Dick.* "Ohne die Seeschilderungen in *Mardi* wären die vollendete Form und grandiose Konzeption der Seebilder in *Moby Dick* kaum möglich gewesen."[12]

In the year 1927 the Knaur Verlag in Berlin published a translation of *Moby Dick* by Wilhelm Strüver and of *Omoo* and *Typee* by Karl Federn. These three works appeared in a low-priced series called "Romane der Welt," under the general editorship of Thomas Mann. The publisher hoped thus to make good novels accessible to a larger class of readers. German publishers, authors, and critics took umbrage at this altruistic endeavor, which, they surmised, would place German originals at a competitive disadvantage. Not only the series but also the included novels were greeted with disfavor, but *Moby Dick* awakened some German interest in Melville. During the nineteenth century the German historians of American literature, Herrig in 1854, Doehm in 1881, Engel and Leixner in 1883, and Evans in 1896, like their American counterparts, had disregarded Melville, and Brunnemann in 1866 and Knortz in 1891 disposed of him as a minor author. But in his *Geschichte der nordamerikanischen Literatur,* Leon Kellner asserted in 1915 that as a realist Melville surpassed Zola and the Goncourts; and Walther

Fischer, in his *Geschichte der englischen Literatur der Vereinigten Staaten*, 1929, called attention to Melville's language which, he said, could be compared with the finest in English.[13]

Toward the end of his years, Melville apparently felt that he had still a message to deliver to the world, and he began to labor with *Billy Budd, Foretopman*. He made several trial beginnings, wrote some continuations and left the work almost finished in 1891, but without directions for completion. The manuscript was preserved, however, and a granddaughter turned it over to Melville's biographer, Raymond Weaver, who edited and published it in 1924. Better editions have appeared later. The appearance of "Benito Cereno" and *Billy Budd* called for a reappraisal of Melville. Both of these were translated in 1938. Forthwith they assumed a political aspect as a prefiguration of the German situation of that time. Billy Budd's struggle was that of the innocent individual with the totalitarian law which leveled all individuality and destroyed the personal element.[14] It was the example par excellence of an innocent man who was sacrificed according to the letter of the law in a world from which every vestige of humanity had disappeared. Similarly Benito, against his will, followed his leader in life and death.[15] That the Nazi regime condemned the works was logical. For the political philosopher Carl Schmitt, Benito Cereno was a symbol of the position of the intelligentsia of the time. This is documented in Schmitt's *Ex captivitate Salus*, 1950, and in Ernst Jünger's reports of discussions and correspondence with Schmitt in *Strahlungen*, 1949.[16]

The short-lived early German interest in Melville, 1846-1850, the long abeyance between 1850 and 1927, and the upsurge of interest since 1927 are mirrored by the statistics of translation, three between 1846 and 1850, none between 1850 and 1927, thirty-six or more between 1927 and today. The translations of the recent period were distributed as follows: *Moby Dick* 8, *Omoo* 7, "Benito Cereno" 6, *Typee* 5, *Billy Budd* 3, *Redburn* and *White Jacket* 2 each, "The Encantados," *Israel Potter* and "Bartleby" one each.

129

Melville's philosophy was variously charged with the pessimism of Schopenhauer and with the existentialism of Kafka and Kierkegaard. Carl Jung called *Moby Dick* the greatest American novel and recommended it as a subject for psychological study.[17] H.G. Oliass said that *Moby Dick*, like the works of Ernst Jünger and Franz Kafka, fulfills a deep metaphysical need for men living in an age wracked by two World Wars.[18] Julius Bab in 1949 described *Moby Dick* as permeated with fanatic pessimism, which, he said, accounts for its vogue among the younger generation after World War II.[19]

In the last year of his life, Thomas Mann was at work editing an anthology to be called *Die schönsten Erzählungen der Welt*. Of a five-page preface fully a half is devoted to *Billy Budd*, leaving little space for Goethe, Kleist, Flaubert, de Maupassant, Cervantes, and Poe. Mann says if he were asked which narrative pleased him best he would have to say *Billy Budd*. In the last sentence of the introduction Mann wrote "nicht dass es nicht auch für jedes andere Stück dieser Sammlung gälte – aber ausdrücklich: Melvilles *Billy Budd* ist wirklich eine der schönsten Erzählungen der Welt."

Leland Phelps, who calls attention to Thomas Mann's preface, adds: "Apparently Thomas Mann discovered Melville's works late in life. There is no indication... that he had read any of Melville's other works." It is strange that he should say this as he is aware of Mann's involvement with the Melville tales in the unwelcome Knaur series *Romane der Welt* as noted above.[20]

Jack London gained his early favor in Germany by his adventure novels rather than by his propagandist works. *The Call of the Wild* and *White Fang* were read with enthusiasm by addicts of such novels. They could compete successfully with the best of the still popular Cooper narratives. Before World War I, London's novels were abundantly translated and Tauchnitz brought out seven reprints between 1911 and 1914. Of these reprints *Martin Eden* alone, 1913, represented a novel of social protest.

Scarcely affected by war and civil turbulence, over thirty of the more than fifty works of London were promptly translated into German. They were prized especially by the Social Democrats. Erwin Magnus began to translate London's works for the Universitas Verlag in Berlin in 1924. The series continued until 1940, and since 1944 the influx of London's tales has diminished but little. The period of the Weimar Republic marked the high plateau of the London vogue in Germany. *Martin Eden* and *The Iron Heel*, despite their crude style, were valuable propagandist works for the socialists. The party was well aware that it did not have London's complete loyalty. From Charmian London's biography of Jack it could learn that he disassociated himself from the German socialists because they lacked fire and the fighting spirit. The German socialists treated his aloofness indulgently. London was not a Marxist, to be sure, but, as Franz Jung said in his essay, *Jack London, Dichter der Arbeiterklasse*, 1924, it was not necessary for Jack London, as it was for Upton Sinclair, to read books in order to become a socialist. The principles of the class struggle were beaten into him. He soon recognized that he was a member of the exploited outcasts, whose only hope lay in the fight of his class against the oppressors.[21]

A controlling fact is that Jack London was by nature an individualist. His best characters are supermen or superdogs. In the split between Nietzsche and Marx, Nietzsche came off with the better part – a fact which is also indicated by the title of W. P. Friederich's chapter on Jack London: "Götter und Proletarier"[7]. London's first works became known when European literature was sated with expressionism, self-searchings, and morbid psychology, and here was an adventurous character, a healthy, robust man of sweat and toil, who wrote from his own experiences. A critic asserted that when one finishes a modern European novel, one exclaims: "Was für ein raffinierter Mensch!" When one finishes a Jack London novel, one exclaims: "Was für ein prächtiger Junge!"[22]

An enthusiastic admirer of London wrote in *Die Literatur* 1933:

Ein Name hat schon lange Klang für uns. Jahr für Jahr ist dieser Klang volltönender geworden zufolge einer sich gleichmässigen Eindeutschung des Gesamtwerkes: Jack London. Bezeichnend, dass dieser Amerikaner, in älteren Lexika nicht auffindbar, erst heute im Nachruhm bekannt wird... Ein Autor für den wirklichkeitshungrigen Menschen unserer Tage! Dass er auch ein Träumer sein kann, macht ihn uns doppelt lieb.[23]

A cooler appraisal of Jack London's work had appeared in the same journal somewhat earlier in the form of an essay by J. E. Poritzky entitled "Jack London, oder das Übermass der Anerkennung." "London," he says, "erzählt temperamentvoll und plastisch. Er gibt wirklich ein Bild von Dingen und Menschen und bringt die Fremdartigkeit des Vorwurfes dem Leser gut nahe," but his anthropological pictures are not valuable to science because they leave in doubt where fact ends and fancy begins, and his romantic works fail to reach the height of true poetry. Fifty works in eighteen years we might say is "des mittelmässigen zu viel." There is not sufficient reason to rank him, as critics have, with Tolstoi, Balzac, and Homer. Even his most readable exotic novels, the critic says, have been surpassed by others – by the Dane Jürgen Jürgensen, by Dauthendey and by Rudyard Kipling. Even a comparison with R. L. Stevenson is out of place. "Ich halte Stevenson für eine reichere Natur und für einen Kerl mit einem ungleich weiteren Horizont."[24]

Frank Norris began his first novel, *McTeague*, 1899, while a student at Harvard. *Octopus* appeared in 1901 and *The Pit* in 1903. These were later combined in one work called *The Epic of Wheat, Octopus*, dealing with the struggle of the ranchers with the railroad barons, and *The Pit* dealing with the Chicago wheat market. Both are novels of protest like those of Upton Sinclair and Jack London. Further works of the kind were prevented by Norris's early death. *Octopus* was translated into German in 1907, *The Pit*, not until 1912, both under the new title *Die Getreidebörse*. This is the work on which Norris's reputation rests. *Octopus* was also translated under the title *Die goldene Frucht*, Berlin, 1940 and 1948, and Wien, 1948, and *The Pit* under the title *Kampf um Millionen*, Berlin, 1935.

The translation of *McTeague*, 1899, did not appear until much later, then first under the title *Gier nach Gold*, Leipzig, 1937, next as *Verfluchtes Gold*, Wien, 1947, then again as *Gier nach Gold*, Berlin, 1958, "aus dem Amerikanischen übersetzt von Paul Bollert." The title indicates the source of interest to the East Berlin Aufbau-Verlag. The recent film version circulating in the United States returns to the original title *McTeague*. The chief scenes are laid in the slums of San Francisco, and the tone of the work is the realism of wretchedness à la Zola. A recent critic refers to the American interest about the year 1900 in the deterministic and evolutionistic theories of Darwin and Spencer, and says:

> Diese Ideen, in der Regel reichlich verwässert oder missverstanden absorbiert, wurden zur Richtschnur einer neuen Generation von Schriftstellern, als deren markanteste Vertreter wir nur Crane, Garland, Norris und Dreiser zu nennen brauchen.

The critic notes that "Goldgier" is treated symbolically in the novel, which does not launch a direct attack on the capitalistic system as did the later *Octopus;* but he also asserts:

> Dennoch bleibt es ein unverkennbares Verdienst Norris', das in Anbetracht der damaligen literarischen Situation Amerikas gar nicht hoch genug eingeschätzt werden kann, in konsequenter Weise einmal den Fluch des Geldes, zu dem es in der kapitalistischen Gesellschaft werden kann, künstlerisch gestaltet zu haben.[25]

Jack London, Frank Norris, Upton Sinclair, and Theodore Dreiser were close contemporaries. Their earliest works all appeared between 1899 and 1906. Of these, Dreiser was the last to make an impression on German readers, for his *Sister Carrie*, 1900, was not translated until 1928, and his chief fame depends on *An American Tragedy*, 1925 (German, 1927). Upton Sinclair might claim to be the second of the group to gain favor in

Germany with his *The Jungle*, and *A Captain of Industry*, 1906, followed by *The Metropolis* and *The Money Changers*, 1908, all four of which were published almost simultaneously in German and English. Upton Sinclair is the only one of the group still living and writing. Not counting collected and selected editions of his works, he can list fifty-two titles translated into German, and his assertion that the largest sale of his works is in foreign languages can not well be challenged.[26]

Hermynia zur Mühlen undertook to translate and Malik in Berlin to publish nearly everything that Upton Sinclair wrote. An edition of *The Jungle* (German, *Der Sumpf*) reached a sale of 65,000 in 1928, of *Oil* (German, *Petroleum*) of 125,000 in 1931, of the anti-nationalistic *100%* of 30,000 in 1923, and of the anti-militaristic *Jimmie Higgins* of 42,000 in 1928. Arthur Holitscher said that nothing like *Jimmie Higgins* had been written in Germany as yet, because the Germans were too close to the events.[27] Upton Sinclair commented in 1933 that books are being burnt in Germany now, but as several million of his works had found their way into Germany, he doubted that all of them would be destroyed.

That Sinclair's works would find favor with the socialists was a foregone conclusion. *Die Aktion* published favorable reviews of *Samuel the Seeker*, of *The Jungle*, and of *They Call Me Carpenter*,[28] *Die Weltbühne* of *Jimmie Higgins*, and *Der Kampf* of *The Jungle* and of *Jimmie Higgins*. The whole question of propaganda literature was at stake, but these socialistic journals defended the genre in principle. Sinclair's works found some favor in other quarters. Thomas Mann and Hermann Hesse indicated indirectly some approval.[29] Georg Brandes wrote an introduction to *König Kohle*, 1918, in which he termed it an American parallel to Zola's *Germinal*, but F.P.Baader said this was at best true as far as the material, but never as far as the artistic mastery was concerned,[30] and Fritz Rosenfeld called Sinclair a great man although not a great artist.[31] E.A.Ackerknecht said that *The*

134

Jungle, Samuel the Seeker, Jimmie Higgins, and *100%* ought all to be included in every "Volksbibliothek."[32]

Upton Sinclair regarded as his best work the two volume polemical novel *Boston,* dealing with the Sacco-Vanzetti case, and this was the opinion of others including A. Ehrentreich[33]; but F. Schönemann maintained that the facts were not as Sinclair represented them and that Sinclair's *Boston* was not the American Boston.[34]

Upton Sinclair had a belated successor in Howard Fast, fifteen of whose works, chiefly novels, were translated into German, most of which, eleven, were published by the East Berlin Verlag, Dietz. The works thus published were written chiefly from 1939 to 1957 and appeared in German chiefly since 1950, but Fast, along with Upton Sinclair, was recently classified as a renegade.[35]

The successor of Upton Sinclair, Frank Norris, and Jack London was chronologically Sinclair Lewis – chronologically but not logically, for Lewis's predecessors wrote of and for the laborers, while Lewis wrote of and for the "white collar class" and "the intelligentsia." Lewis's reputation is founded chiefly on his novels of the years 1920-1936: *Main Street,* 1920; *Babbitt,* 1922; *Arrowsmith,* 1925; *Man Trap,* 1926; *Elmer Gantry,* 1927; *The Man Who Knew Coolidge,* 1928; *Ann Vickers,* 1933; *Dodsworth,* 1934; and *It Can't Happen Here,* 1936, all duly translated into German. The popularity of these novels led to a belated translation of a few less important novels of his earlier period. After 1936, he wrote seven or more novels and saw them translated into German. These did not markedly alter the established picture of Lewis the novelist.

It will suffice here to report the reception of some of the works of the middle period, from *Main Street* to *It Can't Happen Here.* Of these novels *Babbitt* was most frequently translated. A translation published by Wolff in Berlin and München, 1925, reached its 86th thousand in 1931. Later translations have appeared in Berlin, Hamburg, and Leipzig. The Tauchnitz Verlag published reprints of three of Lewis's novels, 1922-1925, and the Albatross Verlag in Hamburg an additional nine between 1932 and 1936. The importance of these novels was well recognized in Germany. Paul Kornfeld wrote: "Es gibt wenige Bücher, deren Erscheinungen ein Ereignis bedeutet; die Bücher von Sinclair Lewis gehören zu ihnen."[36]

Lewis was well grounded in the technique of book publication and advertising. He was especially desirous of translations into German, believing that foreign success was a help to success at home. The "Volksverband der Bücherfreunde" was persuaded to publish a low-priced translation of *Main Street* for its members. Lewis visited the publisher Wolff in München, who in the next year, 1925, issued popular-priced translations of *Babbitt*, 20,000 copies, and of *Arrowsmith*, 15,000 copies.

Lewis also visited Rowohlt: "a truly charming fellow and I am sure he is going to do much more with my books than Wolff did."[37] He was not disappointed: Rowohlt published translations of *Elmer Gantry* and *Man Trap* in 1928, of *The Man Who Knew Coolidge* in 1929, of *Dodsworth* in 1931, and of *Ann Vickers* in 1933. The Knaur Verlag in Berlin offered a new translation of *Main Street* in 1927. This was in the before-mentioned low-priced series "Romane der Welt" of the Knaur Verlag, so ill received by its competitors. The series was prefaced by Thomas Mann. The nationalistic *Türmer*, in an article called "Überfremdung des deutschen Schrifttums," asked why Thomas Mann, the son of a Creole mother, instead of supporting German literature, should sponsor the publication of foreign art, or rather non-art, alien to our nature and our country.[38] *Die schöne Literatur*, edited by Will Vesper, was of a similar opinion, and in a summary of *Elmer Gantry* Karl Martens wrote:

> Die europäische Korruption steckt, gemessen an der der Vereinigten Staaten, erst noch in den primitivsten Anfängen... Ein Vergnügen ist es nicht, sich in die Produktion von Lewis zu ver-

tiefen: instruktiv mag es sein für den, der nordamerikanische Zustände des Studiums für wert hält.[39]

Sinclair Lewis was at first unfortunate in his German translators. Wolff entrusted *Babbitt* and *Arrowsmith* to Daisy Brody, a Hungarian woman who had spent some years in New York. *The Job*, 1917 (German, *Der Erwerb*), was translated by Clarissa Meitner, Wien, 1929. In this abbreviated translation, references to happenings of its period were omitted, thus leaving the impression that the American scene of 1929 was being described, instead of the totally different one of 1917. The Rowohlt Verlag was fortunate in its translator, Franz Fein, who undertook German versions of eight of Lewis's novels between 1927 and 1933 and of *Babbitt* in 1957. One can only sympathize with a translator of these works. A 1922 English edition of *Babbitt* was provided with a glossary of slang and other Americanisms. Most of the German translations were excessively bad. There were unnecessary direct mistranslations of some simple English sentences, and a larger number of unskillful, misleading, or meaningless renderings of American speech, thus obliterating Lewis's chief triumph, the convincing rendering of American conversation. A reviewer of *Babbitt* compiled a five-page list of such inadequacies.[40] *Main Street*, *Babbitt*, and *The Man Who Knew Coolidge* presented the most difficult problems. Compared with these, *Dodsworth* was relatively simple. Franz Fein grappled with Lewis's phrases the most successfully, at times substituting Berliner "Umgangssprache" for American slang and idiom.

F. Schönemann was one of the earliest and staunchest advocates of Lewis. He contributed to *Die Literatur* an essay entitled "Sinclair Lewis, eine neue Verheissung im nordamerikanischen Roman."[41] In another essay he called him a new and representative American author, following Jack London and Upton Sinclair, whose acclaim in Germany, he said, was out of proportion to their literary significance.[42] Similarly, Walther Fischer distinguished Lewis's work from the one-sided propaganda of Upton Sinclair. Unlike his predecessor, Lewis loved his country and felt that he belonged to it.[43] H. Mutschmann recognized that Lewis's works were not the product of class struggle as were Upton Sinclair's, or of frustration as were Theodore Dreiser's.[44]

Upton Sinclair once challenged Lewis to write a proletarian novel even at the risk of offending two million people.[45] Lewis himself said that he did not call for a revolution, but was only trying to interest his countrymen in higher spiritual values. Undiscerning critics, to be sure, could easily contend that *Babbitt* was intended as a true and complete revelation of the soullessness of American life. One critic wrote:

> Das amerikanische Missbehagen über Lewis rührt von der instinktiven Erkenntnis her, dass dieser unbestechliche Beobachter mit Balzac'scher Akribie den standardisierten amerikanischen Menschen bis in die kleinsten Züge durchschaut und angeprangert hat.[46]

It was generally agreed that Lewis was not a literary stylist and that his works were often badly plotted. What he excelled in was the depicting of characters as revealed in their every-day conversations. His treatment of them was good-naturedly satiric. *Main Street*, Schönemann said, established Lewis as the foremost literary critic of American society. Carol Kennicott became the symbol "einer aus dieser Zivilisation herausstrebenden Amerikanerin." To her, Babbitt was "ein glänzendes Gegenstück, der philisterhafte businessman." *Arrowsmith* was also well received. Alois Brandl classified it as an "Entwicklungsroman" with convincing pictures of the American physician and of the philosophical Jew, Max Gottlieb. There was in it, he said, more "Amerikakunde" than could be garnered in a long visit to America.[47]

From these triumphs the majority of the critics felt that *Elmer Gantry* marked a sharp descent. There was no remnant of good nature left in the satire. Schönemann said: "Jeder einzelne Zug an ihm wirkt wissenschaftlich lebenssicher, nur die Häufung wirkt am Ende nicht ganz lebenswahr." This portrait of the unscrupulous religion profiteer was unbelievable to most Germans. "Dass es eine "Main Street" und einen "Babbitt" gibt wird niemand Sinclair Lewis bestreiten. Ob es einen "Elmer Gantry" gegeben hat, wird man bezweifeln können." Schönemann, who had devoted to the church one chapter of his study *Die Kunst der Massenbeeinflussung in den Vereinigten Staaten,* was aware that the portrait of Elmer Gantry was not too far from truthful. In America, church and civic authorities sought to have the book banned as being immoral and irreligious. Schönemann commented "Man kann Sinclair Lewis manche Übertreibungen und Entstellungen vorwerfen, wie sie bei Satiren nicht ausbleiben, aber der Vorwurf der Unreligiosität oder gar Unsittlichkeit trifft ihn nicht." Schönemann was, however, almost alone of the German critics in concluding, that "auch rein literarisch ist *Elmer Gantry* auf der Höhe von Lewis' Schaffen."[48] In its fearless bluntness, W. P. Friedrich compared *Elmer Gantry* to Molière's *Tartuffe* – but he was content to call it "ein ernstes Buch, eine für uns notwendige Warnung" [7].

After the disappointment, *Elmer Gantry,* came *Dodsworth,* which was hailed as a return to the early Lewis. The critical comments were almost uniformly favorable. In some respects it was Lewis's best novel. It was an "Entwicklungsroman" with plausible character development and with a better plot than in most of Lewis's novels. Julius Bab[49] and Paul Kornfeld[50] commended *Dodsworth* understandingly. Even *Die schöne Literatur* could find place for a favorable comment on *Dodsworth:*

> In seinem tiefen Verständnis für Deutschland liegt inhaltlich und zeitkritisch der eigentliche Schwerpunkt des Romans. Lewis' Kritik ist um so treffender als sie vollkommen undoktrinär, dafür aber prachtvoll humoristisch ist.[51]

The awarding of the Nobel Prize to Sinclair Lewis in 1929 found general approbation in Germany. If it was the intention of the judges to seek out a worthy American for the honor, Walther Fischer said, no better choice could have been made. But there were other possible choices. Fischer mentioned Sherwood Anderson, Theodore Dreiser, James Branch Cabell, and Eugene O'Neill. He agreed, however, "dass, alles in allem genommen, Sinclair Lewis als der repräsentativste amerikanische Autor gelten darf, weil er die amerikanische Gegenwart am allseitigsten schildert."[52] Journals like *Das Hochland* and *Der Gral* carried articles on Lewis and his place in American literature. One of the most interesting discussions was that by Arnold Zweig spoken on the Berlin radio and later published in *Die Literatur*: "Improvisation über Sinclair Lewis." Lewis, he said, had won his hearers by producing works which caused embarrassment to critics, but had found masses of readers, "um hinterher von der Kritik und Literaturgeschichte sanktioniert und gewissermassen heilig gesprochen zu werden." He continued:

> Dieser Dichter, Sinclair Lewis,... ist Ihnen bekannt, nicht seines Stils sondern seiner Gestalten wegen... Mit ihm, aber nicht nur mit ihm, hatte sich die amerikanische Literatur von Europa emanzipiert.... Anfang 1918 hielt man alles Amerikanische für Humbug... und heute gewinnt und bereichert uns die amerikanische Literatur, nicht mehr nur durch den herrlichen Edgar Poe und den Vater Walt Whitman, sondern durch eine ganze Schar schöpferischer Dichter, die von einander so verschieden sind wie der prachtvolle Ankläger Upton Sinclair von dem leidenschaftlichen Revolutionär Jack London, oder Ernst Hemingway von Thornton Wilder, Eugene O'Neill von John Dos Passos.
> Sinclair Lewis macht sich tausend Spässe, hält aber den grimmigen Ernst fest, die Welt nicht verschönert, nicht angehasst auszusagen. ... Das tut er im Kampf gegen den bestehenden Gesellschaftsunsinn in Amerika und anderswo, als Künstler, der weiss, dass Tatsache und Spass wundervolle Waffen sind.[53]

With the winning of the Nobel Prize at the age of forty-five, followed by the publication of the much praised *Dodsworth* the following year, Lewis reached the summit of his career and of his reputation at home and abroad. In Germany his marriage with the "Germanophobe" Dorothy Thompson was looked upon askance, and the publication of *It Can't Happen Here*, 1936

(German, Amsterdam, the same year), was a direct declaration of war against National Socialism. In 1938, Lewis's works were entered in the "Reichsschrifttumskammer" list "des schädlichen und unerwünschten Schrifttums."[54] The critic Otto Koischwitz wrote in 1941: "Von Sinclair Lewis, dem einst so gefeierten Schriftsteller, ist schon seit langer Zeit mehr verschrobenes zu hören als geschriebenes zu lesen."[55] Between 1936 and his death, five new novels of Lewis were translated into German. Perhaps the most important one was *Kingsblood Royal*, 1947 (German, 1950), but by this time a new type of American novel was arousing more interest in Germany.

The tardiness of translations of Theodore Dreiser's novels into German worked greatly to his disadvantage. The translation rights of *Jennie Gerhardt*, 1911, and of *The Titan*, 1914, were purchased by a German publisher, who then proceeded to do nothing with them. They were not published in German until *An American Tragedy*, 1925 (German, 1927), had established Dreiser's fame at home and abroad, but several German critics had previously read, admired, and reviewed the American originals – among them Franz Blei, who recommended them to German publishers,[56] F. Schönemann, who was able to affirm that Dreiser's writing technique had greatly improved since the completion of *Sister Carrie* (1900) and *Jennie Gerhardt* (1911)[57] and Erich Posselt, who called *An American Tragedy* a most depressing novel, but second to none in all America.[58] Readers dependent upon translations, however, could easily receive the impression that Dreiser was a follower rather than a forerunner of Sinclair Lewis.

An American Tragedy was Dreiser's sole popular success. Despite a considerable retardation during the years of the Third Reich, when his works were put on the blacklist, the earliest translation, that of Marianne Schön, reached its 364th thousand by 1955. The publisher Zsolnay in Wien recently estimated the total sale of works by Dreiser in the German language at about

647 thousand copies. The best years of Dreiser's works in Germany were between 1927 and 1932, which saw the publication of translations of *An American Tragedy*, of *Jennie Gerhardt*, and of *The Financier*, 1927, of *The Titan* in *Trilogie der Begierde*, 1928, of *Sister Carrie* and *The Genius*, 1929, of *Gallery of Women*, 1930, and of *A Book about Myself* and of *Tragic America*, 1932. Many expected Dreiser to become a Nobel Prize winner in 1930. Edwin Piscator produced a popular German stage and film version of *An American Tragedy*, which was later translated, adapted, and first produced at the Lenox Hill Theater in New York, 1936.

Publishers, and so presumably the readers in Germany, continued to show some interest in Dreiser. His posthumous work, *The Stoic*, 1948, was first translated in 1953 under the title *Der Unentwegte*. Since 1948 there have been new translations of *An American Tragedy, A Book about Myself, The Bulwark (Solon der Quäker), The Financier, Sister Carrie*, and *The Titan*.

The naturalistic *An American Tragedy* came to Germany at a time when Naturalism was already on the wane, yet discoveries of affinities with continental European Naturalism were to be expected. The relationship with Balzac is best authenticated. Dreiser came upon Balzac almost by accident, but then for a period of four or five months he "ate, slept, dreamed and lived him and his characters and his views and his cities."[59] In critical estimates references were made to Flaubert and Balzac, to Tolstoi and Dostoievski, and to Spielhagen and Sudermann. Arnold Zweig said that, thanks to Zola, Germany had outlived Dreiser's type of Realism.[60] Lüdeke asserted that American Naturalism can never be as gruesome as the European type because America has never suffered the depths of misery that Europe has known.[61]

Helpful to Dreiser was the fact of his German descent and his outspoken fondness of Germany and the Germans. He was kindred in spirit to H. L. Mencken and his *American Mercury* colleagues. This group tried to combat the prudery, the Puritan-

142

ism, and the outlived conventions prevalent in American life and letters, which they attributed to the Anglo-Saxon heritage. The German critics were pleased to regard Dreiser as a compatriot. This feeling may have made them more indulgent to his shortcomings. The fact that Dreiser, like Mencken, proclaimed himself an atheist recommended him to the radical thinkers in Germany, though at the cost of Catholic favor.

Not all the comments were favorable. There was something old-fashioned in Dreiser's novelistic work, one critic found. Dreiser could still make use of such time-worn characters as the poor girl, the rich lover, and the stern and honorable father.[62] Opinions varied regarding Dreiser as a writer. In the same journal, *Die schöne Literatur*, and in the same year three different views were expressed. Of *An American Tragedy*, H. Isemann wrote:

> Wenn man bedenkt, dass dieses riesengrosse Amerika geistig so auf dem Hund ist, wie dies Buch, dessen Autor auf dem Umschlag als Genie bezeichnet ist, so möchte man ihnen sagen, dass sie uns mit ihrer "Tragödie" in Frieden lassen sollen.[63]

Hans Knudsen characterized *Ton in des Schöpfers Hand* as "eine erstaunlich schwache Arbeit des angesehenen Amerikaners,"[64] but Richard Grande said apropos of *Jennie Gerhardt*, "Dreiser ist eine grosse und reine epische Kraft."[65]

And reverting to *An American Tragedy*, F. Schönemann added:

> Was immer seine Stärke war, nämlich psychologische Eindringlichkeit, soziales Einfühlungsvermögen, das ist jetzt zur Kunst gereift. Seine Schwächen: stilistische Schwerfälligkeit und journalistische Reportage, treten in dem Rahmen einer grossangelegten menschlichen Tragödie ganz zurück... In seiner Methode ein verspäteter Zola: so ist Dreiser heute einer der wuchtigsten Schriftsteller des modernen Amerikas.[66]

Walther Fischer found *The Financier* and *The Titan* monotonous and lacking art, *The Genius* immature, and he characterized

Dreiser as "schwerblütig" and "schwerartikulierend." The *American Tragedy*, he said, was "kein schlackenloses Kunstwerk zwar, aber ein ehrlicher Versuch, sich mit dem amerikanischen Leben in einem düster gesehenen Durchschnitt auseinanderzusetzen."[67]

Mutschmann quoted with approval Arnold Bennett's estimate of *An American Tragedy:* "It is written abominably by a man who despises style, elegance, clarity, even grammar," but Mutschmann asserted that all this did not detract from the grandeur of the whole composition. Walther Fischer called *An American Tragedy* a simple theme made universally human.[67] A critic in the *Frankfurter Zeitung* said that among his American colleagues Dreiser possessed the most problematical mind. Where Upton Sinclair was a brutal partisan and Sinclair Lewis an acute satirist, Dreiser was a pure artist.[68]

German critics of Dreiser's chief work were pleased to consider its tragedy as possible in the convention-ruled, censorious and prudish America, but not in Germany. Franz Schoenberner felt that this view was too smug and complacent. The chief difference was that Germany did not have any such frightening truth-teller as Dreiser.[69]

While Sinclair Lewis was still living and writing, a new group of American novelists was coming to the front. These writers were less concerned than their predecessors with problems of social significance. They were interested in man the individual rather than in collective groups of men. Furthermore, most of them were more interested than the preceding group in good style and the art form of the novel. Their works soon became known in Germany through translations and reviews. Among those whose names came to have the highest prestige were John Dos Passos, Thomas Wolfe, and the Nobel Prize winners William Faulkner, 1949, and Ernest Hemingway, 1954. Karl Korn wrote in 1937: "Hemingway, Faulkner, Wolfe haben die Dreiser und Sinclair Lewis abgelöst."[70] German critics recognized this varied group of writers as representing a new direction and referred to them

144

as "Die Jüngsten" in distinction from their socially-minded pre-decessors.

In his list of "Ablöser," Korn might well have included John Dos Passos although, to be sure, Dos Passos was a transitional novelist – for his first important success, *Three Soldiers*, 1921 (German, 1922), like Upton Sinclair's *Jimmie Higgins*, 1919, was a pacifistic, anti-war novel. It was also the most widely circulated of his works. The German translator was Julian Gompertz and the publisher was Malik in Berlin (1922), who printed twenty-one thousand copies, but who was not interested in the later novels, for he saw in them too little of propagandist value. Later works of Dos Passos were translated and published as follows: *Manhattan Transfer*, 1925, translated by Paul Baudisch, Berlin, 1929, and München, 1948; *The 42nd Parallel*, 1930, translated by Baudisch, Berlin, 1930; *1919*, again by Baudisch under the title *Auf den Trümmern, Roman zweier Kontinente*, Berlin, 1932; *The Big Money*, 1936, by Klaus Lambrecht under the title *Der grosse Schatten*, Zürich, Prag, 1939; and *Grand Design*, 1949, by Harry Kahn under the title *Das hohe Ziel*, Zürich, 1950. *The Big Money, The 42nd Parallel*, and *1919*[71] were published as a trilogy under the title *U.S.A.* Furthermore, Tauchnitz in the thirties issued reprints of four earlier Dos Passos novels.

Three Soldiers was favorably reviewed by A. Busse, Georg Kartzke, Walther Fischer, and Hans Joachim. Ehrenzweig liked Dos Passos best of all the great "anti-American" novelists as he called them. Dos Passos lacks the humor of Sinclair Lewis, he said, but he is a greater artist.[72]

In his earliest years Dos Passos was regarded by the pacifists, the socialists, and other reformers as the most hopeful ally in the new generation of writers, but he proved a disappointment as a propagandist. It became clear quite early that he was more interested in artistry than in ideology. When on one occasion in New York a group of Communists tried to break up a gathering of Socialists, Dos Passos lodged a complaint. He made a further

145

protest at the time of the Russian invasion of Hungary, and thereafter was referred to as a renegade. In his essay, *The Ground We Stand On*, 1941, he defined his position as fully to the right of what is fast becoming the center.

In *Manhattan Transfer*, Dos Passos uses narrative passages, broadcasts, news reels, and camera-eye descriptions to follow the fortunes of six or seven commonplace New Yorkers through the vicissitudes of their lives. We meet them at random times and places and find them at the end a generation later no happier or wiser than before. Life is drab, but nothing can be done about it. Jean-Paul Sartre said that Dos Passos' persons do not have lives, but only destinies. The subjects are drawn from the downtrodden class, and a few from the class in control. In other works Dos Passos takes account of the early struggles of trade unionism, but he sees no panacea in Marxism, and the Socialists, who once called him comrade, were later at pains to disown him. *Manhattan Transfer* found unqualified favor with F. Schönemann, who praised it, as he said, without disparagement of other great American realists such as Howells and Edith Wharton. Like its predecessor *Drei Soldaten*, it was a "Roman des Nebeneinanders," a form known to the Germans from the time of Gutzkow. "Wir leben," he said, "in einer Art internationaler Angst vor dem Ein-Held-Roman, die wir hoffentlich bald überwinden werden." Stylistically he found a marked improvement in *Manhattan Transfer*, which promised well for the future.[73]

The novels of Dos Passos were variously characterized by the censors of the Hitler regime as "zersetzend," "unheroisch," "unerwünscht," and "verboten," and the translations of his next novels, *The Big Money* and *Grand Design*, were therefore published in Zürich.[74]

The prevailing subject matter of Dos Passos' novels is the average being taken from a broad basis of specimens including no heroes or prophets. Dos Passos has no remedy against human stagnation, and is to be judged as an artist rather than as a world

146

reformer. As an artist he has not been without pupils in the Germany of today.

Francis Scott Fitzgerald has been only incompletely publicized in Germany. A collection called *Die besten Stories of Fitzgerald* was published in Berlin in 1954. Only two of his novels have been translated, *The Great Gatsby*, 1925 (Berlin, 1928 and 1953) and *Tender is the Night*, 1934, (German 1952). The facts of his tragic career were well known.[75]

Ernest Hemingway first became known in Germany through short stories published in German magazines. In *The Green Hills of Africa*, 1935, he tells Kandisky he wrote and published some poems and a long story (not specified) in the *Querschnitt*, years before he could sell anything in America. Hemingway was most actively translated during the years 1926-1930 (five novels or stories) and 1935-1940 (five titles). There followed a pause, broken in 1951 by translations of *Across the River and into the Trees* and finally by *The Old Man and the Sea*, a preliminary sketch of which had appeared in *Esquire* in 1936. All the novels referred to above were translated within a year or so after their appearance in America, and most of them were published by the Rowohlt Verlag as translated by Annemarie Horschitz. Of *The Sun also Rises*, 1926 (German under the title *Fiesta*, 1928), Rowohlt published the 203rd thousand in 1955. Next in popularity, to judge by the circulation statistics, were *A Farewell to Arms*, 1920 (German under the title *In einem anderen Land*, 1930), and *For Whom the Bell Tolls*, 1940 (German, *Wem die Stunde schlägt*, Stockholm, 1941). The Tauchnitz Verlag arranged a reprint of *A Farewell to Arms* in 1930 and the Albatross Verlag in 1937 of *Men Without Women*, and of *The Sun also Rises* in 1939. To large masses of the German public, Hemingway may be known chiefly through a film version of *The Snows of Kilimanjaro*, a watered-down version of Hemingway's short story of 1938.

147

The characters in Hemingway's novels are chiefly prize fighters, bull fighters, hunters, fishermen, and soldiers; the scenes of action are often saloons and bars, and religion is regarded as of trivial importance. Hence the reception of these novels was largely unfavorable on the part of *Gral, Hochland,* and other Catholic journals. The working class and the middle class found little interest in Hemingway's works, for their existence was ignored and the characters had no awareness of any class allegiance.

"Das dritte Reich" looked on Hemingway with mixed feelings. His characters were ruthless and fanatically heroic. The Nazis would gladly have claimed them as kindred, but Hemingway's participation in the war against Franco was too well known to be overlooked, and his works were placed on the black list of the "Reichsschrifttumsstelle," along with those of Theodore Dreiser, Michael Gold, Sinclair Lewis, Jack London, and Upton Sinclair.[76]

In East Germany, the acceptance of Hemingway's novels was selective. Schönfelder quoted with approval Thomas Mann's judgment of *A Farewell to Arms* as "ein Buch von grosser Schlichtheit und Aufrichtigkeit, ein wahrhaft männliches Buch, ein Meisterwerk neuen Typs."[77] In *For Whom the Bell Tolls,* 1940, there is still a trace of collective faith in John Donne's answer "it tolls for thee," but the later novel *Across the River and into the Trees,* Schönfelder said, marks "in Inhalt und Form einen künstlerischen Abstieg... An die Stelle von Donne's Ausspruch... ist der Grundgedanke getreten: jeder stirbt für sich allein." This later marked also a return to the "sinnlich triebhaften" tone of the early novel *The Sun Also Rises,* and is dangerously close to "Dekadenziteratur." Furthermore Schönfelder took umbrage at Hemingway's aloofness:

Ein Schriftsteller, der bewusst jede Tendenz meidet, der erklärt, Politik gehe den Künstler nichts an, der das Vorhandensein von Klassen und Klassenkämpfen ignoriert, und in dessen Werk weder ein einziger Arbeiter noch eine Mutter gestaltet werden, vermag bestenfalls ein winziges Segment des gesellschaftlichen Lebens wiederzuspiegeln... mag er auch ein noch so hervorragender Virtuose seines Faches sein.[78]

In conclusion, the critic commends the Aufbau-Verlag for its re-edition of *A Farewell to Arms*, but he adds: "Hinsichtlich der Publikation von *Über den Fluss und in die Wälder* war er schlecht beraten." Schönfelder regrets that "Hemingway hat weder den ersten noch den zweiten Weltkrieg als eine gesetzmässige soziale Erscheinung der kapitalistischen Welt erkannt."[79]

Another East German critic, Waldemar Damp [378], regards Hemingway as unwaveringly and consistently conscious of social problems. His novels show "eine bewusst politische Verantwortlichkeit zu gewichtigen Streitfragen der Zeit" and are a "sozialkritischer Protest gegen den Kapitalismus." Particularly his novels *Haben und Nichthaben* and *Wem die Stunde schlägt* are an "Abrechnung mit dem Faschismus" and at the same time a "Durchsetzung der proletarischen Lebensansprüche in Spanien und Amerika." The usual Marxistic unanimity is lacking at this point.

All of this fails to touch upon the most dynamic element in his work – the Hemingway style. The best examples are in his short stories, but in *The Sun also Rises* as well:

> Die Sprache des Romans zeichnet sich durch gewollte Dürftigkeit aus. Die meist der Umgangssprache entnommenen Wörter sind kurz und einfach. Schmückende Beiwörter fehlen fast völlig. Es gibt keine komplizierte syntaktische Erscheinung. Der Gebrauch der Parataxe überwiegt: Hypotaxe, die erklärt und begründet, ist selten.[80]

Hemingway tells how his characters were mangled or injured – but not how they suffered. He avoids all pathos. His best public was composed of young writers and young critics tired of propagandist works and tired of soul searchings. As in America, so in

149

Germany, it came to be the conviction of young writers that his was the style to be studied and imitated. Consequently the disciples were taken aback when Hemingway showed signs of abandoning the "Askese" of his earlier works. Possibly he felt that he was falling into a mannerism. Moreover, the bare style was more suitable for short stories than for novels. Irene Seligo called the austere style contagious and said, a little too categorically, that Hemingway was the first American to have a definite influence on European letters.

There were some signs of jealousy in Germany over the success of American novels. Curt Hohoff, among others, asserted that Germany doubtless had writers better than Hemingway.[81] Hans Wernher Richter contradicted him flatly, as did others by implication,[82] among them Dolf Sternberger and Kasimir Edschmid. The influx of American literature was welcomed by Elisabeth Langgässer, Ernst Kreuder, Bernt von Heiseler, and Hans Fallada – but the latter also asserted that not more than one fourth of his friends were capable of appreciating fully the quality of Hemingway's work.[83]

Thomas Wolfe began writing plays in 1918 and continued until 1929. Then he turned to novel writing and wrote massively until his death. The titles and contents of his plays can be found conveniently in Frenz [457]. None of them appeared on the professional theater in America, but *Manor House* [*Herrenhaus*] and *Welcome to Our City* [*Willkommen in Altamont*] have been played in Düsseldorf, Zürich, Berlin, Hamburg, and elsewhere.

On the occasion of his receipt of the Nobel Prize in 1930, Sinclair Lewis asserted that Thomas Wolfe bade fair to become the greatest American writer and perhaps one of the world's greatest writers. At that time only Wolfe's first novel, *Look Homeward Angel*, 1929, had appeared. Hermann Hesse more conservatively called *Look Homeward Angel* the most impressive poetic work from present-day America.

Wolfe's novels were translated in rapid sequence after 1932 as follows:

Look Homeward Angel, 1929; German, 1932.
From Death to Morning, 1935; German, 1937.
Of Time and the River, 1935; German, 1936.
Web of Earth, 1935; German, 1948.
The Web and the Rock, 1939; German, 1941.
You Can't Go Home Again, 1940; German, 1942.
The Hills Beyond, 1941; German, 1956.

The first strong impact of Wolfe's novels occurred in the thirties. World conditions interfered for a time, but after 1941 translations were resumed. Wolfe was fortunate in his first translator, Hans Schiebelhuth, who succeeded brilliantly in coping with the varied difficulties of the text. The success of the first four novels listed above is due to his care. The translations of the later novels were inferior to Schiebelhuth's.

Wolfe's novels were non-political. They appealed chiefly to "die Stillen im Lande," but they found disfavor with critics belonging to the dominant party. Under the title "Unerwünschte Einfuhr," a reviewer in Will Vesper's *Die Neue Literatur*, quoted specimens of the extravagant praise prevailing in the current journals: "Das geheimnisvolle Wunder alles Dichterischen" *(Berliner Tageblatt);* "Thomas Wolfes Register reicht von Whitman bis zu Dostojewski, reicht aber von Goethe bis Hamsun und reicht gar von Homer bis Cervantes und Dickens" *(Deutsche Allgemeine Zeitung).* There follows an annihilating summary and critique of *Von Zeit und Strom*, wherein it appears that only one figure, a Jewish character, copes successfully with the untowardness of existence. No German publisher, the reviewer says, would accept such a formless novel if written by a German. The Nazi critic concludes: "Die Klassiker des amerikanischen Romans, Theodore Dreiser, Upton Sinclair, Sinclair Lewis haben alles schon besser gesagt."[84] It may be noted here that these predecessors took a negative view of American life while Wolfe, as another critic maintained, carried on the tradition of Whitman, though with less joyous confidence.[85] This optimistic view of America distinguished him from Mencken, Dreiser, Lewis, and Faulkner.

Several favorable critics bear distinguished names, among them Hermann Hesse (quoted above), Paul Alveredes, Bernt von Heiseler, and Wolfgang von Einsiedel. The unfavorable critics could justly find fault with Wolfe's gigantic and not always successful struggle with the massiveness of his material. They could say that *Look Homeward Angel* has no unity except the passing of time, that *Of Time and the River*, 1,100 pages, is interminable, boring, and repetitious, and that Wolfe is unselective and completely unpoetic. Those who favored him, on the other hand, found his language "poetic," "hymnic," "rhapsodic," "polyphonic," "orphic." Certain it is that the sale of Wolfe's works in Germany has not been commensurate with the acclaim of his more ardent reviewers.

In an essay of 1961, Hagopian looks back upon "ten years of Faulkner studies in America." He says that, although the volume of Faulkner criticism in America and elsewhere has approached the proportions of mass industry, Faulkner is virtually neglected in German circles devoted to "Amerika-Studien." It is well at this point to note certain chronological stages in the growth of the international reputation of Faulkner. In the early years French criticism predominated. One of the earliest discussions was that of Le Breton: "Technique et psychologie chez W. Faulkner," *Études Anglaises*, September, 1937. Persistent criticism, however, first set in in the forties with Malraux, 1943, Coindreau and Pouillon, 1946, Sartre, 1947, and de Magny, 1948. All of these critics were, like Le Breton, chiefly interested in Faulkner's psychology and technique.[86]

Hagopian [344] may be right in saying that American interest in Faulkner first began after the award of the Nobel Prize in 1949 – but he is not justified in saying that Faulkner is virtually neglected in German circles devoted to American studies. A. Busse, in one of his "Amerikanische Briefe" contributed to *Die Literatur*, called German attention to him in 1932, and was one of the first Germans to do so.[87] Between 1932 and 1938 at least five more Germans made contributions to Faulkner lore,[88] the most distinguished of whom were Hermann Hesse and Bernt von Heiseler, but the most solid study was that of Harnack-Fish, 1935.[89]

Of course, between 1938 and 1945 conditions were not favorable for Faulkner in Germany. His works were denounced by the official critics and censors. But with the awarding of the Nobel Prize, a new period of interest in him began in Germany as in America. Monographs came in quick succession from the University Presses of America: Oklahoma, 1951; Duke, 1952; Minnesota, 1954; Louisiana State, 1957; Stanford, 1957; Kentucky, 1959; Cornell, 1960; Michigan State, 1960; and North Carolina, 1961. Hagopian has written a valuable summary of the principal American studies.[90]

He asks unnecessarily why Faulkner has been neglected by German specialists in "Amerikakunde." Perhaps, he says, this is because he is less readily understood in English and not as successfully translated as, say, Thomas Wolfe, Ernest Hemingway, and Thornton Wilder, and also because he appeals less strongly to German readers. On the contrary, Faulkner has been much written about in Germany, and it would seem from the evidence presented that he is now receiving as much attention as his contemporary American novelists. In fact, the German critics have found a particular fascination in interpreting Faulkner's symbols, in clarifying vague passages, and in surmising events that are only implied.

Most German readers first heard of William Faulkner through the words of Sinclair Lewis in his Nobel Prize speech of 1930, in which he said that Faulkner had freed the Southern women from hoop skirts. He was then first seriously introduced to the Germans by the Rowohlt Verlag in Hamburg. The firm published a translation of *Light in August* (1932) in 1935 with an enthusiastic recommendation:

> Neben die schwermütige Verhaltenheit eines Ernest Hemingway und die leuchtende Überschwenglichkeit eines Thomas Wolfe tritt die aufwühlende Psychologie des grossen Moralisten der modernen amerikanischen Literatur: William Faulkner.

and concluded: "Dieser grosse Dichter leitet seine Gestalten von so tief innen her, wie es nur bei Dostojewski und Conrad der Fall war."

In these words the publishers anticipated nearly everything that the later critics were to say regarding Faulkner as a moralist and a psychologist. One critic, however, added to Conrad and Dostoievski the names of James Joyce and Virginia Woolf as predecessors.[91]

Although several of Faulkner's short stories had appeared earlier in German literary magazines, his fame in Germany began with *Licht im August*, translated by Felix Fein, who coped admirably with the dialect, with Faulkner's lexical oddities, and with his opaque style, making but few errors, one of them unfortunately being in the title. Here it may be noted that a French translator made the same error: *Lumière d'août*, traduit de l'américain par Maurice Coindreau, 1955.

Light in August caught the attention of the critics. It was reviewed in *Velhagen und Klasings Monatshefte*, in *Westermanns Monatshefte*, in religious journals such as the Protestant *Eckart* and the Catholic *Hochland* and *Gral*, and in academic, pedagogical and literary journals such as *Anglia Beiblatt*, *Zeitschrift für neusprachlichen Unterricht*, *Die neueren Sprachen*, *Die Literatur*, and *Die neue Rundschau*.

Faulkner's novels also called forth comments from several noted German critics, from Mildred Harnack-Fish [328], Wolfgang von Einsiedel [329], Karl Korn [330], Hermann Hesse [327], and F. Schönemann.

Von Heiseler noted the total lack of humanity and Christianity.[92] Hesse diagnosed Faulkner as suffering from inexorable Puritanism.[93] Schönemann, at first dismayed by Faulkner's seemingly negative and hopeless philosophy of life, was won over by the appearance of *The Unvanquished*, 1936 (German, 1954).[94] H.G.Brenner commended *Intruder in the Dust*, 1948 (German, 1951), saying that it conveyed its message "deutlicher als in dem Roman *Licht im August*, zupackender als in *Absalom, Absalom*."[95] Although several of the most distinguished critics took exception to the unmitigated presentation of evil, the prevailing opinion was that Faulkner was a novelist of the highest order.

Official disfavor, no doubt, restricted the circulation of Faulkner's novels in Germany, but there were traits in his works that appealed even to the detractors. The Nazis had a morbid interest in "race" problems, and together with Wolfe's novels most of Faulkner's took the reader away from Main Street and Babbittry to hidden rural communities, that is to say, they were in their way "Blut und Boden" novels, though not glorifications in the contemporary German intent.

With *Light in August*, Faulkner was firmly established as a major American novelist. His reputation was further enhanced by *Pylon*, 1935 (German, under the title *Wendemarke*, 1936), and by *Absalom, Absalom*, 1936 (German 1938). The 1940's brought no further German translations of Faulkner's novels, but a new activity began in the 50's. His earliest major work, *The Sound and the Fury*, 1929 was belatedly translated in 1956, *Sanctuary* of 1931, in 1951, *The Unvanquished* 1938, in 1957, *Wild Palms* of 1939, in 1957, *The Hamlet* 1940, in 1957, *Go Down Moses* 1942, in 1953, *Intruder in the Dust*, 1948, in 1951, *A Fable*, 1954, in 1955, *Requiem for a Nun*, 1951, in 1956, and *A Mountain Victory*, 1932, in 1956.

After reading Faulkner's novel *Licht im August*, Hermann Hesse still regarded Wolfe as a greater narrator, but *Licht im August* was comparable with Wolfe's first novel:

> Ähnlich wie Wolfes Buch ergreift dieser Roman durch die Kraft und Bilderfülle, durch die grosse Wriklichkeitsnähe und sinnliche

Jugendlichkeit mit welcher auch hier ein Stück amerikanischen Südens Stimme gewinnt... Die nicht überlegene Psychologie des Dichters beglückt nicht. Dafür aber stehen in seinem Buch Bilder, stehen Gestaltungen naiven Schauens, die sich recht wohl mit denen Wolfes vergleichen lassen.[96]

The Swiss Heinrich Straumann regards *A Fable*, 1954, as Faulkner's most important book, more than that as "die bedeutendste Leistung der angelsächsischen Epik seit dem zweiten Weltkrieg." He described it as

ein ergreifendes und starkes Buch in dem Sinne wie Tolstojs *Krieg und Frieden*... ein gedanklich schwer befrachtetes Buch, schwerer wohl als *Moby Dick*... Es verwirrt den Leser, weil Gedanken und Geschehen auf den verschiedenen Ebenen symbolischer, allegorischer und mimetischer Darstellung bald getrennt, bald eng ineinander verzahnt sind.[97]

Most of the translations of Faulkner's novels are seemingly bad, but it is out of order to blame the interpreters. Some of the ablest translators were chosen for the task. Faulkner's bold word-creations presented a challenge to them, and his convoluted sentences, which sometimes break and take a new direction in their course, posed formidable obstacles. Faulkner is reported to have said to a group of students that he wasted no thought on form: "Wenn man eine Geschichte in sich hat, so muss sie heraus." We need to be reminded that he also wrote lyric poetry, in the opinion of one critic, "im Gegensatz zu seiner so anspruchsvollen Prosa, seltsam flach."[98]

On the whole he was favored with ever-increasing esteem at home and abroad, and during the short time between the deaths of Hemingway and Wolfe and his own death in August, 1962, he was probably regarded by most German critics as America's foremost novelist. The award of the Nobel Prize for literature confirmed his high place in world competition. At the time of his death one critic called him "den letzten grossgearteten zeit-genössischen Erzähler."[99]

In a recent essay [348] Rudolf Haas prophesied:

> Dieser Dichter Faulkner wird einen Platz nicht nur in der Ge-schichte des amerikanischen Romans jetzt schon beansprachen dürfen. Er verdient und verträgt es, an der Weltliteratur gemessen zu werden.

It is true, Haas says, that he lacks the precision of Flaubert and the epic breadth of Tolstoi but "er ist tiefer und reicher als Hemingway, vielschichtiger als Dreiser ... [und] breiter als Stephen Crane."

Deviating briefly from strict chronology, let us here refer to the very belated recognition of Henry James in Germany. In a review of a Willa Cather novel, *Sapir,* a critic wrote in 1956:

> Unser Verhältnis zur amerikanischen Literatur wird nicht zuletzt von der Meinung bestimmt, als sei der Roman der "lost generation" oder die soziale Epik der "Chicagoer Gruppe" allein repräsentativ für die Erzählungskunst dieses Landes. Wer heute von ameri-kanischer Epik spricht, meint Hemingway, Dos Passos, Faulkner, Miller, Wolfe, und von der älteren Generation Lewis, Sinclair, Sandburg und Dreiser. Erst jetzt, z.B. lernen die deutschen Leser Henry James kennen."[100]

To be sure, between 1876 and 1880 several works of Henry James had been translated into German – *A Passionate Pilgrim* in 1876, *Roderick Hudson* in 1876, *The American,* in 1877, and *Eugene Pickering,* in 1880. But they failed to arouse lasting interest, perhaps because German readers looked to America for ruder and cruder literature, and perhaps in good part on account of the difficulty of the style. The revival of interest in Germany was sharply marked in the decade following 1946. In Zürich, Köln, and München several translations appeared: The *Altar of the Dead,* Zürich, 1949, *The Portrait of a Lady,* Köln, 1950, *The*

157

Siege of London under the title *Eine gewisse Frau Headway*, München 1952, *The Turn of the Screw*, in *Meisternovellen*, Zürich, 1953, and again under the title *Die sündigen Engel*, München, 1954, *The Princess Cassamassima*, Köln, 1954, *What Maisie Knew*, Köln, 1955, *The Ambassadors*, Köln, 1956. There appeared also in Köln in 1958 a collection of twelve short stories by James. Ruth and Augustus Götz dramatized *Washington Square* under the title *Die Erbin*, 1954, which was broadcast by radio in Switzerland, June 24, 1954, from Stuttgart, July 11, 1954, and elsewhere later.

By the time of the revival of interest in his novels in Germany, James had been a topic of discussion by many English and American critics, among them Van Wyck Brooks, Joseph W. Beach, E. M. Forster, T. S. Eliot, Graham Greene, and W. H. Auden. James has also been compared with Thomas Mann, whom he resembles in his meticulous effort to render his ideas precisely. Like Tonio Kröger he suffered from the feeling of not belonging. The Germans sympathized with James in his feeling of alienation from the crudeness of American culture and his search for the recovery of the lost European values.

Edith Wharton's similar search for European values also received belated attention in Germany. Three of her novels were translated: *The Age of Innocence*, 1920, under the title *Im Himmel weint man nicht*, 1951, *Twilight Sleep*, 1927, under the title *Die oberen Zehntausend*, 1931, *Ethan Frome*, 1911, under the title *Die Schlittenfahrt*, 1948.[101] This masterpiece was also adapted for the stage and played in several German cities.

To return to our contemporaries: in 1958 there appeared the monograph of Hildegard Schumann *Zum Problem des kritischen Realismus bei John Steinbeck*. This may be accepted as an authentic statement of the Marxist attitude toward Steinbeck. The author recognizes three stages in the literary productions of the author, the early works, the period of greatest significance,

1937-1939, followed by a descent to the role of an entertaining story teller. Chapter V is called "Höhepunkt der Gesellschafts-kritik: *The Grapes of Wrath.*" Schuman states at the outset:

> In Steinbecks Gesamtschafften stellt der Roman the *Grapes of Wrath*, 1939, das literarisch beste und volksverbundenste Werk dar. Trotz der ideologischen Widersprüche, die auch hier nicht eindeutig überwunden sind, müssen wir es als eines der fortschrittlichsten Werke der amerikanischen Literatur der dreissiger Jahre bezeichnen.

But unfortunately, the author says, this work is not typical Steinbeck. Typical rather are those works "in denen Steinbeck seiner mystisch-primitiven Religiosität, erwachsen auf einer biologisch-naturalistischen Grundlage, freien Lauf lässt."

In *The Grapes of Wrath* Steinbeck describes realistically the deterioration of the land, and the inroads of the tractor. The farmers foresee their dispossession by the banks, and regard the tractors and the banks as their enemies; but they fail to see that "verantwortlich ist das Eigentum schlechthin, d.h. die Eigentumsverhältnisse im Monopolkapitalismus."

Steinbeck tells of occasions when, under the pressure of outrageous cruelty, the serfs were able to act with proletarian solidarity – but such sporadic defense, Schumann says, is not sufficient. The wage slaves must be organized. They must be indoctrinated with the theories of Marx, must learn the technique of opposition, must learn to be secretive and ready for surprise action. Such organisation requires leadership, and the natural leaders would be the Communists. In his novel *In Dubious Battle* Steinbeck describes such a leader and his activity, but it is not clear that he fully approves of that self-appointed hero. In fact Steinbeck at his most radical stage seems to fall just short of urging an uprising of the masses. Toward the end of *The Grapes of Wrath* several of the characters are beginning to see the need of organization, but take no action. To this Schumann says: "Was mir ausschlagend bei der ideologischen Gesamtwertung des

Romans erscheint, ist die Tatsache, dass diese Erkenntnis gegen Ende des Buches wieder zurücktritt hinter einer Haltung gefühls- betonter Humanität, hinter einem mystischen Glauben an die Unbesiegbarkeit des Menschen."

In the remaining works of Steinbeck, Schumann finds little or nothing of practical value. Steinbeck is a self-professed individualist. He has a fondness for primitive or half-educated characters, who are unfit for leadership toward progressive goals. The denizens of *Cannery Row* are poor but content. Mysticism and allegory are harmful in so far as they soften the impact of serious realism. And so Schumann concludes:

> Angesichts der Entwicklung Steinbecks seit Ende des zweiten Weltkrieges, angesichts der politischen Entwicklung im heutigen Amerika [muss man es] als unwahrscheinlich bezeichnen, dass [Steinbeck] eine Wandlung zum Positiven und Fortschrittlichen zeigen wird.

[1] Vollmer excludes authors whose reputations were well established before 1871.
[2] Blanke [283].
[3] Effelberger [257].
[4] Schönemann [81].
[5] Schönemann [304].
[6] *Loc. cit.*, XLIV (1903), 181-190.
[7] Kühnelt [231] 199.
[8] Kühnelt [230] 460 f.
[9] Peters [420].
[10] For the following references to Jünger see Peters [420].
[11] Walter [221].
[12] Klaus Lanzinger in DNS, 1960, pp. 1 ff and 15 ff.
[13] Phelps [411].
[14] H. Pongs, *Im Umbruch der Zeit*, 1932, p. 143.
[15] Phelps [412] 297 f.
[16] Phelps [412] 295.
[17] Phelps [411] 349.

18 H. G. Oliass, *Welt und Wort*, IV (1949), 428.
19 Julius Bab, *Amerikas Dichter*, 1949, p. 49.
20 Phelps [411] 298 and [412] 350.
21 *Op. cit.*, p. 61.
22 Thiel [401] 203.
23 Schickert [404].
24 Poritzsky [400].
25 Brüning [416].
26 Bantz [435]; Sinclair [434].
27 Holitscher [428].
28 *Die Aktion*, XIV (1925), 13; XIII (1924), 14.
29 Springer [282] 44.
30 Baader [427] 201.
31 Rosenfeld [424] 342.
32 Ackerknecht, *Bücherei und Bildungspflege*, VI (1926), 273.
33 Ehrentreich [432] 24.
34 Schönemann [422].
35 Schönfelder [269] 55.
36 Kornfeld [389].
37 Harrison Smith, *From Main Street to Stockholm*, New York 1952, p. 250.
38 *Loc. cit.* XXX (1928), 486.
39 *Ibid.*, XXIX (1928), 249.
40 Steiner [388].
41 Schönemann [380].
42 *Der Türmer*, XXXI (1928), 64.
43 Fischer, [392].
44 H. Mutschmann, *Handbuch der Amerikakunde*, Frankfurt, 1931, p. 237.
45 Sinclair [382], 745.
46 Anselm Schlosser, in *Europäische Literatur*, III (1944), 15 f.
47 Brandl [381] 122 f.
48 Schönemann [383] 574 f.
49 Bab [393].
50 Kornfeld [389].
51 Behler-Hagen [386] 243.
52 Fischer [392] 700.
53 Zweig [390].
54 Berendsohn [260] 120.
55 *Die Literatur*, XLIII (1941), 240.
56 Blei [215].
57 Schönemann [320].
58 Erich Posselt, "Zeitchronik," *Die Literarische Welt*, XIX, May 7, 1926.

[59] Theodore Dreiser, *A Book about Myself*, New York 1922, pp. 412 f.

[60] Zweig [390].

[61] Lüdeke [248] 376 f.

[62] Ehrenzweig [321] 151 f.

[63] Isemann [317] 138.

[64] Knudsen [318] 554.

[65] Grande [319] 491.

[66] Schönemann [320] 296.

[67] Fischer [392] 700.

[68] F. Schotthofer, *Loc. cit.*, Dec. 23, 1928.

[69] *Die Literarische Welt*, XLIX (1927), "Buchchronik des Weihnachtsmarktes," p. 15.

[70] *Die Tat*, XXIX (1937); Springer [282] 75.

[71] Mummendey [1] overlooks this translation. 2 d

[72] Ehrenzweig [309] 55.

[73] Schönemann [367].

[74] Berendsohn [260] 170.

[75] Politzer [351]; Irwin (352).

[76] Berendsohn [260].

[77] Schönfelder in ZAA, VII (1954), 216.

[78] *Ibid.*, p. 218 f.

[79] *Ibid.*, p. 218-219.

[80] *Ibid.*, p. 210.

[81] *Süddeutsche Zeitung*, Nr. 58; March 10-11, 1957. *Ibid.*, no. 59.

[82] *Ibid.*, Frey [279].

[83] Fallada [358] 672.

[84] *Loc. cit.* 1937, pp. 501-508. Article "Unerwünschte Einfuhr"; Luther Erdmann in *Das deutsche Wort*, XIV (1938: 147).

[85] "Aspekte der Faulkner-Kritik in Frankreich": JAS, VI (1961), 155-159.

[86] Hagopian [344] 135.

[87] Busse [250].

[88] Lützeler [326].

[89] Harnack-Fish [328]. Mildred Harnack-Fish was a former American exchange student in Germany, a translator, and intermediary of German and American literature. She was hanged for participation in the anti-Nazi underground.

[90] Hagopian [344].

[91] Effelberger [257] 160.

[92] *Deutsche Zeitschrift*, XLIX (1936), 468.

[93] DNR, XLIV (1935), 670.

[94] *Zeitschrift für Neusprachlichen Unterricht*, XXXV (1936), 282, and XXXVIII (1939), 120.

95 Brenner [333].
96 Hesse [327].
97 Straumann [337].
98 DLD, Dec. 1959, p. 9.
99 Busch [347].
100 Haas [348].
101 Schönauer, *Neue deutsche Hefte*, 1956, "Kritische Blätter," p. 6.

VII. THE THEATER

The American drama came into the German purview somewhat later than the contemporary American novel. Not long after the First World War, plays by Robert Sherwood, Maxwell Anderson, and Elmer Rice began to appear on the German stage, accompanied in greater number by such Broadway hits as *Front Page*, *The Trial of Mary Dugan*, *Broadway*, *Burlesque*, and *Abie's Irish Rose*. With concerted discrimination such plays were designated as "Broadway theater" rather than as "American theater." Julius Bab wrote specifically in 1928: "Das Theater der U.S.A. war im ganzen neunzehnten Jahrhundert, war noch vor zehn Jahren, identisch mit dem Broadway-Theater der Zeit."[1] The plays were numerous and many were stage successes in Germany, but there was no threat of "Überfremdung," such as was later to occur, for Germany had at that time an abundance of German playwrights of the highest order, such as Paul Ernst, Franz Werfel, Ernst Toller, Bertolt Brecht, Fritz von Unruh, Max Mell, Reinhold Sorge, Carl Sternheim, Karl Schönherr, Hugo von Hofmannsthal, Hermann Bahr, Arthur Schnitzler, Bruno Frank, Georg Kaiser, Walther von Molo, Gerhart and Carl Hauptmann, Carl Zuckmayer, and several others.

The appearance of Eugene O'Neill marked the beginning of the legitimate American drama. Hans Galinsky wrote:

Dieser Amerikaner... wird zum entschiedenen Wiedererwecker des Tragischen... Er ist der erste, der das amerikanische Drama aus kolonialer Zurückgebliebenheit und Europahörigkeit zu weltliterarischer Wirkung geführt hat.[2]

Other critics were in agreement with Galinsky. Julius Bab wrote: "Mit diesem O'Neill, der weitaus stärksten Physiognomie im Drama des letzten Jahrzehnts, beginnt das amerikanische Theater ein Faktor in der abendländischen Kulturgemeinschaft zu werden."[3] After sketching the discouraging state of the American theater before O'Neill, W. P. Friederich asserted that "An einem solchen fast ganz entmutigenden Hintergrund gemessen, wirkt (sein) dramatisches Genie doppelt eindrucksvoll und überwältigend – schon nur deshalb, weil er den Geld- und Erfolgsinteressen nie auch nur eine Zeile seiner Kunst geopfert hat." [7]. Felix Hollander heralded O'Neill as "ein neuer Mann, der mit frischen unverbrauchten Augen sieht, und eine fremde Welt mit sicheren Strichen hinzustellen weiss."[4] Alfred Kerr claimed "Pate gestanden zu haben" for O'Neill,[5] "denn ich sprach... vielleicht in Europa zuerst von ihm." He was therefore chagrined that the first O'Neill selection for the Berlin stage was *Anna Christie*, made worse by stage production and textual revisions. At the conclusion Anna Christie rather unexpectedly shoots herself. "Eingemottete Dramenmode," Kerr called it.

To be sure, there was little that was autochthonous in O'Neill's early plays. If for America they marked the birth of tragedy, for Europe they signalized the renaissance of the drama of Ibsen, Strindberg, and Wedekind, years ago pronounced dead to the stage and now returning by way of America to haunt the living. To these predecessors some German critics proposed to add the name of Freud, but mistakenly. O'Neill learned German in order to read Wedekind and Nietzsche in the original, but disclaimed any relationship to Freud in his early plays.

One of the earliest German critics to attempt an estimate of O'Neill's dramatic talent was Hugo von Hofmannsthal. He was

165

impressed by O'Neill's strong sense of the theatrical, his use of keynote words, of motifs, and of rhythmically recurrent situations such as he himself used. He described O'Neill's dialogue as "stark, manchmal sehr direkt, manchmal von einem gewissen brutalen und pittoresken Lyrismus." In an interesting comparison he noted that O'Neill's first acts struck an emotional note that was continued rather than intensified in the following ones. Hauptmann, on the other hand, he says, begins with a situation on which he later imposes motives and events and which reach a climax at the end. As a result, Hauptmann's last acts are usually his strongest, O'Neill's strongest are usually the first.[6]

O'Neill's succeeding play, *Emperor Jones*, was only slightly more successful in Berlin. The stage setting was deplorable, and the beating of the tom-toms annoyed the public. It was generally agreed that the production was an artistic failure. Popular successors were *The Hairy Ape*, October 1924, *The Moon of the Caribbees*, December 1924, and *Desire Under the Elms*, 1925, all in Berlin – but none of them made an unqualifiedly favorable impression. *S. S. Glencairn* was played in Essen – "ganz unverhohlener angelsächsischer Kitsch," one critic called it,[7] and *The Great God Brown* was played in Köln, 1928. These were popular successes. The critics were of various opinions, but in general agreed that the primitive O'Neill of *The Hairy Ape* was preferable to the literary O'Neill of *Desire Under the Elms* and *The Great God Brown*. The relation of the latter play to Strindberg was recognized.

The first period of O'Neill representations ended in a popular and literary success. *Strange Interlude*, November 1929, found favor despite its length, and after its shortening by Heinz Hilpert, January 1, 1930, it went on to become a stage hit in Berlin with a hundred representations. The success was due in large measure to the acting of Elisabeth Bergner, and productions might have continued, had she not demanded release from her contract. It was a bold innovation to let the characters of the drama gloss the things they said with the utterance of the subconscious impulses that lay behind. The result was in part belated Ibsenism, and, some critics said, contemporary Freudianism. The role of Nina demanded the most varied talents which Fritz Engel summed up:

> Braunlockig, ein verstörtes, krankes Mädel – dann eine junge Mutter, die es nicht sein soll – dann ein liebendes Weib – dann wiederum Mutter – dann abblühende Reize unter roter Perücke – dann eine alte Dame, der es grob gesagt wird – dann eine sanfte Greisin – und dazwischen noch mehr – neun Akte – neun Rollen – neunmal Frauenliebe, Leiden und Hass – getrieben und treibend durch Enttäuschungen und Entzückungen – neunmal der nämliche Mensch und doch ein anderer.

The invention of such a role was the foundation of its brilliant representation. The achievement, to be sure, was epic rather than dramatic. Engel called it "ein Romandrama."[8]

Soon after the defeat of the Hitler regime, O'Neill was restored to his deserved place in the theater programs. The Frankfurt production of *Mourning Becomes Electra*, April 1947, was hailed as the greatest theatrical event since the end of the war. The tragedy was in the main line of modern drama, connected as it was with Strindberg and Ibsen. It was disassociated from the plays of Thornton Wilder and of Robert Ardrey by its lack of "American" optimism. The public was enthralled despite the length of the play: "Sechs Stunden lang vorgelebtes Menschengeschick, immer neu verdichtet, immer anders gesteigert." One critic called attention to the "ungeheure Reichweite des Stückes":

> Vom Reisser bis zur Tragödie, vom Kriminalstück zur psychologisierenden Gesellschaftsanalyse, von kräftigen Naturalismus bis ins Mythisch-Surreale. Es gibt Mörder und Gespenster, Hintertreppenklatsch und Romantik, uralte Kenntnis menschlicher Verstricktheit, rein tragische Momente neben theatralischer Dramatik.[9]

The interpretation of Heinz Stroux, the director, the stage

167

settings of Herta Bohm, and the acting of Maria Pierenkämper as Elektra were all admired. For some reason the production of the same play in Hamburg was less successful. One cause of the failure may have been the severe pruning.

In this same period two other abortive attempts were made to fashion *Anna Christie* for the theater of the day, in Berlin, November, 1945, and in Hamburg, January, 1950. Portrayers of Anna Christie had to vie with the success of Greta Garbo in the film version of the play, which was its only real success in Germany, but so altered that it was no longer pure O'Neill. His early version was already outmoded.

Ah, Wilderness had its German première in Esslingen, where it was well received, but its appearance in this small city was scarcely noted beyond its confines. A year later, 1947, it was played in Berlin under the direction of Boleslaw Barlog. The selection of this family idyll, this out-of-fashion portrait album, this nostalgic recollection of the days of youth, was criticized by the reporters, for why should Barlog choose just this piece as representative of O'Neill? Walter Lennig called it "ein herzhafter Rückfall in das bürgerliche und sentimentale Theater, gegen das O'Neill sonst so unbarmherzig Krieg geführt hat."[10] Despite the truth of this observation, the play found the favor of the public, as did also a production in Hamburg seven years later, October, 1954. Now it found some critics who commended it. One of them said: "Ein herrliches Stück, in dem reiche Erfahrung, unbändiges Jungsein, zarteste Poesie und trockener Humor... beieinander wohnen."[11]

The Iceman Cometh, New York, 1946, Dublin, 1948, Zürich, 1950, was produced in Hannover, March, 1954. Most of the critics were favorably impressed. Hermann Stresau found that it approached the tragic Greek drama in grandeur.[12] Another compared its effect rather with that of a "Jedermann-Spiel." A critic who sought to assess the effect of the drama on the public concluded that the reaction was not "stürmisch" but rather "bedächtig," and that it belonged to the group of dramas "die man zunächst mit Reserve aufnimmt, deren Wirkung aber von Tag zu Tag tiefer wird."[13]

The critics were fairly well agreed regarding *A Moon for the Misbegotten*, this revelation of the "unbarmherzige Zucht des antiken Schicksals auf dem Schauplatz einer heruntergewirtschafteten amerikanischen Farm."[14] One of the earliest and best of the productions took place at Bochum during the "Woche amerikanischer Dramatik," March, 1955. It was Greek in the hopeless gloom of irresistible Fate and also in its absolute maintenance of the unities of time, place, and action. One reporter spoke of the "stundenlange Atemlosigkeit eines gebannten Hauses."[15]

O'Neill's plays seem to have found a permanent place in the German repertories. In 1954 began an O'Neill renaissance. There were two German "Erstaufführungen" in that year, two "Neuinszenierungen," and a dozen other productions, including *Desire under the Elms* in Heidelberg, and *The Great God Brown* in Stuttgart. In 1955 were produced *Ah, Wilderness* in Wiesbaden and *Desire under the Elms* in Hildesheim and in Düsseldorf. In the season 1960-1961 O'Neill was represented in Wien at the Burgtheater with *A Touch of the Poet* and *A Moon for the Misbegotten*, at the Theater in der Josefstadt with *Ah, Wilderness* and *The Great God Brown*. In the same season *Hughie* was played in Hamburg. In 1962 *Ah, Wilderness* was played in Linz. These examples demonstrate continued interest in O'Neill's plays in West Germany and Austria.

One might conclude from the evidence that the general public was quicker to appreciate the plays of O'Neill than were the critics. One might note also that the critics who rejected certain "Erstaufführungen" sometimes changed their opinions at the appearance of later revivals, and finally that while individual plays were often sharply criticized, admiration for the dramatist remained. The greatness of O'Neill was greater than the sum of his dramas. The critics could well be confused by O'Neill, who never let himself fall victim of a "Schablone," and every new drama in regard to form was unexpected. The constant element in the dramas is the helpless submission to inevitable fate. The nostalgic *Ah, Wilderness,* by contrast, serves only to present a picture of transient content.

It will have been seen that O'Neill's activity as a playwright fell into two periods. The first extended from about 1919 to about 1933. During these years appeared *Beyond the Horizon, Emperor Jones, Anna Christie, The Hairy Ape, Desire under the Elms, Strange Interlude, Mourning Becomes Electra,* and *Ah, Wilderness.* These plays were duly and for the most part promptly produced on the Berlin and various other German stages. During the next twelve years O'Neill was inactive as a playwright. The early plays soon ceased to be accepted on the German stage, and had O'Neill written new ones, they would surely have been banned by the Nazi regime.

The second period began about 1945 with *A Moon for the Misbegotten* and did not end with O'Neill's death in 1953. *A Moon for the Misbegotten* was followed by *The Iceman Cometh,* New York, 1946, the last play that O'Neill lived to see produced. O'Neill expressed the wish that another group of plays, obviously because of their more intimate nature, should not be made public until long after his death. To this group belong *A Touch of the Poet, Hughie,* and *A Long Day's Journey into Night.* These plays all found a place in the repertoires of Wien, Zürich, Berlin, and West Germany from 1960-1963.

At the end of the Second World War the German economy touched its zero point, but almost the first group to rise from the ruins was the Theater Guild. It did not even have an undamaged stage to start with. In Berlin the actors went into the Grunewald, gathered rushes and, with a high disregard for fire risks, wove them into curtains. Nails cost many cigarettes, but some could be salvaged from ruined buildings; actors fainted at rehearsals from hunger. This was a commonplace; but the show went on.

170

Next came the problem of the repertory. There was an abundance of novelties to choose from. During the preceding years the drama outside of Germany had proliferated and provided an abundant source of choices. From England there were new plays by Eliot, Fry, Coward, and Maugham; from France by Anouilh, Giraudoux, Cocteau, Sartre; from America by Williams, Steinbeck, Saroyan, O'Neill, and Wilder. Then too there were the German classics, for these also were a novelty to the war generation when played in unexpurgated and unedited forms. To the older generation the reappearance of these plays was a nostalgic return to the days of its youth. One of the earliest novelties in Berlin was a production of *Nathan der Weise*.

As a result of all this there was a richness of repertoire which concealed for a time a grave deficiency – the lack of a new generation of German writers for the theater. In the season 1949-1950, Carl Zuckmayer appears to have been "der meist gespielte deutsche Dichter." Curt Götz, a sort of German Noël Coward, continued to produce saucy and entertaining conversation pieces, and Hermann Billinger continued to write his concoctions of "Blut und Boden," folklore, superstition, and dialect. More important and refreshing than these were the experiments of Brecht. But it is to be noted that all of these playwrights had established their reputation before the beginning of the war, and that to find novelties the directors had to look to foreign writers. A few random statistics confirm this fact. The *Frankfurter Allgemeine Zeitung* reported for 1954: "Im Schauspiel stehen 267 deutschsprachige Werke, 337 ausländischen gegenüber." In the season 1948-1949 next after *Hamlet*, Priestley's *Ever Since Paradise* and Coward's *Blithe Spirit* were the most popular plays. In the season 1951-1952 the order of popularity was John Patrick's *Das heisse Herz*, Schiller's *Wilhelm Tell*, Herbert's *Wolken sind überall (Once in a Blue Moon)*, and Curt Götz's *Dr. med. Hiob Prätorius*. Thornton Wilder's *Die Heiratsvermittlerin* was probably the most often produced and most popular play for the 1954-1955 season. In the season 1955-1956, Patrick's

Das kleine Teehaus was played on fifty stages and continued its success the following season. In Vienna, as might have been expected, the foreign element was strong. The Akademietheater, 1952-1953, offered 71 foreign and 41 German plays. Of the foreign plays 19 were French, 17 British and 12 American. Berlin, 1946-1948, offered 34 British and 27 American plays; München, 1946-1951, 16 American and 8 British plays.

Among the British authors who contributed to the German repertoires from 1946-1954 were Shaw with 16 plays, Coward with 11, Maugham with 7, Fry and Priestley with 6 each, Eliot and Rattigan with 5 each. Among the Americans can be noted: O'Neill with 10 plays, Tennessee Williams with 8, Saroyan with 4, Elmer Rice, John Patrick, and Maxwell Anderson each with 3, and Thornton Wilder with probably as many as O'Neill. At least 117 British and American plays were represented during these years. French dramas vied with them in popularity. Next in order seem to have been all Scandinavian authors taken together, followed by Spanish, Italian, and ancient Greek dramatists.

East Berlin has drawn no curtain against Western plays as such. In their repertoires are to be found the names of Abbot and Holm, of Barrie, Beckett, Bridie, Coy, Fry, Henry James, Kingsley, Odets, O'Neill, Priestley, Saroyan, Steinbeck, Van Druten, and Wolfe. Some plays, to be sure, were not favored, among them Wilder's *Our Town*, which was felt to glorify the family too much, and his *The Skin of Our Teeth*, which seemed to acquiesce in the inevitability of war.

Amidst this superabundance of effective foreign successes, young and hopeful new playwrights felt themselves to be overlooked. They said directors preferred to be assured of success by the foreign plays rather than to take risks with untried experiments. They even said that their manuscripts were returned unread, but many critics agreed with the assertion that with the exception of Zuckmayer, Bruckner, Hochwälder, Dürrenmatt, Götz, Frisch, and a few others, German authors

172

were played *"weil* sie deutsche Autoren sind." It may be noted here that of the six exceptions two were Swiss writers and one an Austrian living in Switzerland, and that none of the others was a novice. As a matter of fact efforts were made to encourage new talent. The theaters belonging to the "Bund" undertook to present three plays each year by three as yet undiscovered German playwrights. The competition led to several fiascos. In one city the chosen three were hooted down by the audience. It does not appear that the award succeeded in discovering a single important talent, and to present an unripe drama is to do its author a disservice.

At the end of the Second War and during the first years of the occupation, approximately until 1948, the theater programs of Berlin and of East and West Germany were not dissimilar. Among the American dramatists represented were Ardrey, Behrman, Odets, O'Neill, Irwin, Saroyan, and Steinbeck. The plays of these authors were chiefly written during the thirties. The forties contributed Gow and d'Usseau's *Deep are the Roots*, Lilian Hellman's *Watch on the Rhine*, and Miller's *All my Sons* and *Death of a Salesman*.

Toward the end of the forties, East and West German stages began to drift apart. The East German theaters continued to present "progressive" plays, among them Odet's *Golden Boy*, Herb Tank's *Tanker Nebraska*, Howard Fast's *Dreissig Silberlinge*, and repeated *Deep Are the Roots* and *All my Sons*. At the same time the West German theaters were gradually deteriorating in the view of East German critics.

In the season 1947-48 there appeared in West Germany not only the defensible *Three Men on a Horse* of Holm and Abbot and *The Voice of the Turtle* of Van Druten, but also Wilder's *Our Town* and Saroyan's *The Time of Your Life*, both of them detrimental, according to East German standards, as were also Emmet Lavery's Jesuit drama, *Die erste Legion* and the "kitschig" *Boy Meets Girl* of the Spivacs. In the season 1949-50 appeared Tennessee Williams' *A Street Car Named Desire*, regarded as morbid, and Garson Kanin's *Born Yesterday*, to which was conceded the merit of exposing the crudities in high American political circles.

Sometimes, though but rarely in the annals of literature, a historical crisis, a deeply involved public, and a drastic dramatization of the situation come in total conjunction. Such was the timeliness of Thornton Wilder's most powerful play, *The Skin of Our Teeth*. Only the Germans have seen it in its proper setting – out-of-doors before the background of ruins. The spectators sitting there with collars turned up and with lap robes, if they had them, shared the misery of human life, and they could feel themselves as actors in a timeless world drama.

In America, as Schimming said, rightly or wrongly, the play was looked upon "wie ein gesellschaftskritischer Scherz ohne tiefere Bedeutung," in Germany "als etwas unendlich Ernsthafteres: nämlich ein prophetisches Gedicht von beklemmender Zielsicherheit, eine Schau des sich in der Geschichte entfaltenden Bösen und des von Mal zu Mal näherkommenden Unterganges." It was a play "dessen Seelenlage in dem vom Grauen der Apokalypse geschüttelten Nachkriegsdeutschland eine viel echtere Resonanz als drüben finden konnte."[16] Seelmann-Eggebert wrote:

> Vielleicht gibt uns der tiefste Sinn, der in der modernen amerikanischen Dramatik von Wilder bis Ardrey und von Osborn bis Behrman liegt, eine Lösung: Das Leben ist schwer, das Leben ist aber auch schön; man muss den Kampf aufnehmen, muss sich resignieren können und zuletzt doch ja sagen zu ihm. Ist das nicht eine Einstellung, ist das nicht ein Geist, die heute in unseren Theatern wirklich leben und aus ihnen sprechen müssten?[17]

Thornton Wilder was well known in Germany before the war, but as a novelist rather than as a playwright. His *Cabala*, 1926, was translated in 1929, *The Bridge of San Luis Rey*, 1927, in 1929, *The Woman of Andros*, 1930, and *Heaven's My Destination*, 1934, in 1935. The *Bridge of San Luis Rey* met with the same critical

174

praise in Germany that it reaped elsewhere in Europe as well as in America. Hans Egon Holthusen found that in his first three novels Wilder made his ideas clearer from one work to the next.[18]

Immediately after the war Wilder won acclaim in Germany as a dramatist with his two most important plays: *Our Town*, 1938 (German, 1944) and *The Skin of Our Teeth*, 1942 (German under the title: *Wir sind noch einmal davongekommen* (1944). Since that time nearly all his plays were translated and most of them staged within a year or two after their publication in America. The prevailing tone is of doughty defiance of hardship. The wide choice of subject matter, and the great divergence of form could not fail to interest the critics, the stage directors, and the public. Meanwhile Wilder has presented himself frequently before the German public. He received the "Ordre pour le mérite" in 1937, later an honorary degree from the Goethe University in Frankfurt, and the German Book Trade's annual peace prize. He has made several trips to Germany. During the air lift he won the favor of the West Berliners by flying into their city on a cargo plane, and he has frequently made public addresses to the Germans in their own language.

The reception of Wilder's works by the German critics has been as favorable as by the American, but the favor has been prevailingly for different reasons. With the Germans the entertaining element is of secondary importance and the "Weltanschauung" is the chief value. The German critics sometimes see allegories and hidden meanings of which the American authors are possibly unaware.

In their first season, 1945-46, *Our Town* and *The Skin of Our Teeth* were played in several German theaters, and in the following season by most of the remaining important ones. *Our Town* was received favorably in München, December 2, 1945, as well as in Berlin the following spring. The lack of success in the Hebbel Theater in Berlin, 1949, may have been due to unskillful staging. It is true that one of the women in *Our Town* chooses a return to death rather than to a renewed struggle with

175

life, but the whole tone of the play is "lebensbejahend," and that tone continued to be dominant in Wilder's plays. *Our Town* still remains in the programs of German theaters. The German "Uraufführung" of *The Skin of Our Teeth* took place in Darmstadt in April, 1946 under the direction of Harl-Heinz Stroux, one of the leading directors of the time. It came immediately under lively discussion, and Stroux took it on a "Gastreise" in July of that year to Wiesbaden, Frankfurt, and elsewhere. Other productions took place in München, Hamburg, Köln in 1947, and in Frankfurt, 1953.

The astonishing feature of the play was the time and place of its origin. Written in 1941, it was prophetic rather than reportorial, and written in undevastated America. Yet its atmosphere was that of post-war Germany. A minority of the German critics called it pessimistic, but most of them saw in it faith and hope for the future through tenacity – "Katastrophenoptimismus." Wilder's most notable plays were unacceptable in East Berlin, but the Eastern critics saw the West Berlin productions. Their verdicts followed, for the most part, the line of the official displeasure. Wilder was called an apologist for an unsatisfactory social order, and *Our Town* was charged with dallying with an unprogressive belief in a future life.

The most popular play of the 1954-1955 season and the most popular of all Wilder's plays in Germany was *The Matchmaker*, 1954 (German under the title *Die Heiratsvermittlerin*, 1955). This was also the least original of Wilder's works for the theater. In 1835 John Oxenford had written a play called *A Day Well Spent*, and its plot was then taken over and adapted to Viennese life by Johann Nestroy under the title *Einen Jux will er sich machen*, 1842. Wilder first tried to adapt it to old New York life with a version called *The Merchant of Yonkers*. This was not particularly successful on Broadway. His second version, *The Matchmaker*, drew full houses in America, Britain, and Germany. Some of the German critics were loath to believe that Wilder had stepped out of his role to write a play of mere entertainment value, but attempts to point out deeper meanings were not particularly successful. The Burgtheater in Wien, and some of the German theaters as well, revived Nestroy's comedy in order to allow the public to make comparisons.

In 1947 Wilder was invited to take part in the dedication of the Kongresshalle in Berlin. He presented three one-act plays in English. Ethel Waters played the title role of Bernice, the wise and understanding supporter of a freed convict on his return to the world. The production of the *Wreck of the Five Twenty-Five* was a "Welturaufführung." *The Happy Journey to Trenton and Camden* was already known to the Germans, but this version gained interest by being played by an all-Negro cast.

Wilder's *Life in the Sun* was received coolly at the Edinburgh Festival, 1955, but productions in Zürich and Frankfurt under the title *Alkestiade* found favor with the German critics, if not with the German public. Perhaps a symbolic interpretation is not wholly out of order here. A reviewer in the *Frankfurter Allgemeine Zeitung* formulated it: Hercules (America) snatches Alcestes (Europe) from the snares of death.

Paul Fussell, in a recent essay, called Wilder's success in Germany undeserved and said the German canonization of Wilder was having a pernicious effect in Germany: "After wallowing from 1933 until 1945 in brutal political realities (Germany) now hankers as violently after the spiritual and the ideal."[19] But other critics have pointed out that it is fallacious, on the basis of a single strong preference, to draw conclusions regarding the German psyche as a whole: "The Germans accepted plays of widely divergent styles, subjects, and intellectual climates."[20]

Heinrich Straumann, a Swiss, considers Eugene O'Neill as the most important American dramatist. His dramas have more intensity and weight, he says, than Thornton Wilder's. "Trotzdem hat O'Neill bei uns viel weniger Fuss gefasst. O'Neill scheint das abzugehen, was als Botschaft bezeichnet und interpretiert werden kann." The European reader of today desires such a "Botschaft," and finds it in Thornton Wilder's conviction "dass im blossem Mut, im immer wieder von vorn Anfangen, ein ewiger Wert liege, zusammen mit der Idee, dass jeder von uns mit einem Stück Verantwortung behaftet ist." In this connection he observes that the more recent dramatists Tennessee Williams and Arthur Miller have been more favored than O'Neill, even though their achievements are less original than his.[21]

The East German critic Schönfelder derides Straumann's ethical interpretation of Wilder's *The Skin of Our Teeth*. He declares that it is a rude self-deception to believe "dass die Millionen amerikanischer Arbeitslosen nichts Wichtigeres zu tun haben, als sich jeden Augenblick mit dem Weltschicksal unmittelbar verantwortlich verbunden zu fühlen." Wilder's popularity at the end of the war was explicable, he says, but "der gegenwärtige Wilder-Rummel, der im Jahre 1957 mit der Verleihung des Friedenspreises in Frankfurt seinen Höhepunkt erreichte, hat nicht so sehr literarische als kulturpolitische Gründe." He also condemns Wilder's "platte Sonntagsschule-Weisheiten, seinen blassen Ästhetizismus, seine Flucht aus der Gegenwart in die Vergangenheit... und seine Beschäftigung (oder ist es eine Spielerei?) mit christlichem Gedankengut."

Schönfelder also takes exception to Straumann's use of the term "Europäische Leserschaft." Actually Straumann, he says, discusses chiefly the German public with some reference to English and French readers, but in fact there is no such thing as a national reading public. Teen-age boys read adventure tales that are of no interest to girls of the same age.

Ein atheistischer, klassenbewusster Hafenarbeiter aus London liest in seinen Mussestunden andere Bücher als die katholische Oberschwester eines Kölner Krankenhauses... Marxistisch geschulte bulgarische Philosophiestudenten und die Mitglieder eines französischen Existentialistenklubs werden Faulkner's Roman *Sanctuary* ganz verschieden beurteilen.

The taste of reading publics is determined by many factors, of which nationality is but one.

Was wir als Publikum bezeichnen ist die Gesamtheit zahlreicher Leserschichten, die sich nach Temperament, Veranlagung, Geschlecht, Alter, sozialer Herkunft, Erziehung, Bildungsgrad, Klassenzugehörigkeit, politischer oder religiöser Anschauung, Nationalität und den daraus resultierenden Interessen und Geschmacksrichtungen von einander unterscheiden.[22]

One of the earliest of Tennessee Williams' scenarios was called *Twenty-Seven Wagons Full of Cotton*. Williams combined this with another outline called *The Long Stay Cut Short* or *The Unsatisfactory Supper*. With some added material a play was produced which appeared in several German repertoires under the more convenient American film scenario title *Baby Doll*.

Between 1946 and 1954 he produced several plays which appeared promptly on various German stages.

Glass Menagerie, 1944, Basel, 1946, Hamburg, 1949.
A Street Car Named Desire, 1947, Zürich, 1949, Pforzheim, 1950.
The Rose Tattoo, 1950, Hamburg, 1952.
Cat on a Hot Tin Roof. Düsseldorf, 1955.
Camino Real, 1953, Darmstadt, 1954.
Summer and Smoke, 1948, (German, *Der steinerne Engel*), Stuttgart, 1951.

By this time the German critics were able to evaluate Williams' products not only separately but as a group. The first two of these plays had in common the theme of unsatisfied love – but of *The Rose Tattoo* a critic wrote: "Er ist doch wohl nicht tot, der grosse Pan; er ist nur ausgewandert an das Mississippi Delta."[23] For the first two plays an awareness of the decadent phases of the Old South is helpful, and the German directors were not always successful in conveying this picture.

Glass Menagerie and *A Street Car Named Desire* were totally unlike in structure. The substance of the *Menagerie* is made up of retrospect and dreams of the future. It is therefore of necessity static. *A Street Car Named Desire*, leading from hysteria to insanity, is pathological and more sensational. Williams seems to urge compassion and understanding for all the characters in these plays, as well as for those in *Cat on a Hot Tin Roof*.

It was clear that Williams had read widely and creatively. A tinge of Hemingway and of Thomas Wolfe has been detected in his work, and slightly more of the playwright Saroyan, but European masters predominate. One critic observed:

> Es ist reizvoll zu beobachten, wie das, was das alte Europa einmal vor reichlich fünfzig Jahren erregt hat, nun von Amerika aus mit Psychoanalyse durchsetzt als letzter Schrei zu uns zurückkommt.[24]

Another critic described *A Street Car Named Desire* as a "naturalistischer Reisser à la Zola oder Sudermann."[25] Still another observer said of *Glass Menagerie:* "Es ist eine mit dichterischer Kraft gezeichnete Seelenstudie auf der Linie zwischen Strindberg und Saroyan, mit einem Schuss Wilderischer Skepsis in einer Atmosphäre von Maeterlinckischer Zartheit."[26] Maurois called *A Street Car Named Desire* the best of those imported from America, and was reminded of Strindberg and Chekhov.[27] Frequent also was the comparison with Hauptmann and Ibsen and, where sex is involved, with Wedekind. One critic called Blanche a late descendant of Ibsen's and Hauptmann's feminine characters. The Germans were quick to see that the motif of the "Lebenslüge" reappeared in *Cat on a Hot Tin Roof*. *The Rose Tattoo* brought other predecessors into consideration. Serafina delle Rose was compared with Hauptmann's Mutter Wulff and the Spanish *Celestina*.[28] *Summer and Smoke (Der steinerne Engel)* was one of the least admired of William's theater pieces. A critic asserted that there lies "über dem Ganzen ein wenig erstickend der Problemstaub der Jahrhundertwende."[29] Heinz Rode called it a "Sudermanniade" and added, "Der Vielgelästerte konnte auch mehr."[30]

With *Camino Real,* Williams confronted the German directors with difficult stage problems. Williams himself said that he regarded his texts only as architect's sketches, the details of which were to be filled out by the producer, but Berthold Viertel wrote to Williams' representative:

Obwohl Tennessee Williams behauptet hat, nichts sei einfacher und klarer als Text und Wege dieses Monster-Dramas und ihm sei keine Dunkelheit aufgefallen, kommt es mir doch so vor, als ob ein Fremdenführer durch die Symbolismen dieser Dichtung nicht überflüssig wäre. Es ist eine Heraklesarbeit, die ich übernehme, aber wie ich unsere Deutschen kenne, werden sie gerade für dieses Stück sein.[31]

Camino Real was first staged at the Landestheater in Bertold Viertel's translation in the "entfesseltem Theater" style under the direction of Gustav Rudolf Sellner, "Piscator's heir in the German theater."[32] The pageant has been called Williams' *Faust II,*[33] a twentieth century "Purgatorio,"[34] a *Grosses Welttheater* after the manner of Hofmannsthal,[35] but above all a play in the style of the Spanish Baroque. As one critic said:

Seit alters her ist es das Grundprivileg des spanischen Theaters gewesen, das Leben als Traum, das Sein als Schein darzustellen und dabei Traum, Allegorie, und Abstraktion in blutvollste Dynamik zu verwandeln.[36]

Karl Korn describes *Camino Real* as

Allegorisches Welttheater, ein ferner Nachhall aus Hofmannsthal und Claudel; es ist episches Theater zwischen Wilder und Brecht, eine Phantasmagorie, worin Spuk, Traum und Wirklichkeit auf einer Ebene zusammentreffen . . . Was Sellner[37] zu diesen aus dem Worttext erkenntlichen Urbildern aufgewiesen hat, ist der grosse Hintergrund: Kafka.

He sums it up by saying: "Das Stück kann man als ein mit bewundernswerter Naivität gemachtes Abfallprodukt aus der

dramatischen Weltliteratur der letzten fünf Jahrzehnte ansehen."[37] In its form *Camino Real* seemed to promise a new
direction in Williams' creative work, but in that respect it
remained alone. Otherwise it is pure Tennessee Williams conveying its message constantly in symbols which German critics
have been quick to interpret.[38]

After the panoramic *Camino Real*, Williams returned to the
narrower stage and produced further plays in rapid succession.
Since then have appeared *Rise in Flames Said the Phoenix,
Orpheus Descending, Suddenly Last Summer, Period of Adjust-
ment, Sweet Bird of Youth, The Night of the Iguana,* and *The
Milk Train Doesn't Stop Here Any More.* These plays have met
with varying favor in Germany.

An East German critic, Jutta Friedrich [509], found no
missionary value in Tennessee Williams' plays. Williams, she
admits, is with Arthur Miller "der bedeutendste zeitgenössische
amerikanische Dramatiker." (One notices here the omission of
Thornton Wilder's name.) She also adds that Williams is an
author without development:

> Es ist eigentlich nur ein Thema, das seinen Dramen zugrunde liegt –
> die Unfähigkeit der Zentralgestalten, Dasein und Wirklichkeit zu
> ertragen. Alle seine Stücke handeln vom Versagen; sie sind durch-
> zogen von Resignation, verlorenen Hoffnungen, Einsamkeit,
> Gewalt und Tod. Es gibt – vielleicht mit der Ausnahme der *Rose
> Tattoo* – kein echtes "Happy End". Alle Gestalten sind äusserlich
> und innerlich gescheitert.

From 1937 on Williams' work was autobiographic. This means
not only that his scenes were laid in the lower Mississippi and
other regions well known to him, and that his characters are
near-portraits of relatives and acquaintances, but, more impor-
tantly, it means that Williams suffers from the same maladjust-
ments as thwart his characters "und so müssen wir die Ursache
für das Scheitern der Helden in Williams selbst suchen. Denn er
ist gescheitert trotz seines äusseren Erfolges und des Ruhmes,

den er im In- und Auslande besitzt." Williams recognized that capitalism was the cause of the maladjustment of his characters and their destruction, but the lamentable fact was that their downfall was not the result of a battle, but of a "kampflose Kapitulation." He has never placed an optimistic forward-striving character in an important position in any one of his plays. They depict few healthy, normal human beings. And so the Marxist critic concludes:

> Die private Thematik und die Darstellung der Wirklichkeit aus der Sicht der nicht alltäglichen, abnormalen und neurotischen Individuen hat Williams den Vorwurf der Dekadenz eingetragen. Er wird damit zu einem hervorstehenden Vertreter des Escapismus und Psychologismus, der an den Bühnen der DDR keinen Platz hat.[38]

That Tennessee Williams suffers from some maladjustment need not be doubted, but the "Dramaturg" and critic Kurt Klinger who admires his ability to create dramatic moments, his mastery of analytical dialogues, and his "nicht nur raffinierten sondern genialer Theatersinn,"[39] diagnoses it otherwise. Williams, he says, is torn between two impulses, the desire simply to enjoy life and the impulse to write – and the impulse proved more powerful than the desire. Williams' analyst is reported to have said: "Sie schreiben nichts als gewaltsame Melodramen, die nur wegen der Gewaltsamkeit der Zeit in der wir leben Erfolg haben." This did not deter Williams from writing, as was his intention, but there may have been an element of truth in the psychiatrist's blunt declaration. Williams' plays are somewhat timebound. *A Street Car Named Desire* in a revival does not carry the impact it once wielded, and the later dramas are less shattering than the earlier ones. At the age of fifty, after twenty-five years of success, he finds himself in a precarious position. Merely to continue on the same level is not enough. He must surpass himself in a less congenial era or be thought of as antiquated.

183

The season 1961-1962 foreshadowed a decrease of new plays from America, but Tennessee Williams' plays were staged as they appeared, including *Zeit der Anpassung* and *Orpheus steigt heraus*, and *Die Nacht der Leguan* was scheduled for the next year in Zürich. The same season, however, brought forth two interesting American novelties. In his earlier years, after his apprenticeship with the Playmakers of the University of North Carolina, Thomas Wolfe attended George Pierce Baker's school of drama at Yale. Here he wrote as a semester work a play called *Welcome to Our City*, which was duly played at the "47 Workshop." After that, it lay dormant for forty years. Then it was translated by Susanna Rademacher and placed in the repertoire of the Zürich theater for the season 1962-1963. Second, Faulkner's *Requiem for a Nun* was dramatized and played chiefly in smaller theaters such as in Bielefeld, Bremen, Heidelberg, Iserholm, and in the Zimmertheater in Hamburg.

The plays of O'Neill and of Thornton Wilder still interested the directors and the public. In Wien, 1961-1963, O'Neill was especially well represented. The Burgtheater offered *A Long Day's Journey into Night*. The Theater in der Josefstadt produced *Ah, Wilderness* 52 times in 1960-61 and continued it into the next season; the Volkstheater produced *Beyond the Horizon* 43 times in 1960-61; and the Akademietheater played *A Moon for the Misbegotten* 29 times in 1960-61. *Straws* and *A Touch of the Poet* ran only for a short time. Theaters in the smaller cities, among them Linz, Kassel, Aachen, Bremen, Cuxhafen, Essen and Dortmund, welcomed O'Neill plays, Stuttgart reproduced *Hughie*, and Wupperthal *All God's Chillun Got Wings* and *The Great God Brown*.

Of Thornton Wilder's plays, *Our Town* was most frequently played. *Glückliche Reise* appeared frequently in the repertoires, but *The Skin of our Teeth* has lost its timeliness. Arthur Miller's *Der Tod eines Handlungsreisenden*, 1945, still holds attention. It was played many times in Wien and elsewhere. A critic called it "ein bürgerliches Trauerspiel von nahezu klassischer Strenge" and "eine Tragödie von zeitloser Gültigkeit."

In December of 1963, the theaters of Wien offered six "Novitä-ten." One was a Grillparzer play, one was translated from the French and the remainder were of English or American origin. Since then other American plays have been added to the repertoire, among them Albee's *Wer hat Angst vor Virginia Woolf?*, Arthur Miller's, *Seit dem Sündenfall*, and Ustanov's *Endspurt* (American title *Photo Finish*).

There is still a dearth of native German playwrights, and new talent is slow in coming forward. The German theaters are still dependent on foreign lands to fill out their repertoires, but the American contributions are becoming scarcer. Most numerous of these are works by Tennessee Williams, Thornton Wilder, and the posthumous plays of O'Neill – but if statistics were available, they might perhaps show that the works of these three were surpassed by the contributions of the two leading Swiss and an Austrian playwright, Friedrich Dürrenmatt, Max Frisch, and Fritz Hochwälder, together with those of the Swiss citizen Curt Götz.

Despite the popularity of American plays in Germany, the German playwrights have remained unaffected by them. Horst Oppel [286] suggests that *Our Town* may be an exception, but he adds that not a single German writer can be regarded as a follower of Wilder nor of Tennessee Williams, Saroyan, nor Steinbeck.

Straumann [268] comments on a new evaluation of American literature which has been taking place in Europe since about 1920. Throughout the nineteenth century and later, European readers looked toward America for adventure literature (Poe, Cooper, Bret Harte, Jack London), and for accounts of man's successful struggle with his environment, his urge to rectify injustice and inequality (*Uncle Tom's Cabin*, Jack London), and its glorification of material success. Mark Twain, Sinclair Lewis, and a few others revealed the hollowness of the quest for success. To be sure, there had always existed in American literature a more idealistic and less earthbound element (Emerson, Melville, Hawthorne, Henry James, Whitman), but their message fell upon stony ground in a Germany which was becoming materialistic, and appreciation was belated and only partial. Hemingway was first regarded in Germany as a materialist, with no sense of the past and future, and a view of man as an exclusively physical being. It was not until the appearance of *The Snows of Kilimanjaro*, 1938, and *The Old Man and the Sea*, 1952, that the German critics began to recognize in Hemingway's novels a wrestling with deeper problems of human psychology. In line with the new interpretation of Hemingway was the new assessment of Melville.

CONCLUSIONS

What, then, is the German opinion of American literature today? Long after America had freed herself gradually from English standards in other respects, England still preserved her hegemony in the field of literature as a last stronghold, and this continued throughout the nineteenth century. An essay of 1938 calls attention to the new situation at that time and sums up what might still be called the German majority view of American literature.

> Erst seit Beginn des Jahrhunderts kann das literarische Schaffen Amerikas die Bezeichnung einer Nationalliteratur beanspruchen. Um diese Zeit schwindet die letzte Spur einer Abhängigkeit vom englischen Einfluss... Die Schriftsteller, die diesen Wandel bewirkten, verschafften dem amerikanischen Schrifttum gegen Ende des Weltkrieges auch innerhalb der Weltliteratur einen gleichberechtigten und gleichwertigen Platz neben den anderen Literaturen der grossen Kulturstaaten... Allerdings sind gerade sie keine nationalen Dichter, wenigstens im Sinne eines Nationalismus, wie wir ihn verstehen. Patriotisch wie ihre Vorläufer sind sie auch nicht... Sie schreiben nichts, um ihr Vaterland zu verherrlichen... Es fehlt ihnen die nationale Vitalität eines Longfellow,... der leidenschaftliche Patriotismus eines Emerson, Walt Whitmans Vision von der Grösse, der Tiefe, der Weite der "Staaten," sein so grenzenloser Glauben an die Zukunft eines einigen Volkes und eines einigen Amerikas, der ihn zum ersten Künder eines echten Amerikas machte.[40]

Walther Fischer greeted the award of the Nobel Prize to Sinclair Lewis, 1939, as a "weithin sichtbare Geste, durch die die Literatur der Vereinigten Staaten gewissermassen amtlich in die Gemeinschaft der modernen Weltliteratur aufgenommen wurde" and he concluded his essay on "Das amerikanische Theater der Gegenwart," 1948, with the observation:

> Ein Land, das gleichzeitig dreier Autoren von der Bedeutung Eugene O'Neills, Maxwell Andersons und Thornton Wilders sich rühmen kann, darf wohl für sich den Anspruch erheben, mit an der Spitze der dramatischen Produktion der Weltliteratur vorwärts zu schreiten.[41]

Werner Ross recalled in 1953:

> Es ist noch nicht lange her, dass in den Literaturgeschichten die amerikanische Literatur als ein blosses Anhängsel der englischen im Anhang behandelt wurde. Ihr haftete... das Vorurteil an, es handle sich um einen kolonialen Abklatsch, um Literatur aus zweiter Hand für kulturelle Hinterwäldler.[42]

There was, to be sure, he said, evidence enough to the contrary, but Poe was regarded as an exception and Melville was overlooked at home and abroad. The independence of Whitman's *Leaves of Grass*, 1855, however, was not to be denied, and the literature of the following century was of conscious independence. This is not merely a matter of originality of subject matter and plot; it is also an independence of style. The leading authors of the twentieth century write in an American style, and with an American word usage that is not to be confounded with English.

---

[1] Julius Bab, *Das Theater der Gegenwart*, Leipzig, 1920; p. 210.
[2] Galinsky [485] 237 f.
[3] Bab, *Op cit.*, p. 212.
[4] Felix Hollander, *Lebendiges Theater*, Berlin, 1932; p. 24.
[5] Alfred Kerr, *New York and London*, Berlin, 1923; *Berliner Tageblatt*, Oct. 1 1923.
[6] Hofmannsthal [479] 888-892.

187

[7] Karl Arns. *Die schöne Literatur*, XXXIX (1928), 61.
[8] Fritz Engel, *Berliner Tageblatt*, Nov. 5, 1929.
[9] Kyra Stromberg, *Der Kurier*, Berlin, April 16, 1947.
[10] *Sonntag*, Berlin, July 13, 1947.
[11] Dr. B. *Hamburger Echo*, Oct. 1954.
[12] Stresau, *Frankfurter Allgemeine Zeitung*, April 23, 1954.
[13] C. E. Lewalter, *Die Zeit*, April 8, 1954.
[14] Gerhart Weise, *Die neue Zeitung*, Berlin, April 4, 1954.
[15] Albert Schulze-Vellinghausen, *Frankfurter Allgemeine Zeitung*, March 24, 1955.
[16] Wolfgang Schimming, *Theater Almanack*, II (1947), 307.
[17] Ulrich Seelmann-Eggebert, *ibid.*, II (1947), 358.
[18] Holthusen [445].
[19] Fussell [500].
[20] Frenz [501].
[21] Straumann [268].
[22] Schönfelder [269].
[23] Christian Lewalter, *Die Zeit*, Oct. 9, 1952.
[24] Werner Fiedler, *Der Tag*, May 1950.
[25] Julius Zerfass, *Die Neue Zeitung*, Dez. 1947.
[26] Heinz Joachim, *Die Welt*, Feb. 15, 1949.
[27] Gerhard Sanden, *Die Welt*, April 15, 1959.
[28] Frenz and Weisstein [507], 269.
[29] *Die Zeit*, Dec. 13, 1951.
[30] *Die Neue Zeitung*, Dec. 14, 1954.
[31] *Hamburger Abendblatt*, Nov. 20, 1959.
[32] Frenz and Weisstein [507], 259.
[33] Willy Haas, *Die Welt*, Nov. 16, 1954.
[34] Gerhard Sanden, *Hamburger Anzeiger*, Nov. 15, 1954.
[35] Rudolf Grossmann, *Die Rampe*, Hamburg, 1954-55, Heft 7, p. 53.
[36] Buchloh [506].
[37] Korn, *Frankfurter Allgemeine Zeitung*, Nov. 8, 1954.
[38] Friedrich [509].
[39] Kurt Klinger, "Zwischenruf zur Toleranz: Zum Werk von Tennessee Williams...," *Forum*, XI (1964), 266-268.
[40] Demmig [258] 527.
[41] Fischer [262].
[42] Ross [276].

BIBLIOGRAPHY

ABBREVIATIONS

AB	Anglia Beiblatt
AG	Americana-Germanica
AGR	American-German Review
AL	American Literature
APS	American Philosophical Society
ASNS	Archiv für das Studium der neueren Sprachen
BLU	Blätter für literarische Unterhaltung
CL	Comparative Literature
DA	Dissertation Abstracts
DLD	Das literarische Deutschland
DNR	Die Neue Rundschau
DNS	Die Neueren Sprachen
DVLW	Deutsche Vierteljahrsschrift für Literaturwissenschaft und Geistesgeschichte
ES	Englische Studien
GAA	German-American Annals (New Series)
GJ	Grillparzer Jahrbuch
GQ	German Quarterly
GR	Germanic Review
GRM	Germanisch-romanische Monatsschrift
JAS	Jahrbuch für Amerikastudien
JEGP	Journal of English and Germanic Philology
MDU	Monatshefte für deutschen Unterricht
MFLA	Magazin für die Literatur des Auslandes
MLF	Modern Language Forum
MLJ	Modern Language Journal
MLN	Modern Language Notes
MLQ	Modern Language Quarterly

MLR	Modern Language Review
MP	Modern Philology
NEQ	New England Quarterly
NLW	Neue literarische Welt
NPZ	Neuphilologische Zeitung
PMLA	Publications of the Modern Language Association of America
RG	Revue Germanique
RLC	Revue de Littérature comparée
UCP	University of California Publications
ZAA	Zeitschrift für Anglistik und Amerikanistik
ZDP	Zeitschrift für deutsche Philologie

INTRODUCTION
COMPREHENSIVE BIBLIOGRAPHIES AND SURVEYS

See also [27] - [31], [65] - [84], [244] - [288].

MUMMENDEY, RICHARD, "*Die schöne Literatur der Vereinigten Staa-* [1]
ten von America in deutschen Übersetzungen, eine Bibliographie,"
Bonner Beiträge zur Bibliotheks- und Bücherkunde, VI
(1961); 199 pp.

ROEHM, ALFRED I., *Bibliographie und Kritik der deutschen Über-* [2]
setzungen aus der amerikanischen Dichtung, Univ. of Chicago
Diss., Leipzig, 1910; 62 pp.
Bryant, Longfellow, Poe, Whittier, Lowell, Holmes, Emerson,
Whitman, Taylor, Joaquin Miller, Bret Harte, *et al.*

BAGINSKY, PAUL BEN, "German Works Relating to America, 1493- [3]
1800; A list compiled from the collections of the New York
Public Library," New York, *The New York Public Library*,
1942; xv, 217 pp.

ROHRER, MAX, ed., *Amerika im deutschen Gedicht, 1774-1945,* [4]
München, 1948; 173 pp.

PALMER, PHILIP MOTLEY, *German Works on America, 2492-1800,* [5]
UCP in Modern Philology, XXXVI (1952), 271-412.

LOCHER, K. T., *German Histories of American Literature, 1800-* [6]
1950, Univ. of Chicago Press, 1955; 268 pp. on microcards.
See also [65]. E. E. Doll, AGR, XXX³ (1958); 37-38.

FRIEDERICH, WERNER PAUL, *Werden und Wachsen der USA in* [7]
300 Jahren; politische und literarische Charakterköpfe von
Virginia Dare bis Roosevelt, Bern, Francke, 1939; 271 pp.

LESSING, O., "American Literature Conquers Europe," AGR, III [7a]
(1937), 12-14, 56.

POCHMANN, HENRY A., L. M. PRICE, J. R. FREY, *et al.*, "Anglo-German [8]
[Literary] Bibliography, 1936-1941, 1946-1963," annually in
JEGP, 1937-1942, 1947-1963.

ZUCKER, A. E., D. CUNZ, F. REICHMANN, et al., "Bibliography Ameri-   [9]
cana-Germanica," AGR, April, Hefte, 1942-1965.

Varia, "Deutsche amerikakundliche Veröffentlichungen," 1956-   [10]
1961; yearly in JAS, 1956 ff.

STAMMLER, HEINRICH, Amerika im Spiegel seiner Literatur, Stutt-   [11]
gart, 1949; 152 pp.

OPPEL, HORST, "Amerikanische Literatur," pp. I, 47-60 in Real-   [12]
lexikon der deutschen Literatur, ed. Merker and Stammler, 2 ed.,
Berlin, 1955.
With special references to its relations with German literature.

JANTZ, HAROLD, "Amerika im deutschen Dichten und Denken,"   [13]
columns 146-203 in Deutsche Philologie im Aufriss, ed. Wolfgang Stammler, Berlin, 1955.
Columns 309-372 in 2. Auflage, 1960.

OPPEL, HORST, "Die amerikanische Literatur in Deutschland und   [14]
das Problem der literarischen Wertung," pp. 127-144 in Festschrift für Walther Fischer, Heidelberg, Winter, 1960.

GOEBEL, JULIUS, "Amerika in der deutschen Dichtung bis 1832,"   [15]
Vortrag, New York, 1890; pp. 102-127 in Forschungen...
Rudolph Hildebrand, Leipzig, 1894, and pp. 55-74 in Goebel's
Der Kampf um die deutsche Kultur in Amerika, Leipzig, 1914.
Klopstock, Herder, "Sturm und Drang," Lenau, the aged
Goethe.
J. Minor, Göttingische Gelehrte Anzeigen, 1896, 662-666.

DESCYZK, GERHARD, "Amerika in der Phantasie deutscher Dichter,"   [16]
Deutsch-Amerikanische Geschichtsblätter, XXIV (1894), 7-142.

FRAENKEL, ERNST, Amerika im Spiegel des deutschen politischen   [17]
Denkens, Köln, 1959; 333 pp.
80 German political scientists, philosophers, poets, statesmen,
from Christian Schubart to Theodor Heuss. C.V.Easum,
American Historical Review, LXV (1959), 158.
E. Fraenkel, "Selbstanzeige", JAS, VII (1962), 348-349.

BLUME, BERNARD, "Amerika und die deutsche Literatur," in   [18]
Deutsche Akademie für Sprache und Dichtung [Darmstadt],
Jahrbuch für 1959; 137-148.

JANTZ, HAROLD, "The Myths about America: Origins and Ex-   [19]
tensions," JAS, VII (1962), 6-18.

LINK, FRANZ H., "Theorien zur amerikanischen Literatur."   [20]
DVLW, XXXVI (1962), 401-429, 583-613.

Switzerland

WILDI, MAX, *Der angelsächsische Roman und der Schweizer Leser,* [21]
Zürich, 1944; 81 pp.

MARJASCH, SONIA, *Der amerikanische Bestseller, sein Wesen und seine* [22]
Verbreitung unter besonderer Berücksichtigung der Schweiz,
Schweizer anglistische Arbeiten, Bern, Francke, 1946; 176 pp.

FELLER, MAX KARL, *Die Aufnahme amerikanischer Literatur in der* [23]
deutschsprachigen Schweiz, Diss., Humboldt University, Berlin
[1949?].

MÖHL, GERTRUD, *Die Aufnahme amerikanischer Literatur in der* [24]
deutschsprachigen Schweiz während der Jahre 1945-1950,
Zürich [1951].

GRAF, EMIL, *Die Aufnahme der englischen und amerikanischen* [25]
Literatur in der deutschen Schweiz, 1800-1830, Zürich [1951].

KEISER, ROBERT, *Die Aufnahme englischen Schrifttums in der*
deutschen Schweiz, 1830 bis 1860, Zürcher Beiträge zur
vergleichenden Literatur, X (1962); 111 pp. [26]

PART I. FROM COLONIES TO INDEPENDENCE

I. THE COLONIAL PERIOD

JANTZ, HAROLD, "German Thought and American Literature in [27]
New England, 1620-1820," JEGP, XLI (1942), 1-83.

JANTZ, HAROLD, "The First Century of New England Verse; [28]
Verzeichnis amerikanischer Bücher in deutscher Übersetzung,"
U.S. Information Agency, 1954 ff.

BENZ, ERNST, "Ecumenical Relations between Boston Puritanism [29]
and German Pietism: Cotton Mather and August Hermann
Francke," *Harvard Theological Review,* LIV (1961), 159-193.

RIESE, TEUT, *Das englische Erbe in der amerikanischen Literatur:* [30]
Studien zur Entstehungsgeschichte des amerikanischen Selbst-
bewusstseins im Zeitalter Washingtons und Jeffersons, Beiträge
zur englischen Philologie, Heft 39, Bochum-Langendreer, 1958;
xiii + 240 pp.

BRUMM, URSULA, *Die religiöse Typologie im amerikanischen Denken;* [31]
Ihre Bedeutung für die amerikanische Literatur und Geistes-
geschichte, Leyden, 1863.
Sewall, Cotton Mather, Edward Taylor, Jonathan Edwards,
Emerson, Hawthorne, Melville. Ilse Blumenstengel, DNS,
1965; 149-151.

The American Revolution

BIEDERMANN, KARL, "Die nordamerikanische und französische [32] Revolution in ihren Rückwirkungen auf Deutschland," *Zeitschrift für deutsche Kulturgeschichte*, III (1958), 483-495.

HATFIELD, JAMES TAFT, and ELFRIEDA HOCHBAUM, "The Influence [33] of the American Revolution upon German Literature," AG, III (1899-1900), 333-385.
References to Goethe, Gleim, Klinger, Klopstock, Schiller, Schubart, Stolberg, Wieland, Voss.

GALLINGER, HERBERT P., *Die Haltung der deutschen Publizistik* [34] *zu dem amerikanischen Unabhängigkeitskriege, 1775-1783,* Diss., Leipzig, 1900; 77 pp.

WALZ, JOHN A., "The American Revolution and German Literature," [35] MLN, XVI (1901), 336-351, 411-418, 449-462.

WALZ, JOHN A., "Three Swabian Journalists and the American [36] Revolution," AG, IV (1901-1902), 95-129, 267-291, and GAA, I (1903), 209-224, 257-274, 347-356, 406-419, 593-600.
Schiller, Weckherlin, Schubart.

KING, HENRY SAFFORD, *Echoes of the American Revolution in* [37] *German Literature*, UCP in Modern Philology, XIV (1929); 192 pp.
E. H. Zeydel, MDU, XXII (1930), 150 f.
C. A. Williams, JECP, XXXV (1936), 433 f.

WERTHEIM, URSULA, "Der amerikanische Unabhängigkeitskampf im [38] Spiegel der zeitgenössischen deutschen Literatur," *Weimarer Blätter*, III (1957), 429-470.
Also in E. Braemer and Ursula Wertheim, *Studien zur deutschen Klassik* (Germanistische Studien) Berlin, 1961; 71-114 and 426-433.

GERMAN NAMES

Brentano, S.

VON HOFE, HAROLD, "Sophie Mereau Brentano and America," [39] MLN, LXXV (1960), 427-431.

Halberstadt Poets

—, "The Halberstadt Poets and the New World," GR, XXX [40] (1957), 243 f.

Heinse

—, "Heinse, America, and Utopianism," PMLA, LXXII (1957), [41] 390-402.

Herder

CLARK, ROBERT THOMAS, "Herder and the Noble Savage," *Stanford* [42]
University Bulletin, Abstracts of Dissertations, VIII (1930-
1933), 53-55.

SCHMITT, ALBERT R., *Herder and America,* Diss., Univ. of Penn- [43]
sylvania, 1961-62.

Jacobi, F.H.

VON HOFE, HAROLD, "Jacobi, Wieland, and the New World," MDU, [44]
XLIX (1957), 187-200.

La Roche

LANGE, VICTOR, "Visitors to Lake Oneida: An Account of Sophie La [45]
Roche's Novel, *Erscheinungen am See Oneida,*" *Symposium,*
May, 1948, 48-78.

Lessing

SCHNEIDER, HEINRICH, "Lessing and America," MDU, XXX (1938), [46]
424-432 and in H. Schneider, *Lessing...* Bern, 1951; 198-240.

Schiller

CARRUTH, WILLIAM HERBERT, "Schiller and America," AGR, IV [47]
N.S. (1908), 131-146.

JANTZ, HAROLD, "*William Tell* and the American Revolution," [48]
pp. 65-81 in *A Schiller Symposium,* ed. A. L. Williams, Austin,
Texas.

Schlegel, A.W.

VON HOFE, HAROLD, "August Wilhelm Schlegel and the New [49]
World," GR, XXXV (1960), 279-287.

Schlegel, Friedrich

—, "Friedrich Schlegel and the New World," PMLA, LXXVI [50]
(1961), 63-87.

Tieck

MATENKO, PERCY, *Ludwig Tieck and America,* Chapel Hill, Uni- [51]
versity of North Carolina Press, 1954; 120 pp.

Wieland [33], [37].

AMERICAN NAMES

Franklin

VICTORY, BEATRICE M., "Benjamin Franklin and Germany," AG, [52]
XXI (1915); 180 pp.

HAUSEL, HELMUT, *Benjamin Franklin, 1706-1790, im literarischen* [53]
Deutschland seiner Zeit, Diss. Erlangen, 1952.
HEGEMANN, DANIEL U., "Franklin in Germany. Further Evidence [54]
of his Reputation in Germany," GQ, XXXVI (1954), 187-194.
VAGTS, ALFRED, "Benjamin Franklin, Influence and Symbol," [55]
AGR, XXIII² (1957), 1-2.

Franklin and Forster
KAHN, ROBERT L., "An Account of a Meeting with Benjamin [56]
Franklin at Passy on October 9, 1777 from Georg Forster's
English Journal," The William and Mary Quarterly, XII (1955),
472-474.
—, "Georg Forster and Benjamin Franklin," Proceedings, APS, [57]
CII (1958), 1-6.

Franklin and Grimm
"Franklin, Grimm and J.H.Landolt," Proceedings, APS, XCIX [58]
(1955), 401-404.

Franklin and Herder
SUPHAN, BERNHARD, "Benjamin Franklin's *Rules for a Club Es-* [59]
tablished in Philadelphia, übertragen und ausgelegt als Statut
für eine Gesellschaft von Freunden der Humanität von J.G.
Herder, 1792...," Berlin, 1883; 36 pp.
Cf. *Briefe zur Beförderung der Humanität* in Herder, *Werke,*
(ed. Suphan, Berlin, 1877-1913), XVII and XVIII.

Franklin and Lichtenberg
KAHN, ROBERT, L. "A Meeting between Lichtenberg and Franklin?," [60]
German Life and Letters, IX (1955), 64-67.

Franklin and Raspe
—, "Some unpublished Raspe-Franklin Letters," *Proceedings* [61]
APS, XCIX (1955), 127-132.
—, "Three Franklin-Raspe letters," *Proceedings,* APS, XCIX [62]
(1955), 398-400.

Paine
GABRIELLI, VITTORIO, "Thomas Paine fra l'America e l'Europa," [63]
Studi Americani, I (1955), 9-53.
ARNOLD, HANS, "Die Aufnahme von Thomas Paines Schriften in [64]
Deutschland," PMLA, LXXIV (1959), 365-386.

PART II:
FROM POLITICAL TO LITERARY INDEPENDENCE

III. VARIOUS GERMAN VIEWS OF AMERICA

Surveys:

LOCHER, KASPAR T., *The Reception of American Literature in German* [65]
Literary Histories in the Nineteenth Century. Diss., University
of Chicago, 1948; 459 pp.
See also [6]

BAKER, T. S., "America as the Political Utopia of Young Germany," [66]
AG I: 2 (1897), 62-102.

BARBA, PRESTON A., "Emigration to America as Reflected in [67]
German Fiction," GAA, XXI (1914), 193-227.
See also [84]

PECKHAM, H. HOUSTON, "Is American Literature Read and Re- [68]
spected in Europe?," *South Atlantic Quarterly*, XIII (1914),
382-388.
Translations of Bryant, Clemens, Cooper, Emerson, Franklin,
Harte, Hawthorne, Irving, Longfellow, Lowell, Motley, Park-
man, Poe, Prescott, Whitman, and Whittier.

BREFFKA, CONST., *Amerika in der deutschen Literatur*, Köln, [69]
1917; 27 pp.

SCHÖNEMANN, FRIEDRICH, *Das Amerikanertum in der Literatur*, [70]
Amerikakunde, Bremen, 1921.

BARBA, PRESTON A., "The American Indian in German Fiction," [71]
GAA, XI (1933), 143-174.

WEHE, W., "Das Amerika-Erlebnis in der deutschen Literatur," [72]
Geist der Zeit, XVII (1934), 96-104.

SCHRÖDER, S., *Amerika in der deutschen Dichtung von 1850-1890.* [73]
Diss., Heidelberg, 1934; 95 pp.

WAGNER, LYDIA ELIZABETH, "The Reserved Attitude of Early [74]
German Romanticists toward America," GQ, XVI (1943),
8-12.

POCHMANN, HENRY S., *New England Transcendentalism and St. Louis* [75]
Hegelianism, Philadelphia, 1948.
Ward Miner, AGR, April, 1948, 31-32.

HEWETT-THAYER, HARVEY, *American Literature as Viewed in Ger-* [76]
many, 1828-1851, University of North Carolina Studies in
Comparative Literature, XXII (1958); 86 pp.

CRONHOLM, (geb. KUBE), ANNA-CHRISTIE, *Die nordamerikanische* [77]
Sklavenfrage im deutschen Schrifttum des 19. Jahrhunderts, Diss.,
Berlin, Freie Univ., 1958; 107 pp.

FRANZ, ECKHART G., *Das Amerikabild der deutschen Revolution von* [78]
1848-1849. Zum Problem der Übertragung gewachsener Ver-
fassungsformen. Beiheft 2, zum JAS, Heidelberg, 1958;
154 pp.

TIMPE, EUGENE F., *The Reception of American Literature in Germany,* [79]
1862-1872, Diss., University of Southern California, 1961.
University of North Carolina Studies in Comparative Literature, XXXV (1964); 95 pp.

The Novel

VON KROCKOW, LIDA, "American Characters in German Novels," [80]
Atlantic Monthly, LXVIII (1891), 824-838.

SCHÖNEMANN, F., "Deutsche und amerikanische Romane," *Ger-* [81]
manistic Society Quarterly, III (1916), 96-105 and 158-177.

VOLLMER, CLEMENT, "The American Novel in Germany, 1871- [82]
1913," GAA, new series, XV (1917), 113-144, 165-219.
With bibliography of translations.

WEBER, PAUL CARL, *America in Imaginative German Literature of* [83]
the 19th Century, New York, Columbia Univ. Press, 1926;
xv + 301 pp.
E. H. Zeydel, MLN, XLII (1927), 204-207.

VAN DE LUYSTER, NELSON, *Emigration to America as Reflected in* [84]
the German Novel of the 19th Century: Especially in the fiction
of Bitzius, Laube, Gutzkow, Auerbach, Freytag, Storm, Keller,
Spielhagen, Heyse, Raabe, Diss., University of North Carolina,
unpublished, 1943.
See also [66] f.

Switzerland [21] - [26].

Fontane

CORRELL, ERNST, "Theodor Fontane's *Quitt*," *Mennonite Quarterly* [85]
Review, XVI (1942), 221-222.

ZIEGLSCHMID, A. J. F., "Truth and Fiction and Mennonites in the [86]
Second Part of Theodor Fontane's Novel *Quitt*," *Mennonite*
Quarterly Review, XVI (1942), 223-246.

DAVID, ARTHUR L., "Theodor Fontane's Interest in America as [87]
Revealed by his Novel, *Quitt*," AGR, XIX³ (1953), 28-31.

Freiligrath

LEARNED, M. D., "Ferdinand Freiligrath in America," AG, I (1897), [88]
54-78.
Acquaintance with Longfellow *et al.*

Gerstäcker

See also [154], [182] ff, [225].
O'DONNELL, GEORGE H. R., "Gerstäcker in America, 1837-1843," [89]
PMLA, XLII (1927), 1036-1043.
PRAHL, AUGUSTUS J., "America in the Works of Gerstäcker," MLQ, [90]
IV (1932), 213-224.
EVANS, CLARENCE, "Friedrich Gerstäcker, Social Chronicler of the [91]
Arkansas Frontier," *Arkansas Historical Quarterly*, VI (1948),
440-449.

—, A Cultural Link between Nineteenth Century German [92]
Literature and the Arkansas Ozarks," MLJ, XXXV (1951),
523-530.
The town of Combs in the Ozarks as the setting of *Germels-*
hausen.
LANDA, BJORNE, *The American Scene in Gerstäcker's Fiction*, Diss., [93]
University of Minnesota, 1952.
DA, XII (1952), 424.
VAN DE LUYSTER, NELSON, "Gerstäcker's Novels about Emigrants [94]
to America," AGR, XX⁵ (1954), 22 f., 36.

Goethe

MACKALL, LEONARD, *Briefwechsel zwischen Goethe und Amerikanern*, [95]
GJ, XXV (1904), 1-37.
Everett, Lyman, Cogswell, Kirkland, Bancroft, Calvert.
WADEPUHL, WALTER, "Amerika, du hast es besser," GR, VII (1932), [96]
186-191.

—, *Goethe's Interest in the New World*, Jena, Frommann, 1934; [97]
84 pp.
H. Pfund, AGR, I⁴ (1935), 45 f.
C. D. Vail, JEGP, XXXV (1936), 611 f.
O. W. Long, GR, XI (1936), 60-62.
LONG, ORIE WILLIAM, *Literary Pioneers. Early American Explorers* [98]
of European Culture, Cambridge, Harvard University Press,
1935; 267 pp.
Ticknor, Everett, Cogswell, and Bancroft visit Goethe.

BEUTLER, ERNST, *Von der Ilm zum Susquehanna. Goethe und Ame-* [99]
rika in ihren Wechselbeziehungen, Goethe-Kalender auf das
Jahr 1935, pp. 86-153, and in *Essays um Goethe,* Wiesbaden,
1946; I, 462-520.

REINSCH, FRANK H., "Goethe and American Freedom," MLF, XXI [100]
(1936), 122-127.

HELLERSBERG-WENDRINER, ANNA, "America in the World View of [101]
the Aged Goethe," GR, XIV (1939), 270-276.

PFUND, HARRY W., "Amerika, du hast es besser," *Yearbook of the* [102]
German Society of Pennsylvania, I (1950), 33-43.

RILEY, THOMAS A., "Goethe and Parker Cleaveland," PMLA, LXVII [103]
(1952), 350-374.

HAMMER, CARL, JR., "Goethe, Prévost, and Louisiana," MLQ, XVI [104]
(1954), 332-338.

URZIDIL, JOHANNES, *Das Glück der Gegenwart, Goethes Amerikabild* [105]
Goethe Schriften, VI, Zürich and Stuttgart, 1958; 58 pp.
Dieter Cunz, *Books Abroad,* XXXIII (1959), 58.
H. W. Pfund, AGR, XXVI⁴ (1960), 39.
E. Bianquis, *Études Germaniques,* XVI (1960), 282.

ARNDT, KARL, J. R., "The Harmony Society und *Wilhelm Meisters* [106]
Wanderjahre," CL, X (1958), 349-355.

Hohenhausen

HACKENBERG, FRITZ, *Elise von Hohenhausen: Eine Vorkämpferin* [107]
und Übersetzerin englischer und nordamerikanischer Dichtung...
Diss., Münster, 1912; 107 pp.

Humboldt

PFEIFFER, GOTTFRIED, "Alexander von Humboldt's Entwicklungs- [108]
jahre und amerikanische Reise," *Ruperto Carolo Mitteilungen*
der Vereinigung der Freunde der Studentenschaft der Universität
Heidelberg, 1945; pp. 128-150.

Knortz

FRENZ, HORST, "Karl Knortz, Interpreter of American Literature [109]
and Culture," AGR, III³ (1946), 27-30.

Kürenberger [112]

MULFINGER, GEORGE A., "Ferdinand Kürenbergers Roman, *Der* [110]
Amerikamüde, dessen Quellen und Verhältnis zu Lenaus
Amerikareise," GAA, V (1903), 315-346, 385-405.

MEYER, HILDEGARD, *Nordamerika im Urteil des deutschen Schrift-* [111]
tums bis zur Mitte des 29. Jahrhunderts. Eine Untersuchung
über Kürenbergers "Amerikamüden", mit einer Bibliographie,
Hamburg, 1929; vi + 166 pp.

Lenau, [110] - [111]
CASTLE, EDUARD, "*Amerikamüde*, Lenau und Kürnberger," JGG, [112]
XII (1902), 15-42.
BLANKENAGEL, J. C., "Deeds to Lenau's Property in Ohio," GR, [113]
II (1927), 210-212.
ROUSTAN, L., "Le Séjour de Lenau en Amérique," RLC, VIII [114]
(1928), 62-86.
ARNDT, KARL J. R., "Nikolaus Lenau's American Experience," [115]
MDU, XXIV (1932), 241-243.
—, "The Effect of America on Lenau's Life and Work." [116]
GR, XXXIII (1958), 125-142.
BERGES, RUTH, "Lenau's Quest in America," AGR, XXVIII[4] (1962), [117]
14-17.

Liliencron
LOEWENBERG, ERNST L., "Liliencron und Amerika," MDU, [118]
XXXVII (1945), 428-433.

Mackay
RILEY, THOMAS, "New England Anarchism in Germany," NEQ [119]
XVIII (1945), 25-38.

May [184], [186]
LOHR, OTTO, "Stimmt Karl Mays Amerikabild?", *Mitteilungen, In-* [120]
stitut für ausländische Beziehungen, II (1958), 274-278.
Möllhausen [184].

Ruppius [155]
GRAEWERT, THEODOR, *Otto Ruppius und der Amerikaroman im 19.* [121]
Jahrhundert, Diss., Jena, 1935; 70 pp.
SCHRADER, FREDERICK F., "Otto Ruppius, *A Career in America*," [122]
AGR, IX[3], 1943; 28-33.

Sealsfield [190]
FAUST, ALBERT B., *Charles Sealsfield, der Dichter beider Hemisphären*, [123]
Weimar, 1897; 295 pp.
DJORDJEWITSCH, J., *Charles Sealsfields Auffassung des Amerikaner-* [124]
tums und seine literarhistorische Stellung.
FNL, LXIV (1932): 312, 5.

DALLMANN, WILLIAM P., *The Spirit of America as Interpreted in the* [125]
Works of Charles Sealsfield, Diss., Washington University, St.
Louis, 1937; xii + 125 pp.

BAUERNFEIND, LISELOTTE, *Karl Postl-Charles Sealsfield: Die Demo-* [126]
kratie im Lichte seines literarischen Schaffens und seiner Per-
sönlichkeit, Diss., Wien, 1948.
Microfilm in University of California library.

JANTZ, HAROLD, "Charles Sealsfield's Letter to Joel R. Poinsett," [127]
GR, XXVII (1952), 155-164.

ARNDT, KARL J. R., "Sealsfield and Strubberg at Vera Cruz," MDU, [128]
LXIV (1952), 225-228.
CASTLE, EDUARD, *Der grosse Unbekannte: Das Leben Charles* [129]
Sealsfields, Wien, 1952; 720 pp.
ARNDT, KARL J. R., "Charles Sealsfield in Amerika," ZDP, LXXII [130]
(1953), 169-182.
—, "Charles Sealsfield and the *Courrier des États Unis*," PMLA, [131]
LXVIII (1953).
—, "Recent Sealsfield Discoveries," JEGP, LIII, (1954), 577-581. [132]
WILLEY, NORMAN L., "Sealsfield's Unrealistic Mexico," MDU, [133]
XLVIII (1956), 126-156.
KRUMPELMANN, JOHN T., "Sealsfield Vindicated," MDU, L [134]
(1958), 257-259.

Sealsfield - Sources

HELLER, OTTO, "The Source of Chapter 1 of Sealsfield's *Lebensbilder* [135]
aus der westlichen Hemisphäre," MLN, XXIII (1908), 172-173.
A Sketch from Life in "New York Mirror and Ladies' Literary
Gazette," November 7, 1829.
Identical plots.
BORDIER, PAUL, "Sealsfield, ses idées, ses sources d'après le *Kajüten-* [136]
buch," RG, V (1909), 273-300 and 369-421.
Accounts of explorations, Chateaubriand, Irving's *Astoria*.
THOMPSON, GARRETT W., *An Inquiry into the Sources of Charles* [137]
Sealsfield's Novel "Morton oder die grosse Tour," Diss., Univer-
sity of Pennsylvania, 1910; 56 pp.
Personal observation, Cooper, Irving, Scott.
Cf. *Zeitschrift für französischen und englischen Unterricht*,
XXII (1923), 170-174.

202

HELLER, OTTO, "Some Sources of Sealsfield," MP, VII (1910), [138] 587-592.
Samuel Lover *et al.*
See also O. Heller, MLR, III (1908), 360-365.

BARBA, PRESTON A., "Sealsfield Sources," GAA, IX (1911), 31-39. [139]
A Journey to Texas, anon., N.Y., 1834, and *Das Kajütenbuch.*

UHLENDORF, B. A., "Two Additional Sources of Sealsfield," JEGP, [140] XX (1921), 417-18.
McKinney's *Sketches of a Tour to the Lakes*... and *Der Legitime und die Republikaner*, Zürich, 1823.

WILLEY, NORMAN, "Charles Sealsfield as a Realist," MDU, XXXIV [141] (1942), 295-306.
K. J. R. Arndt, MDU, XXXV (1943), 271-285.
N. J. Willey, MDU, XXXV (1943), 365-377.

KRUMPELMANN, JOHN T., "A Source for Local Color in Sealsfield's [142] *Kajütenbuch*," JEGP, XLIII [1944], 428-433.
J. H. Ingraham's *The Southeast by a Yankee*, 1831.

AUFDERHEIDE, ELFRIEDE, *Das Amerika-Erlebnis in den Romanen* [143] *von Charles Sealsfield*, Diss., Göttingen, 1946.

SCHROEDER, ADOLF, E., "New Sources of Charles Sealsfield," JEGP, [144] LXVI (1947), 70-74.

WILLEY, NORMAN L., "Sealsfield's Working Methods," *Papers of* [145] *the Michigan Society of Science, Arts and Letters*, XXXIV (1948), 299-315.
Das Kajütenbuch

KRUMPELMANN, JOHN T., "Sealsfield's 'China Trees,'" MDU, XLIII [146] (1951), 44-45.

—, "Sealsfield and Sources," MDU, XLIII (1951), 324-326. [147]

ARNDT, K. J. R., "Plagiarism, Sealsfield or Simms?," MLN, LXIX [148] (1954), 577-581.

Sealsfield Americanisms

SCHMIDT, MAX L., *Amerikanismen bei Charles Sealsfield*, Deutsche [149] Studien zur Geistesgeschichte, V, Würzburg, 1937; iii + 82 pp. Diss., Bonn, 1937.

DILKEY, MARVIN CHARLES, "A Critical Investigation of Charles [150] Sealsfield's Literary Style," *Cornell University Abstracts of Theses*, Ithaca, N.Y., 1938; pp. 46-48.

HELLER, O., and THEODORE H. LEON, *The Language of Charles* [151] *Sealsfield, a Study in Atypical Usage*, St. Louis, Washington University Studies, New Series, Language and Literature XI (1941); xi + 144 pp.

KRUMPELMANN, JOHN T., "Charles Sealsfield's Americanisms," [152]
American Speech, XVI (1941), 26-31 and 104-111.
See also J.B.Macmillan in *American Speech*, XVIII (1943),
117-127.

ARNDT, KARL, J. R., "Sealsfield's Command of the English [153]
Language," MLN, LXVII (1952), 310-313.

Strubberg [155]

WOODSON, LEROY H., *American Negro Slavery in the Works of* [154]
Friedrich Strubberg, Friedrich Gerstäcker, and Otto Ruppius,
Diss., Catholic University of America, Washington, D.C.,
1949; 340 pp.

Zchokke

OPPEL, HORST, "Die deutsche Siedelung in Louisiana im Spiegel des [155]
Amerika-Romans der Goethe-Zeit: Heinrich Zschokkes *Prin-*
zessin von Wolfenbüttel." In: *Die Wissenschaft von deutscher*
Sprache... Festschrift für Friedrich Maurer, Stuttgart (1963),
347-360.

IV. POETS AND POETRY OF AMERICA

For this chapter see Roehm [2], Rohrer [4], the footnotes to the chapter,
Poe [418] ff., and Lyric Poetry [510]-[544].

V. THE PROSE WRITERS OF AMERICA

AMERICAN NAMES

Bellamy

BOWMAN, SYLVIA, *et al., Edward Bellamy Abroad: An American* [156]
Prophet's Influence, New York, Twayne, 1963.

Channing

PUKNAT, SIEGFRIED B., "Channing and German Thought," Publi- [157]
cations, APS, I (1957), 195-202.

Channing and Auerbach

—, "Auerbach and Channing," PMLA, LXXII (1957), 962-978. [158]

Clemens

ENGEL, EDUARD, "Mark Twain. Ein amerikanischer Humorist," [159]
MFLA, Oct. 9, 1880, 375-379.

SCHÖNBACH, ANTON E., "Über die amerikanische Romandichtung [160]
der Gegenwart," *Deutsche Rundschau*, XLVI (1886), 416-433.

VON THALER, CARL, "Mark Twain in Deutschland," *Die Gegenwart*, [161] LX (1899), 376-378.

HENDERSON, ARCHIBALD, "Mark Twain – wie er ist," *Deutsche* [162] *Revue*, XXXIV (1909), 195-205.

—, "The International Fame of Mark Twain", *North American* [163] *Review*, CXCII (1910), 805-815.

—, "Mark Twain als Philosoph, Moralist und Sociologe," *Deutsche* [164] *Revue*, XXXVI (1911), 184-205.

SCHÖNEMANN, FRIEDRICH, "Amerikanischer Humor," GRM, VIII [165] (1920), 152-164, 216-227.

—, "Mark Twains Weltanschauung," *ES*, LV (1921), 53-84. [166]

—, *Mark Twain als literarische Persönlichkeit*, Jena, 1925; 119 pp. [167]

A. Brandl, *Die Literatur*, XXVII (1924-25), 627 ff.

J. Ellinger, AB, XXXVI (1925), 372-374.

W. Fischer, ES, LXI (1926), 135-139.

H. Lüdeke, *Deutsche Literaturzeitung*, II (1925), 1802-1813.

FISCHER, WALTHER, "Mark Twain zu seinem 100. Geburtstag," [168] DNS, XLIII (1935), 471-480.

SCHÖNEMANN, F., "Mark Twain und Deutschland," *Hochschule und* [169] *Ausland*, XIV (1936), 37-43.

Reprinted in *Auslese*, Feb. 1936.

WEST, V. ROYCE, "Mark Twain and Germany," AGR, XI[4] 32-37. [170]

HEMMINGHAUS, EDGAR H., *Mark Twain in Germany*, Columbia [171] University Germanic Studies, New Series, IX (1939); 170 pp.

H. A. Pochmann, MDU, XXXIII (1941), 234 f.

ASSELINEAU, ROGER, *The Literary Reputation of Mark Twain from* [172] *1920 to 1950*, Paris, 1954; 241 pp.

The text deals only with American criticism, but the bibliography, pp. 68 to 226, contains many entries of German criticism.

SCHÖNEMANN, FR., "Mark Twain's *Huckleberry Finn*," ASNS, [173] CXCII, 1955-56, 273-289.

SCHÖNFELDER, KARL HEINZ, *Mark Twain; Leben, Persönlichkeit* [174] *und Werk*, Halle, 1961; 118 pp.

With list of reprints and translations that have appeared in East Germany.

KLOTZ, GÜNTHER, "Mark Twain's *Letters from the Earth*," [Rev.] [175] ZAA, XI (1963), 281-287.

Clemens and the German Language

HUBLER, LEO, "Mark Twain und die deutsche Sprache," *Anglia*, [176] LXV (1941), 206-223.

KRUMPELMANN, JOHN T., *Mark Twain and the German Language*, [177]
Baton Rouge, Louisiana State Univ. Press, 1953; ii + 21 pp.

Clemens and Austria

LEDERER, MAX, "Mark Twain in Vienna," *Mark Twain Quarterly*, [178]
VII¹ (1944), 1-12.

MICHEL, ROBERT, "The Popularity of Mark Twain in Austria," [179]
Mark Twain Quarterly, VIII (1950), 5-6, 19.

STIEHL, KARL, *Mark Twain und die Wiener Presse zur Zeit seines* [180]
Aufenthalts in Wien, 1897-1899, Diss., Wien, 1953.

Clemens and Switzerland

HÜPPY, A., *Mark Twain und die Schweiz. Dem grossen Freund und* [181]
Bewunderer unseres Landes... gewidmet, Zürich, 1935; 90 pp.

Cooper

BARBA, PRESTON A., "Cooper in Germany," GAA, XII (1914), [182]
3-60, and in *Indiana University Studies*, XXI (1914), 52-104.

ZAECKEL, EUGENE, *Der Einfluss J. F. Coopers und W. Irvings auf* [183]
die deutsche Literatur, Diss., Wien, 1944.

PLISCHKE, H., *Von Cooper bis Karl May, Geschichte des völkerkund-* [184]
lichen Reise- und Abenteuerromans, Düsseldorf, 1951; 208 pp.
Cooper, Ruppius, Sealsfield, Gerstäcker, Möllhausen, Strubberg, May, *et al.*

THORP, W., "Cooper beyond America," *New York History*, XXXV [185]
(1954), 522-539.

Cooper and Gerstäcker, [184]
Cooper and Goethe

WUKADINOVIĆ, SPIRIDION, *Goethes "Novelle": der Schauplatz*, [186]
Cooper'sche Einflüsse, Halle, 1909; 127 pp.

Cooper and Hauff

BRENNER, C. D., "The Influence of Cooper's *The Spy* on Hauff's [187]
Lichtenstein," MLN, XXX (1915), 207-210.

Cooper and May [184]

READ, HELEN APPLETON, "Karl May, Germany's Fenimore Cooper," [188]
AGR, II⁴ (1936), 4-7.

Cooper and Möllhausen [182]

BARBA, PRESTON A., *Balduin Möllhausen, the German Cooper*, [189]
AG, Monograph Series, XVII (1914); 188 pp.
Cooper and Ruppius [121].

206

Cooper and Sealsfield

ARNDT, KARL J., "The Cooper-Sealsfield Exchange of Criticism," [190]
AL XV (1943), 16-24.

KOZELUH, ALFONS, *Charles Sealsfield und James Fenimore Cooper,* [191]
Diss., Wien, 1949.

Cooper and Stifter

SAUER, AUGUST, "Über den Einfluss der nordamerikanischen [192]
Literatur auf die deutsche," JGG, XVI (1906), 21-51. and
pp. I, 104-138 in A. Sauer, *Probleme und Gestalten*, Stuttgart,
1933.

Cooper and Strubberg

BARBA, PRESTON A., "Friedrich Armand Strubberg," GAA, X [193]
(1912), 175-225, XI (1913), 3-63, 115-142 and AG, Monograph
Series, XVI (1913); 151 pp.

Cooper and Switzerland

LÜDEKE, H., "James Fenimore Cooper and the Democracy of [194]
Switzerland," ES, XXVII (1946), 33-44.

Emerson

FRANCKE, KUNO, "Emerson and German Personality," *The Inter-* [195]
national Quarterly, VIII (1903), 92-107.
Grimm, J. Schmidt, Fr. Spielhagen.

VON ENDE, A., "Emerson-Übersetzungen," *Literarisches Echo,* [196]
V (1903), 1324-1326.

SIMON, J., *Ralph Waldo Emerson in Deutschland, 1851-1932*, Neue [197]
deutsche Forschungen, Abt.: Amerikanische Literatur- und
Kulturgeschichte, III (1937); 180 pp.

WELLEK, RENÉ, "Emerson and German Philosophy," NEQ, XVI [198]
(1943), 41-63.

MARCUSE, LUDWIG, "Emerson in Modern Germany," *Emerson* [199]
Society Quarterly, Nov. 12, 1958, pp. 50-51.

Emerson and Grimm

HOLLS, FRIEDRICH WILLIAM, ed., *Correspondence between R. W. Emer-* [200]
son and H. Grimm, Boston, 1903; iii + 90 pp.
In *Atlantic Monthly*, XVI (1903), 467-479.

DUFFY, CHARLES, "Material Relating to R. W. Emerson in the [201]
'Grimm Nachlass,'" AL, XXX (1959), 523-525.

Emerson and Nietzsche

HAMMEL, H. "Emerson and Nietzsche," NEQ, XIX (1946), 63-84. [202]

207

BAUMGARTEN, EDUARD, "Mitteilungen und Bemerkungen über den [203] Einfluss Emersons auf Nietzsche," JAS, I (1956), 93-152.

HUBBARD, STANLEY, *Nietzsche und Emerson*, Philosophische For- [204] schungen, Neue Folge, Basel, VIII (1958); 195 pp.

BAUMGARTEN, EDUARD, *Das Vorbild Emersons im Werk und Leben* [205] *Nietzsches*, Hadelberg, 1958

Harte

KINDT, HERMANN, "Freiligrath und Bret Harte," *Gegenwart*, IX [206] (1876), 393-394.

TIMPE, EUGENE F., "Bret Harte's German Public," JAS, X (1965), [206a] 215-220.

Hawthorne

LINK, H., *Die Erzählkunst Nathaniel Hawthornes*, Frankfurter [207] Arbeiten... Anglistik- und Amerika-Studien, VII (1962), 196 pp.
H. Larrass, ZAA, XI (1964), 420-423.

TIMPE, EUGENE F., "Hawthorne in Germany," *Symposium*, XIX [207a] (1965), 171-179.

Howells

WIRZBERGER, KARL-HEINZ, "The Simple, the Natural and the [208] Honest: William Dean Howells als Kritiker, und die Durch- setzung des Realismus in der amerikanischen Literatur des ausgehenden 19. Jahrhunderts," ZAA, IX (1961), 1-48.

Irving [183].

REICHART, WALTER, A., "The Early Reception of Washington [209] Irving's Works in Germany," *Anglia*, LXXIV (1956), 345-363.

—, "Washington Irving's Influence on German Literature," MLR, [210] LII (1957), 536-553.

—, "The Earliest German Translations of Washington Irving's [211] Writings. A Bibliography," *Bulletin of the New York Public Library*, LXI, 491-498.

—, *Washington Irving and Germany*. University of Michigan [212] Publications in Language and Literature, Univ. of Michigan Press, 1957; 212 pp.
E. Teichmann, RLC, XXXIV (1960), 745-749.

Irving and Hauff

PLATH, OTTO, "Washington Irvings Einfluss auf Wilhelm Hauff," [213] *Euphorion*, XX (1913), 459-471.

Irving and Heine

KABEL, P., "Die Quellen für Heines 'Bimini' und 'Mohrenkönig,'" [214]
ASNS, CXVII (1906), 256-267.
*Voyages and Discoveries of the Companions of Columbus,
Conquest of Granada.*

Irving and Raabe

BRANDES, WILHELM, "Raabe und Washington Irving," *Mitteilungen* [215]
für die Gesellschaft der Freunde Wilhelm Raabes, XIII³ (1923),
75-79.

Irving and Reuter

SPRENGER, R., "Zu Fritz Reuters Dichtungen," *Jahrbuch des* [216]
Vereins für Niederdeutsche Sprachforschung, XXVII (1901),
150-151.
Knickerbocker's History of New York and *Urgeschicht von
Mekelnborg.*

KEERL, F., *Die Quellen zu Fritz Reuters "Urgeschicht von Mekeln-* [217]
borg," Diss., Greifswald, 1915; 78 pp.

James

HAERDTER, R., "Henry James," *Die Gegenwart*, VIII⁴ (1953), 117 f. [218]

UHLIG, H., "Henry James, deutsch," *Texte und Zeichen*, I (1955), [219]
262-266.

BAUMGAERTEL, GERHARD, "The Reception of Henry James in [220]
Germany," *Symposium*, XII (1959), 19-31.

Melville [409]-[412]

Melville and Gerstäcker

WALTER, JOSEF, *Hermann Melville's Influence upon Gerstäcker's* [221]
South Sea Novels, Diss., Freiburg (Schweiz), 1952.

Poe [418]-[423]

BETZ, LOUIS P., "Edgar Poe in Deutschland," *Die Zeit*, XXXV [222]
(1903), 8-9, 21-23.

EDWARD, GEORGE, "Poe in Germany," pp. 73-99 in *The Book of* [223]
the Poe Centenary, University of Virginia, 1909.

EWERS, HANNS HEINZ, "E. Poe und sein Einfluss," *Zeitgeist*, 1909, [224]
299, No. 3; and *Eckart*, III (1908-1909), 345 ff.

HIPPE, FRITZ, *Edgar Allen Poes Lyrik in Deutschland*, Diss., Leipzig, [225]
1913; xi + 91 pp.

TANNENBAUM, LIBBY, "'The Raven' Abroad," *Magazine of Art*, [226]
XXXVII (1914), 123-127.

LANG, SIEGFRIED, "Edgar Poe und die neuere Dichtung," *Neue* [227]
Schweizer Rundschau, XXI (1928), 188-197.
BABLER, OTTO F., and TH. VODIČKA, "Die deutschen Raben-Über- [228]
setzungen; Versuch einer Bibliographie," *Zeitschrift für Bücher-*
freunde, XXXVIII (1934), 80-82.
—, "German translations of Poe's 'Raven'", *Notes and Queries*, [229]
CLXXIV (1938), 9.
See also *Notes and Queries*, 1938, pp. 88 and 106.
KÜHNELT, HARRO H., "Deutsche Erzähler im Gefolge von E. A. Poe," [230]
Rivista di letterature moderne, I (1950-51), 457-465.
—, "Die Aufnahme und Verbreitung von E. A. Poes Werken im [231]
Deutschen," pp. 195-224 in *Festschrift für Walther Fischer*,
Heidelberg, 1959.
BANDY, WILLIAM T., "The Influence and Reputation of Edgar [232]
Allan Poe in Europe." [Pamphlet] Baltimore, *Edgar Allan*
Poe Society, 1962; 15 pp.

Poe and Spielhagen
COBB, PALMER, "Edgar Allan Poe and Friedrich Spielhagen; Their [233]
Theory of the Short Story," MLN, XXV (1910), 67-72.
MITCHELL, ROBERT MCBURNEY, "Poe and Spielhagen; Novelle and [234]
Short Story," MLN, XXIX (1914), 36-41.
A reply to [233].

Poe and Winterfeld
ANDRAE, AUGUST, "Zu Edgar Allan Poes Geschichten," ES, [235]
XLVIII (1915), 479.

Stowe
MACLEAN, GRACE E., "*Uncle Tom's Cabin in Germany*," Diss., Hei- [236]
delberg, 1910, and AG, X, Monograph Series (1910); 102 pp.
Hackländer, Auerbach, Hesslein.
JAFFE, ADRIAN, "Uncle Tom in the Penal Colony; Heine's View of [237]
Uncle Tom's Cabin," AGR, XLX³ (1953), 5-6.

Taylor
PRAHL, AUGUSTUS J., "Bayard Taylor in Germany," GQ, XVIII [238]
(1945), 16-25.
KRUMPELMANN, JOHN T., "Bayard Taylor as a Literary Mediator [239]
between Germany and the South Atlantic States," DNS, 1955,
415-418.
—, *Bayard Taylor and German Letters*, Brittannica et Americana, [240]
IV (1959); 234 pp.
P. A. Shelley, MP, LIX (1962), 71-75.

FRENZ, HORST, and PHILIP ALLISON SHELLEY, eds., "Bayard [241]
Taylor's German Lecture on American Literature," JAS, II
(1950), 89-133.

Thoreau

RYSSEL, FRITZ HEINRICH, "Henry Thoreau: Die Welt und ich," [242]
NLW, July 10, 1952, p. 11.

URZIDIL, JOHANNES, "Weltreise in Concord," NLW, May 10, 1953, [243]
p. 6.

Twain, see Clemens

- PART III: FROM LITERARY INDEPENDENCE TO
LITERARY COMMONWEALTH

VI. THE NOVEL

Surveys

HEWETT-THAYER, HARVEY W., "America and Americans in Recent [244]
German Fiction," *Bookman*, XLIII (1916), 95-112 and in
The Modern German Novel, Boston, 1924; 1-25.

PHELPS, WILLIAM LYON, "Amerikanische Schriftstellerinnen," [245]
Die Literatur, XXVIII (1926), 522-526.
Wharton, Cather, Sedgwick, Gale, Ferber.

WILLIAMS, BLANCHE COTTON, "Die amerikanische Novelle," *Die* [246]
Literatur, XXVIII (1926), 515-520.

HARTEN-HOENKE, TONI, "Die Überschüttung Deutschlands mit [247]
amerikanischer Literatur," *Der Türmer*, XXX (1928), 373-
376.

LÜDEKE, HENRY, "Der europäische Naturalismus im amerikani- [248]
schen Roman," *Zeitschrift für deutsche Bildung*, V (1929), 57 ff.

JOACHIM, HANS, "Romane aus Amerika," DNR, XLI: 2 (1930), [249]
396-409.
Dos Passos, Hemingway, Wilder.

BUSSE, A., "Amerikanischer Brief," *Die Literatur*, XXXIV (1932), [250]
339-341.
O'Neill, Cather, Ferber, Faulkner, Jeffers.

EHLE, RALPH V., *America Reflected in Two German Periodicals*, [251]
*"Die deutsche Rundschau" and "Die Neue Rundschau," 1900-
1923*, Diss., Johns Hopkins University, 1933.

MOHRMANN, H., *Kultur- und Gesellschaftsprobleme des amerikanischen* [252]
Romans der Nachkriegszeit, (1920-1927), Diss., Giessen, 1933,
Düsseldorf, 1934.

LÜDEKE, HENRY, "American Literature in Germany; a Report of [253] Recent Research," AL, VI (1935), 168-175.

—, "Neuhumanismus und Demokratie im amerikanischen Geistes- [254] leben," GRM, XXI [1933], 220-233.

FRISÉ, ADOLF, "Der junge amerikanische Roman," *Die Tat*, XXVII [255] (1936), 639 f.

VON HEISELER, BERNT, "Neue Amerikaner," *Deutsche Zeitschrift*, [256] XLIX: 1 (1936), 468-469.
Wolfe, Faulkner, Wilder

EFFELBERGER, HANS, "Neue Entwicklungstendenzen in der [257] amerikanischen Literatur der Gegenwart," DNS, 1936, 154-161.
Hemingway, Wilder, Wolfe, Faulkner, Pearl Buck, Dos Passos.

DEMMIG, CHARLOTTE, "Neue Kräfte in der amerikanischen Gegen- [258] wartsliteratur," *Die Literatur*, XL (1938), 527-530.
Bromfield, Wilder, Cabell, James, London, *et al.*

HARNACK-FISH, MILDRED, *Entwicklung der amerikanischen Literatur* [259] *der Gegenwart in einigen Vertretern des Romans und der Kurz-geschichte.* Diss., Giessen, 1941.
Sherwood Anderson, Wilder, Wolfe, Faulkner.

BERENDSOHN, WALTER A., *Die humanistische Front: Einführung in* [260] *die deutsche Emigrantenliteratur*, Zürich, 1946.

GREGG, CATHERINE, "Die neuere Literatur in USA," *Die Literarische* [261] *Welt*, 1946, 213-233.
Dreiser, Lewis, Hemingway, Cather, Wolfe, Buck, Saroyan, Wilder, O'Neill, Sandburg, Millay.

FISCHER, WALTHER, *Hauptströmungen des modernen amerikani-* [262] *schen Schrifttums.* In *Abhandlungen und Vorträge*, hrsgg. von der Wittheit zu Bremen, XVII: 4 (1948).
I "Der moderne amerikanische Roman und seine geistigen Grundlagen," pp. 3-26.
II "Das amerikanische Theater der Gegenwart," pp. 27-54.

FREEMANTLE, ANNE, "Romane in Amerika," *Frankfurter Hefte*, [263] V (1950), 1328-1331.

BRÜNING, EBERHARD, Rev. of Alva Bessie, *The Un-Americans*, [264] N.Y., 1947, ZAA VI (1959), 316-328.
Howard Fast, *et al.*

DODERER, HANS, "Zur Technik des modernen amerikanischen [265] Romans," DNS, 1958, 257-264.

ROGGE, HEINZ, "Die amerikanische Negerfrage im Lichte der [266] Literatur von Richard Wright und Ralph Ellison," DNS, 1958, 56-65, 103-113.

212

LEITEL, ERICH, *Die Aufnahme der amerikanischen Literatur in* [267] *Deutschland: Übersetzungen der Jahre 1942-1944, mit einer Bibliographie*, Diss., Jena, 1958; 276 Bl.

STRAUMANN, HEINRICH, "Amerikanische Literatur in Europa: [268] Eine geschmacksgeschichtliche Überlegung," *Anglia*, LXXVI (1958), 208-216.

SCHÖNFELDER, KARL-HEINZ, "Amerikanische Literatur in Europa: [269] Methodologisches zu geschmacksgeschichtlichen Überlegungen," ZAA, VII (1959), 35-57.
Reply to Straumann, above.

LINK, FRANZ, H., "Über das Geschichtsbewusstsein einiger ameri- [270] kanischen Dichter des 20. Jahrhunderts," JAS, IV (1959), 143-160.

BALLINGER, SARA ELIZABETH, *The Reception of the American Novel* [271] *in German Periodicals, 1945-1957*. Diss. Indiana Univ., 1959. *Die Neueren Sprachen, Merkur, Frankfurter Hefte, Deutsche Rundschau.*

DICKSON, P., *Das Amerikabild in der deutschen Emigrationsliteratur* [272] *seit 1933*, Diss., München, 1951; 138 pp.

OPPEL, HORST, "Forschungsbericht der deutschen Amerikanistik," [273] DNS, 1952, 292-302.

GRAMES, BERNICE D., "The American Story," DNS, 1952, 140-143. [274] Capote, McCullers, Faulkner, Caldwell, Wolfe, Chase, Kantor, Hemingway, Dos Passos.

DODERER, KLAUS, "Die angelsächsische Short Story und die deutsche [275] Kurzgeschichte," DNS, 1953, 417-424.

ROSS, WERNER, "Der amerikanische Roman der Gegenwart," [276] *Hochland*, XLVI: 1 (1953), 153-163.

FREY, JOHN R., "America and her Literature Reviewed by Post- [277] War Germany," AGR, XX⁵ (1954), 4-6, 31.

—, "Post-war Germany. Enter American Literature," AGR, [278] XXI¹ (1954), 9-12.

—, "Post-War German Reactions to American Literature," [279] JEGP, LIV (1955), 173-194.

BLANK, GUSTAV H. "Der amerikanische Schriftsteller und die [280] Gesellschaft; zum amerikanischen Roman des 20. Jahrhunderts," DNS, 1955, 153-164.

Deutsche Akademie für Sprache und Dichtung, Darmstadt, ed., [281] "Befruchtung oder Überschwemmung: Wie wirkt die Übersetzung in Deutschland? Eine Rundfrage," DLD Nov. 1, 1950, p. 5; Nov. 20, 1950, p. 9; Dec. 5, 1950, p. 48.

SPRINGER, ANNE M., *The American Novel in Germany: A Study of the* [282] *Critical Reception of Eight American Novelists Between the Two World Wars.* (Brittannica et Americana) VII (1960); 116 pp.
London, Sinclair, Dreiser, Lewis, Dos Passos, Hemingway, Faulkner, Wolfe; Bibliography.

BLANK, GUSTAV, "Das Verhältnis von Dichtung, Dichter und [283] Gesellschaft in der amerikanischen Literatur des 20. Jahrhunderts," JAS, VI (1961), 32-74.

LINK, FRANZ H., "Tendenzen in der amerikanischen Literatur- [284] geschichtsschreibung der letzten zwanzig Jahre," JAS, VI (1961), 48-58.

SINDE, WOLFGANG, "Englische und amerikanische Literatur in [285] Reclams *Universal-Bibliothek*," ZAA, X (1962), 279-288.
Contains "Bibliographie aller seit 1945 in Reclams *Universal-Bibliothek* erschienenen Übersetzungen aus der englischen und amerikanischen Literatur". 15 translations "aus dem Amerikanischen".

OPPEL, HORST, "American Literature in Post-War Germany: [286] Impact or Alienation?" *Studies in Comparative Literature*, VII (1962), 259-272; and in DNS, 1962, 1-10.

LANG, HANS JOACHIM, *Studien zur Entstehung der neueren amerika-* [287] *nischen Literaturkritik*, (Brittannica et Americana,) VIII (1961); 276 pp.
Ursula Brumm, *Anglia*, LXXX (1963), 286-287.

BRUMM, URSULA, "Über den amerikanischen Roman der Gegenwart," [287a] DNR LXXIV (1963), 633-646.

GERMAN NAMES

Hauptmann

HEUSER, F. W. J., "Gerhart Hauptmanns Amerikafahrt, 1932," [288] *Gerhart Hauptmann-Jahrbuch*, II (1937), 111-131.

—, "Gerhart Hauptmann's Trip to America, 1894," GR, XIII [289] (1938), 3-11.

MILLER, SIEGFRIED H., "Gerhart Hauptmann's Relation to [290] America," MDU, XLIV (1952), 332-339.

Hesse

FIELD, G. WALLIS, "Hermann Hesse as Critic of English and [291] American Literature," MDU, LIII (1961), 147-158.

214

Kafka

HEUER, HELMUT, *Die Amerikavision bei William Blake und Franz* [292]
Kafka, Diss., München, 1959.

RULAND, RICHARD E., "A View from Back Home: Kafka's *Amerika*," [293]
American Quarterly, XII (1961), 33-42.

Mann [540]

SUHL, ABRAHAM, "Anglizismen in Thomas Manns *Doktor Faustus*," [294]
MDU, XL (1948), 391-397.
H. G. Haile, MDU, LI (1959), 262-269.

POLITZER, HEINZ, "America in the Later Writings of Thomas Mann," [295]
MLF, XXVII (1952), 91-100.

BRINER, ANDRES, "Conrad Beisel and Thomas Mann," AGR, XXVI [296]
(1959), 24-25, 38.

Rilke

JONAS, K. W., "Rilke and America," *Etudes germaniques*, IX (1954), [297]
55-59.

Werfel

FREY, JOHN R., "America and Franz Werfel," GQ, XIX (1946), [298]
121-128.

ARLT, GUSTAV O., "Franz Werfel and America," MLF, XXXVI [299]
(1951), 1-7.

AMERICAN NAMES

Anderson, (Sherwood)

CLARK, EDWARD, "*Weinsberg, Ohio:* Eine Interpretation," DNS, [300]
1959, 547-552.

Bierce

PIRA, GISELA, "Ambrose Bierce," DNS 1963, 425-430. [301]

Buck

MAGNUS, ILSE, *Pearl S. Buck*, Diss., Kiel, 1954. [302]

Caldwell

ROSENTAL, GISELA, *Erskine Caldwell: Wesen und Grenzen seiner* [303]
Kunst. Diss., Berlin, 1952.

Cather

F. SCHÖNEMANN, "Willa Cather, *Antonia*" [Rev.], *Die Literatur*, [304]
XXXI (1929), 354.

KAZIN, ALFRED, "Willa Cather," *Monat*, I (1948), 70-81. [305]

215

REISCH, INGEBORG, *Das Pionierideal in der Darstellung der ameri-* [306] *kanischen Gesellschaft bei Willa Cather und Sinclair Lewis.* Diss. Berlin, Freie Univ.; 97 pp.

Dos Passos [249], [257], [352].

SCHÖNEMANN, F. [Review], "John Dos Passos. *Manhattan Transfer,* [307] Roman einer Stadt, mit einem Vorwort von Sinclair Lewis," Berlin, 1935, *Die Literatur*, XXX (1928), 296.

WELTMANN, LUTZ, "Der 42. Breitengrad," *Die Literatur*, XXXIII [308] (1931), 291 f.

EHRENZWEIG, STEPHAN, "Der 42. Breitengrad," *Das Tagebuch*, XI [309] (1930), 13 ff.

NEUSE, WERNER, *Die literarische Entwicklung von John Dos Passos,* [310] Diss., Giessen, Glasgow, 1931.

TÜRK, WERNER, "Dos Passos," *Die Literatur*, XXXV (1933), [311] 377-380.

PORTER, JOHN, *Bibliography of John Passos*, Chicago, Normandie [312] House, 1950.

HICKS, GRANVILLE, "Der Romancier und die Macht: Über John [313] Dos Passos als politischen Schriftsteller," *Monat*, IV (1952), 414-420.

BLUM, KARL, *Amerikanismen der Regionalmundart und des Slang* [314] *in John Dos Passos' Romantrilogie, "U.S.A."* Diss., Mainz, 1958.

Dreiser [261], [282].

BLEI, FRANZ, "Tisch mit Büchern," *Prager Presse*, Feb. 20, 1924. [315]
RUNDT, FRANZ, "Besuch bei Dreiser," *Prager Tageblatt*, Sept. 26, [316] 1928.
ISEMANN, H., "Eine amerikanische Tragödie," *Die schöne Literatur*, [317] XXXIX (1928), 438.
GRANDE, RICHARD, "Jennie Gerhardt," *Die schöne Literatur*, [318] XXXIX (1928), 491.
KNUDSEN, HANS, "Ton in des Schöpfers Hand," *Die schöne Literatur*, [319] XXXIX (1928), 554.
SCHÖNEMANN, FR., "Eine amerikanische Tragödie," *Die Literatur*, [320] XXX (1928), 296.
EHRENZWEIG, STEPHAN, "Theodore Dreiser, Jennie Gerhardt," [321] *Das Tagebuch*, IX (1928), 761 f.
WIRZBERGER, KARL HEINZ, "Die neueste amerikanische Dreiser- [322] forschung," ZAA I (1963), 186-195.
—, "Dreisers Amerikanische Tragödie," ZAA, I (1953), 224-230. [323]

—, "Das Leben und Schaffen Theodor Dreisers: Eine biographi- [324]
sche Skizze," ZAA, II (1954), 6-42.

WENTZ, JOHN C., "An American Tragedy as Epic-Theater: The [325]
Piscator-Dramatization," Modern Drama, IV (1962), 365-376.

Faulkner, [256], [257], [259], [274], [276], [279], [282].

LÜTZELER, HEINRICH, "Neue Romane," Hochland, XXXIII: 1 [326]
(1935), 266-270.

Licht im August

HESSE, HERMANN, "Notizen zu neuen Büchern," DNR, XLVI: 2 [327]
(1935), 664-672.

Licht im August, p. 670.

HARNACK-FISH, MILDRED, "William Faulkner, ein amerikanischer [328]
Dichter aus grosser Tradition," Die Literatur, XXXVIII
(1935), 64-67.

VON EINSIEDEL, WOLFGANG, "William Faulkner," Europäische [329]
Revue, XI² (1935), 707-708.

KORN, KARL, "Moira und Schuld...," DNR, XLIX: 2 (1938), 603- [330]
609.

BRAEM, H. M., "Das Scandalon William Faulkners," Deutsche [331]
Rundschau, LXXXIV (1948), 944-950.

SKULIMA, LONI, "Der Nobelpreisträger für Literatur: Versuch [332]
einer Darstellung. Der Dichter William Faulkner," DLD,
Nov. 20, 1950, p. 4.

BRENNER, HANS GEORG, "Faulkners Nobelpreis-Roman," DLD, [333]
Dec. 20, 1951, p. 9.

Intruder in the Dust.

FRANZEN, ERICH, "William Faulkners puritanischer Mythos," [334]
Merkur, V (1951), 629-641.

SEYPPEL, JOACHIM, "Faulkners Dichtung: Der Weg in die Sack- [335]
gasse; zu seinem Roman Intruder in the Dust," NPZ, IV (1952),
369-373.

PUSEY III, WILLIAM WEBB, "William Faulkner's Works in Germany [336]
to 1940: Translation and Criticism," GR, XXX (1955), 211-
226.

STRAUMANN, HEINRICH, "Eine amerikanische Seinsdeutung: [337]
Faulkners Roman, A Fable," Anglia, LXXIII (1956), 484-
515.

VON EINSIEDEL, WOLFGANG, "Revolte des Menschensohnes: Zu [338]
William Faulkners 'Eine Legende,'" Merkur, X (1956), 282-290.

NOLTING-HAUFF, LORE, Sprachstil und Weltbild bei William [339]
Faulkner, Diss., Freiburg, 1958; 252 Bl.

BLUMENBERG, HANS, "Mythos und Ethos Amerikas im Werk [340] William Faulkners," *Hochland*, L: 1 (1958), 234-250.

GRENZMANN, WILHELM, "Nobelpreisträger William Faulkner: [341] Sein Weg und seine Dichtung," *Universitas*, XIV: 2 (1959), 909-920.

CHRISTADLER, MARTIN, *Natur und Geschichte im Werk von William* [342] *Faulkner*, Diss., Tübingen, 1959; 381 Bl.

HAGOPIAN, JOHN V., "Style and Meaning in Hemingway and [343] Faulkner," JAS, IV (1959), 170-179.

—, "The Aydt and the Maze: Ten Years of Faulkner Studies in [344] America," JAS, VI (1961), 134-151.

KAHN, LUDWIG W., "William Faulkner: Das Romanwerk des [345] Dichters als geistige Antwort auf unsere Zeit," *Universitas*, XVI (1961), 1307-1318.

HAPPEL, NIKOLAUS, "William Faulkner's *A Rose for Emily*," DNS, [346] 1962, 396-403.

BUSCH, GÜNTHER, "Zum Tode William Faulkners," *Merkur*, XVI [347] (1962), 897-899.

HAAS, RUDOLF, "Faulkner und die Humanität," *Universitas*, XVIII [348] (1963), 347-363.

BUNGERT, HANS, "William Faulkners letzter Roman," DNS 1963, [349] 498-506.
The Reivers.

Fitzgerald

BOVERI, MARGRET, "Francis Scott Fitzgerald; Traum und Jazz," [350] *Frankfurter Hefte*, VII (1952), 144-145.

POLITZER, HEINZ, "Ein Held der Hilflosigkeit; Zur Wiederent- [351] deckung Francis Scott Fitzgeralds," *Monat*, VI (1952), 194-195.

IRWIN, WILLIAM R., "Dos Passos and Fitzgerald as Reviewers of the [352] American Social Scene," DNS, 1960, 417-428.

HÖCKER, URSULA, *Darstellung und Kritik der Gesellschaft in den* [353] *Werken von F. Scott Fitzgerald*. Diss., Freiburg, 1961.

MILLGATE, M., "Scott Fitzgerald as Social Novelist. Statement and [354] Technique: *The Last Tycoon*," *English Stiudes*, XLIII (1962), 29-34.

Hemingway, [257], [261], [274], [279], [282], [343].

POLGAR, ALFRED, "Der neue Hemingway," *Das Tagebuch*, XI (1930), [355] 1646.

MANN, KLAUS, "Ernest Hemingway," *Die Neue Schweizer Rund-* [356] *schau*, XXIV (1931), 272.

218

COHN, L. H., *A Bibliography of the Works of Ernest Hemingway,* [357]
New York, Random House, 1931.

FALLADA, HANS, "Ernest Hemingway, oder woran liegt es?", *Die* [358]
Literatur, XXXIII (1931), 672-674.

—, "Gespräch zwischen ihr und ihm über Ernest Hemingway," [359]
Die Literatur, XXXV (1932), 21-24.

DIETRICH, MAX, "Ernest Hemingway," *Hochland,* XXX: 2 (1933), [360]
89-91.

SKULIMA, LONI, "Ein neuer Hemingway, aber nicht der Heming- [361]
way," DLD, Nov. 1, 1950, p. 13.
Across the River and into the Trees.

KRÄMER-BADONI, RUDOLF, "Geburt und Tod literarischer Stile," [362]
DLD, Dec. 5, 1950, p. 5 and Dec. 20, 1950, p. 3.

VON EINSIEDEL, WOLFGANG, "Ein Komet verblasst" [Hemingway], [363]
Merkur, IV (1950), 1220-1225.

POLITZER, HEINZ, "Der neue Hemingway," DNR, LXII: 1 (1951), [364]
136-139.

BRANDSTÄTTER, DIETER, *Ernest Hemingway.* Diss., Kiel, 1951. [365]

GURTLER, LEA, *Der Bestseller Hemingway,* Diss., Innsbruck, 1950. [366]

PAPAJEWSKI, HELMUT, "Die Frage nach der Sinnhaftigkeit bei [367]
Hemingway," *Anglia,* LXX (1951), 186-209.

OPPEL, HORST, *"Across the River and into the Trees."* [Rev.] DNS, [368]
1952, 473-486.

FREY, JOHN R., "Hemingway as a Literary Force in Post-War [369]
Germany," Prog., MLA, Chicago, Dec. 1953.

FRANZEN, ERICH, *"Der alte Mann und das Meer,"* NLW, March [370]
25, 1953; p. 3.

HENSEL, GEORG, "Filmtod eines Schriftstellers," NLW, March 25, [371]
1953; p. 3.
Schnee am Kilimanscharo.

SCHULZE, MARTIN, *Ernest Hemingway: Werden und Wesen seiner* [372]
Kunst, Diss., Halle, 1954; 249 Bl.

GRONKE, ERICH, "Das jüngste Buch Hemingways," ZAA, II (1954), [373]
118-123.

HAPPEL, NIKOLAUS, "Äusserungen Hemingways zur Darstellung der [374]
Wirklichkeit und Wahrheit," ASNS, CXC (1954), 204-213.

MUCHAROWSKI, HANS-GÜNTER, *Die Werke von Ernest Hemingway.* [375]
Eine Bibliographie der deutschsprachigen Hemingway-Literatur
und der Originalwerke von 1923-1954, Hamburg, 1955; 48 Bl.

STRESAU, HERMANN, "Ernest Hemingway: Von der Kunst des [376] Weglassens," *Deutsche Universitätszeitung*, XII (1957), Heft 23-24, 24-26.

PLIMPTON, GEORGE A., "Gespräch mit Ernest Hemingway," [377] *Merkur*, XIII (1959), 526-544.

DAMP, WALDEMAR, Individuum und Gesellschaft in Hemingways [378] Romanen, Diss., Greifswald, 1964.
"Selbstanzeige," Weimarer Beiträge, 1965, 317.

WELLERSHOFF, DIETER, "Hemingway und seine Dichtung," *Uni-* [378a] *versitas*, XIX (1964), 1057-1068.

Henry

PIRA, GISELA, "O. Henry," DNS, 1962, 374-479. [379]
H. Wustenhagen, ZAA, XI (1963), 423-426.

James [218]-[220].

Lewis [261], [282].

SCHÖNEMANN, F., "Sinclair Lewis, eine neue Verheissung im nord- [380] amerikanischen Roman," *Die Literatur*, XXV (1923), 683-688.

BRANDL, A., "*Arrowsmith*," ASNS, CLI (1926), 129-131. [381]

SINCLAIR, UPTON, "Sinclair Lewis," *Weltbühne*, XXIII (1927), 745. [382]

SCHÖNEMANN, F., "Ein neuer Sinclair Lewis," *Die Literatur*, XXIX [383] (1927), 574.

—, "Sinclair Lewis – Gesamtbesprechung," *Der Türmer*, XXXI [384] (1928), 64-66.

KRIESI, HANS, *Sinclair Lewis*, Frauenfeld und Leipzig, 1928, [385] 217 pp.

BEHLER-HAGEN, MALLY, "Sam Dodsworth," *Die schöne Literatur*, [386] XXXI (1930), 293 f.

LETTENBAUR, J. A., Sinclair Lewis und die Neuen in Amerika," [387] *Hochland*, XXVII: 2 (1930), 317-328.
Upton Sinclair, Theodore Dreiser, Sherwood Anderson.

STEINER, ARPAD, "Sinclair Lewis in Germany," pp. 134-140 [388] in *Curme Volume of Linguistic Studies*, Urbana, Illinois, 1930.

KORNFELD, PAUL, "Babbitts Frau," *Das Tagebuch*, XI (1930), [389] 382 ff.

ZWEIG, ARNOLD, "Improvisation über Sinclair Lewis," *Die* [390] *Literatur*, XXXIII (1930), 185-186.

DEMMIG, CHARLOTTE, "Sinclair Lewis," *Der Gral*, XXV (1931), [391] 637 ff.

FISCHER, WALTHER, "Sinclair Lewis, der Nobelpreis-Dichter," [392]
Neue Jahrbücher für Wissenschaft und Jugendbildung, VII
(1931), 700-709.

BAB, JULIUS, "Sam Dodsworth und das kommende Amerika," [393]
"Vorwort" to Sinclair Lewis's *Sam Dodsworth*, Berlin, 1932.

STORCH, WILLY, *Sinclair Lewis und das amerikanische Kultur-* [394]
und Sprachbild, Diss., Marburg, 1938.

SCHÖNFELDER, KARL-HEINZ, *Sinclair Lewis als Sozial- und Kultur-* [395]
kritiker, Diss., Leipzig, 1950; 144 Bl.

KOPKA, HANS W. K., *Grundlagen und Grenzen der Gesellschaftskritik* [396]
bei Sinclair Lewis. Diss., Berlin, 1951.

EDENER, WILFRIED, *Die Religionskritik in den Romanen von* [397]
Sinclair Lewis, Beiheft 10 zum JAS, Heidelberg, 1963; 216 pp.

London

JUNG, FRANZ, *Jack London, ein Dichter der Arbeiterklasse*, Wien, [398]
1924.

BEHL, F. W., "Jack London," *Die Gegenwart*, LIV (1925), 10-13. [399]

PORTIZSSKY, J. E., "Jack London oder das Übermass der Anerken- [400]
nung," *Die Literatur*, XXX (1927), 84, 85, 88.

THIEL, RUDOLF, "Charmian London, *Jack London, sein Leben und* [401]
sein Werk," 1928 [Rev.] *Die Literatur*, XXXI (1928), 362-363.

REIFFERSCHEIDT, F. M. "Der Schriftsteller Jack London," *Hochland*, [402]
XXV: 2 (1928), 329-332.

HOLITSCHER, ARTHUR, "Jack London"; "Vorwort" to Charmian [403]
London, *Jack London, sein Leben und sein Werk*, Berlin, 1928.

SCHICKERT, WERNER, "Jack London. *An der weissen Grenze*," [404]
[Rev.] *Die Literatur*, XXXV (1933), 633.

RENTMEISTER, HEINZ, *Das Weltbild Jack Londons*, Halle, 1960; [405]
256 pp.
K.-H. Wirzberger, JAS, IX (1961), 318-320.

Mailer

WILLE, HANS-JÜRGEN, "Norman Mailers neues Buch," NLW, [406]
May 12, 1952, p. 12.
Am Rande der Barbarei.

Malz [264], [476], [477].

Marquand

FREY, ALEXANDER M., "Ein amerikanischer Roman," NLW, [407]
September 25, 1953, p. 8.
Das Leben ist zu kurz.

RICHTER, WERNER, "John P. Marquand und das Problem der [408] Kontinuität," *Hochland*, XLIX, 2 (1957), 274-280.

Melville

KÜHNELT, HARRO, "The Reception of Melville's Works in Germany [409] and Austria," *Innsbrucker Beiträge zur Kulturwissenschaft*, IV (1956), 111-121.

MANGOLD, CHARLOTTE WEISS, *Herman Melville in German Criticism* [410] *from 1900-1955*, Diss., Univ. of Maryland, 1959. DA, XX (1959), 4114.

PHELPS, LELAND R., "*Moby Dick* in Germany," CL, XI (1959), 349- [411] 355.

PHELPS, LELAND R., "The Reaction to *Benito Cereno* and *Billy Budd* [412] in Germany," *Symposium*, XX (1959), 294-299.

Melville and Gerstäcker [221].

Miller, Henry,

DONAT, ANTOINE, "Henry Miller," *Monat*, XIV (1961), 27-39. [413]

Mitchell

PUSEY, W. W., "*Gone with the Wind* in Germany," *Kentucky* [414] *Foreign Language Quarterly*, V (1955), 180-188.

Norris

KLEIN, KARL HEINZ, *Frank Norris' Erzählungstechnik im Ver-* [415] *hältnis zu seiner Kunsttheorie*. Diss., Marburg, 1952; 143 pp.

BRÜNING, EBERHARD, [Review] "Frank Norris' *Gier nach Geld* [416] [*Mc Teague*], aus dem Amerikanischen übersetzt von Paul Böllert," Berlin, Aufbau Verlag, 1958; ZAA, VII (1959), 212-215. See also ZAA, III (1955), 205-206.

LANZINGER, KLAUS, "Der epische Grundplan in Frank Norris' [417] Weizen-Trilogie," DNS, 1963, 437-451.

Poe [222]-[235]

KÜHNELT, HARRO H., "E. A. Poe und die phantastische Erzählung [418] im österreichischen Schrifttum von 1900-1920," *Schlern-Schriften*, CIV (1953), 131-143.

SCHUHMANN, KUNO, *Die erzählende Prosa Edgar Allan Poes: Ein* [419] *Beitrag zu einer Gattungsgeschichte der "Short Story,"* Diss., Frankfurt, 1957; Frankfurter Arbeiten... Anglistik- und Amerika Studien, VI (1958); 166 pp. K. Lanzinger, DNS, 1964, 151-152.

Poe and Jünger
PETERS, H. F., "Ernst Jünger's Concern with Poe," CL, X (1958), [420]
144-149.

Poe and Kafka
HOFRICHTER, LAURA, "From Poe to Kafka," *University of Toronto* [421]
Quarterly, XIX (1961), 405-419.

Poe and Kubin
KÜHNELT, HARRO H., "E. A. Poe und A. Kubin – zwei künstlerische [422]
Gestalter des Grauens," *Wiener Beiträge zur englischen*
Philologie, LXV (1957), 121-141.

Poe and Meyrink
WOLFRAM, KLAUS, "Gustav Meyrink and E. A. Poe," *St. Peters-* [423]
berger Zeitung, 1909, p. 276.

Prescott and Wassermann
STEINER, ARPAD, "William H. Prescott and Jakob Wassermann," [424]
JEGP, XXIV (1925), 555-559.
The Conquest of Peru and *Das Gold von Caxamalca*.

Salinger
BUNGERT, HANS, "J. D. Salingers *The Catcher in the Rye: Isolation* [425]
und Kommunikationsversuche der Jugendlichen," DNS, 1960,
208-216.

Sinclair
BRANDES, GEORG, Introduction to Upton Sinclair, *König Kohle*, [426]
Zürich, 1918.
BAADER, F. P., "*König Kohle*," *Das literarisches Echo*, XXI (1919), [427]
1201.
HOLITSCHER, ARTHUR, "*Jimmie Higgins*," [rev.], *Weltbühne*, XVI [428]
(1920), 494.
ROSENFELD, FRITZ, "Upton Sinclair," *Der Kampf*, XV (1922), [429]
342 f.
MANN, KLAUS, "Besuch bei Upton Sinclair," *Das Tagebuch*, IX [430]
(1928), 25 f.
SCHÖNEMANN, F. [rev.], "Upton Sinclair, *Boston*," *Die Literatur*, [431]
XXXII (1929), 174.
EHRENTREICH, ALFRED, "Literarische Auswirkungen des Falles [432]
Sacco und Vanzetti," *Zeitschrift für französischen und englischen*
Unterricht, 1931, p. 29.
SINCLAIR, UPTON, *Books by Upton Sinclair in Translation and* [433]
Foreign Editions, Pasadena, 1938.

BANTZ, ELIZABETH, "Upton Sinclair: Book Reviews and Criticism [434] Published in German and French Periodicals," *Bulletin of Bibliography*, XVIII (1946), 204-206.

SCHUSTER, HANNS, "Der Wandel des amerikanischen Bildes seit [435] Upton Sinclair," *Eckart*, XXVIII (1960), 336-344.

Steinbeck

KUTZ, HERMANN, *John Steinbeck*, Diss., Kiel, 1952. [436]

BACHMAN, C. H., "Erstaufführungen," NLW, March 10, 1953, [437] p. 7.

SCHÖNAUER, FRITZ, "John Steinbecks neuer Roman," NLW, [438] July 10, 1953, p. 15.

East of Eden

GÄRTNER, HEINZ, *John Steinbeck...* Diss., Berlin, Freie Univ., 1956. [439]

SCHUMANN, HILDEGARD, *Zum Problem des kritischen Realismus* [440] *bei John Steinbeck*, Halle, 1958; 348 pp.

K. H. Schönfelder, ZAA, IX (1962), 105-108.

MICKEL, WOLFGANG, "Die Mächtigkeit des Dinges... *The Pearl*," [441] DNS, 1960, 369-384.

RAUTER, HERBERT, *Bild und Symbol im Werke John Steinbecks*, [442] Diss., Köln, 1960.

MAIER, WOLFGANG CHRISTIAN, *Die Grundformen der menschlichen* [443] *Existenz in den Romanen von John Steinbeck*. Diss., München, 1960; 240 pp.

FELDGES, ALFRED, "John Steinbecks *The Raid*: Eine Interpre- [444] tation," DNS, 1963, 234-239.

Warren

POENICKE, KLAUS, *Robert Penn Warren; Kunstwerk und kritische* [445] *Theorie*, Diss., Berlin, Freie Universität, Heidelberg, 1959, and Beiheft 4, JAS, 1959; 160 pp.

K. Poenicke, JAS, V (1960), 349-351.

Wharton

VON HOLLANDER, WALTHER, "*Zeitalter der Unschuld*," NLW. Feb. [446] 25, 1952, p. 14.

Wilder [249], [256], [257], [258], [478-506].

HEINRICH, GREGOR, "Das Werk des amerikanischen Dichters [447] Thornton Wilder," *Hochland*, XXX: 1 (1932), 176-180.

HOLTHUSEN, HANS EGON, "Thornton Wilder," *Hochland*, XXXV: 2 [448] (1938), 196-204.

Wilder's prose narratives.

GÜNTHER, JOACHIM, "Thornton Wilder, *Dem Himmelbin ich aus-* [449] *erkoren*," DLD, August 5, 1951, p. 10.

NEILL, WOLFGANG, "*Der Zirkel der Villa Horaz*," NLW, Jan. 10, [450] 1952, p. 11.
Wilder's *Cabale*.

STOCK, GISELA, *Das Erzählwerk Thornton Wilders: Entwicklung* [451] *seines Weltbildes von "The Cabale" bis "The Ides of March*," Diss., Mainz, 1956.

NEIS, EDGAR, "Thornton Wilders Novelle, *The Bridge of San Luis* [452] *Rey:* Versuch einer Interpretation," DNS, (1956), 18-26.

PAPAJEWSKI, HELMUT, "Die Problemschichtung in Wilders *The* [453] *Bridge of San Luis Rey*," GRM, XXXVIII (1957), 370-383.

Wolfe

KARSTEN, OTTO, "Geburt der Kunst aus dem Schicksal; Bemer- [454] kungen zu Thomas Wolfe." ASNS, XXXVIII (1936), 308-311.

PUSEY, WILLIAM W., III, "The German Vogue of Thomas Wolfe," [455] GR, XXIII (1948), 131-148.

SEBAIS, H. W., "Angelsächsische Romane," NLW, Dec. 19, 1952, [456] p. 12.
Wolfe, *Von Zeit und Strom*.

FRENZ, HORST, "Bemerkungen über Thomas Wolfe," DNS, 1953, [457] 371-377.

KRACHT, FRITZ ANDREAS, *Die Thomas Wolfe Kritik in den Ver-* [458] *einigten Staaten und Deutschland*, Diss., München, 1953; 161 pp.

PFISTER, KARIN, *Zeit und Wirklichkeit bei Thomas Wolfe*, Diss., [459] Marburg, 1953, Anglistische Forschungen, LXXXIX (1954), Heidelberg; 140 pp.
E. Gronke, ZAA, III (1955), 115-117.

REEVES, G., *Thomas Wolfe et l'Europe*, Paris, 1955; 158 pp. [460]

VOIGT, WALTER, *Die Bildersprache Thomas Wolfes mit besonderer* [461] *Berücksichtigung der Metaphysik des amerikanischen Engli-schen.* Mainzer amerikanische Beiträge, III (1960); xii + 280 pp.

LARRASS, HORST, *Thomas Wolfe: Zur Problematik des bürgerlichen* [462] *Dichters im Zeitalter des Imperialismus*, Diss., Greifswald, 1961; 181 pp.

LANZINGER, KLAUS, "Die Reise im Zug als Vorwurf und Sinnbild [463] bei Thomas Wolfe," DNS, 1962, 293-307.

FUCHS, KONRAD, "Thomas Wolfe, der suchende Realist," DNS, 1963, [464] 110-117.

225

FRENZ, HORST, "Thomas Wolfe als Dramatiker," DNS, 1956, 153-157. [465]

VII THE THEATER

Surveys

VOLLMER, LULA, "Das amerikanische Drama," *Die Literatur,* [466]
XXVIII (1926), 520-524.

GAITHER, MARY AND HORST FRENZ, "German Criticism of American [467]
Drama," *American Quarterly*, 1955, 111-122.

PRICE, LAWRENCE M., "'Überfremdung' and 'Nachwuchs' in the Ger- [468]
man Theater Today," MLF, XLII (1957), 146-151.

SAUTER, HERMANN, "Das moderne amerikanische Drama," [469]
Deutsche Universitätszeitung, XIII (1958), 541-551, 589-606.

BRÜNING, EBERHARD, "Amerikanische Dramen an den Bühnen der [470]
Deutschen Demokratischen Republik und Berlins von 1945-
1955," ZAA, VII (1959), 246-269.

HAAS, RUDOLF, "Das Menschbild im modernen amerikanischen [471]
Drama," *Universitas*, XV (1960), 561-572.

BRÜNING, EBERHARD, *Haupttendenzen des amerikanischen Dramas* [472]
der dreissiger Jahre. Ein Beitrag zur Literaturgeschichte der
Vereinigten Staaten unter Berücksichtigung des Einflusses ameri-
kanischer Dramatik auf die Spielplangestaltung deutscher
Bühnen nach dem zweiten Weltkrieg; Habilitationsschrift. Leipzig, 1961.

KARSCH, WALTHER, "American Drama and the German Stage," [472a]
pp. 64-88 in *The German Theater Today; a Symposium*, Univ.
of Texas Press, Austin, Texas, 1963.

AMERICAN NAMES

Albee

NAGEL, IVAN, "Requiem für die Seele"; Über Albees *Wer hat Angst* [472b]
vor Virginia Woolf, DNR LXXIV (1963), 646-651.

Ahlgren

HOCHE, KLAUS, "Reportage oder Zeitkritik?," NLW, Nov. 10, [473]
1952, p. 13.
The Man with the Golden Arm.

Anderson, (Maxwell), Stalling and Zuckmayer

STEINER, PAULINE and HORST FRENZ, "Anderson and Stalling's [474]
What Price Glory? and Carl Zuckmayer's *Rivalen*," GQ, XX
(1947), 239-252.

226

Fast [264]

KOPKA, HANS W. K., "Eine erste ausführliche Fast-Bibliographie," [475]
ZAA, I (1953), 97-107.

Malz [264]

BRÜNING, EBERHART, "Albert Malz, Leben und Werk im Überblick," [476]
ZAA, IV (1956), 19-63.

—, *Albert Malz, Ein amerikanischer Arbeiterschriftsteller*, Halle, [477]
1957.

Miller

VAN ALLEN, H., *An Examination of the Reception and Critical* [477a]
Evaluation of the Plays of Arthur Miller in West Germany,
1950-1961. Diss. Univ. of Arkansas.
DA, **XXV**, 1901.

GEORGE, MANFRED and HENRY KRANZ, "Neues Meisterwerk der [478]
modernen Dichtung. Arthur Millers Drama *After the Fall*
als Spiegel unseres Daseins," *Universitas*, XIX (1964), 349-
353.

O'Neill

VON HOFMANNSTHAL, HUGO, "Eugene O'Neill," *Das Tagebuch*, IV [479]
(1923), 888-892.

FRENZ, HORST, "List of Foreign Editions and Translations of [480]
Eugene O'Neill's Dramas," *Bulletin of Bibliography*, XVIII
(September-December, 1943), 33-34.

—, "Eugene O'Neill's Plays Printed Abroad," *English Journal*, V [481]
(1944), 340-341.
In Germany, England, France, Italy, Spain, Sweden, etc.

KIRCHNER, GUSTAV, "Eugene O'Neill, *The Iceman Cometh*," NPZ, [482]
II (1950), 28-31.

—, "Das Lustspiel O'Neills *Ah, Wilderness*," DNS, 1952, 3-10. [483]

—, "Eugene Gladstone O'Neill (1888-1953): Ein Rückblick..." [484]
ZAA, II (1954), 137-184.

GALINSKY, HANS, "Eugene O'Neill: Die Wendung des modernen [485]
amerikanischen Theaters zur Tragödie," DNS, 1953, 233-246
and pp. 140-152 in Galinsky, *Sprache und Sprachkunstwerk in*
Amerika, Heidelberg, 1961.

FRENZ, HORST, "Eugene O'Neill on the German Stage," *Theatre* [486]
Annual, XI (1953), 24-34.

—, "Eugene O'Neill in Deutschland," *Euphorion*, L (1956), 307- [487]
327.

SPILLER, ROBERT E., "Nobelpreisträger Eugene O'Neill und die [488]
Weltliteratur unserer Zeit," *Universitas*, XII (1957), 1277-
1280.

KRUTCH, JOSEPH WOOD, "Die Wiederentdeckung Eugene O'Neill's," [489]
Deutsche Universitätszeitung, XIV (1959), 286-289.

PIRA, GISELA, "Eugene O'Neill, *Where the Cross is Made:* Versuch [490]
einer Interpretation," DNS, 1960, 179-182.

STAMM, RUDOLF, "Das Spätwerk O'Neills," DVLW, XXXIV, [491]
(1960), 101-118.

DEIBER, HANS, "Der Tragiker der neuen Welt: Anspruch und [492]
Leistung Eugene O'Neills," *Neue deutsche Hefte*, LXXXI
(1961), 16-35.
See also pp. 163-168 of NDH, 1961.

BRYER, JACKSON H., "Forty Years of O'Neill Criticism, a Selected [493]
Bibliography," *Modern Drama*, IV (1961), 196-216.

DONNER, A. S., "Tragedy and the Pursuit of Happiness: *Long Day's* [494]
Journey into Night," JAS, VI (1961), 115-121.

ROHDE, (geb. KLEINHUBBERT) MARIANNE, *Bedeutung und Zusam-* [495]
menhang der vier Spätdramen Eugene O'Neills, Diss., Freiburg in
Br., 1961; 226 pp.

SCHUHE, OSCAR FRITZ, "Eugene O'Neill und seine Dramen," [496]
Universitas, XVII (1962), 235-244.

LACHMANN, "Meisterwerke des Films: O'Neill: *Eines langen Tages* [497]
Reise in die Nacht," *Universitas*, XVII (1962), 1369-1370.

Wilder [447]-[453].

BRAUN, HANNS, "Das Mysterium Iniquitatis bei Thornton Wilder," [498]
Hochland, XXXIX: I (1947), 473-475, 572-579.

STÜRZL, ERWIN, "Weltbild und Lebensphilosophie Thornton [499]
Wilders," DNS, 1953, 341-351.

FUSSELL, PAUL, "Thornton Wilder and the German Psyche," [500]
Nation, CLXXXVI (1958), 394-395.

FRENZ, HORST, "American Playwrights and the German Psyche," [501]
DNS, 1961, 170-178.
Reply to Fussell above.

—, "The Reception of Thornton Wilder's Plays in Germany," [502]
Modern Drama, III (1960), 123-137.

PIXBERG, HERMANN, "*Die Alkestiade* von Thornton Wilder," [503]
Eckart, XXIX (1960), 281-283.

VIEBROCK, HELMUT, "Thornton Wilder's Hauptmotiv," DNS [504]
(1961), 349-363.

PAPAJEWSKI, HELMUT, *Thornton Wilder*, Frankfurt am Main, 1961; [505]
166 pp.
P. F. Günther, *Books Abroad*, XXXVII (1963), 175 f.
H. Kosok, DNS, 1964, 53-54.

Williams

BUCHLOH, PAUL C., "Verweisende Zeichen in Tennessee Williams' [506]
Camino Real," *Anglia*, LXXVII (1959), 173-203.
FRENZ, HORST and ULRICH WEISSTEIN, "Tennessee Williams and his [507]
German Critics," *Symposium*, XIV (1960), 258-275.
MACHTS, WALTER, "Das Menschbild im den Dramen Tennessee [508]
Williams," DNS, 1961, 445-455.
FRIEDRICH, JUTTA, "Individuum und Gesellschaft in den Dramen [509]
Tennessee Williams," ZAA, XIII (1965), 45-60.

Wolfe [465]

VIII. LYRIC POETRY

GOLL, CLAIR, "Junge amerikanische Dichtung," DNR, XXXI: 1 [510]
(1920), 707-714.
BRUNNER, KARL, "Amerikanische Lyrik der Gegenwart," GRM, XI [511]
(1923), 33-43.
Walt Whitman, Amy Lowell, Ezra Pound, Babette Deutsch,
Vachel Lindsay, Carl Sandburg, Bliss Carman, Richard Hovey,
Edgar Lee Masters, Paul Laurence Dunbar.
VAN DOREN, MARK, "Die neue Dichtkunst Amerikas," *Die Literatur*, [512]
XXVIII (1926), 511-514.
Emerson, Whitman, Dickinson, Robinson, Pound, Masters,
Lindsay, Sandburg, Frost, Jeffers, Leonard.

Dickinson

RIESE, TEUT ANDREAS, "Emily Dickinson und der Sprachgeist [513]
amerikanischer Lyrik," DNS, 1963, 145-149.

Frost

LICHTENSTEIN, ERICH, [rev.], "*Lyrik von Robert Frost*, deutsch," [514]
NLW, Oct. 30, 1953, p. 6.

Millay

BORCHARDT, RUDOLF, "Die Entdeckung Amerikas: Die Poesie [515]
von Edna St. Vincent Millay," DNR, LXII: 4 (1951), 82-100.

Robinson

SCHÖNEMANN, F., "Der Lyriker der amerikanischen Skepsis," [516]
Die Literatur, XXXV (1933), 446-448.
Edw. Arlington Robinson.

BAUMGÄRTNER, ALFRED, *Das lyrische Werk Edwin Arlington* [517]
Robinsons, Diss., Mainz, 1953; 146 Bl.

Whitman

LESSING, O. E., "Whitman and his German Critics," JEGP, IX [518]
(1910), 85-98.
THORSTENBERG, EDWARD, "The Walt Whitman Cult in Germany," [519]
The Sewanee Review, XIX (1911), 71-86.
KNORTZ, KARL, *Walt Whitman und seine Nachahmer*, Leipzig, 1911; [520]
159 pp.
LESSING, O. E., "Die Botschaft Walt Whitmans," *The Open Court*, [521]
Aug. 1919 and pp. 77-97 in *Brücken über den Atlantik*, Berlin
und Leipzig, 1927.
CLARK, GRACE DELANO, "Walt Whitman in Germany," *Texas* [522]
Review, VI (1921), 125-135.
ZAREK, O., "Walt Whitman und die deutsche Dichtung," DNR, [523]
XXXIII (1922), 1202-1209.
Same in English translation, Little's *Living Age*, CCCXVII
(1923), 333-339.
JACOBSON, ANNA, "Walt Whitman in Germany since 1914," GR, [524]
I (1926), 132-141.
BAB, JULIUS, "Walt Whitman und die Botschaft Amerikas," [525]
pp. 145-156 in *Befreiungsschlacht*, Stuttgart, 1928.
LAW-ROBERTSON, HARRY, *Walt Whitman in Deutschland*, Giessener [526]
Beiträge zur deutschen Philologie, XLII (1935); 91 pp.
LESSING, O. E., "Walt Whitman and his German Critics Prior to [527]
1910," *American Collector*, III (1936), 7-15.
SCHUMANN, DETLEV W., "Enumerative Style and its Significance [528]
in Whitman, Rilke, Werfel," MLQ, III (1942), 171-204.
—, "Observations on Enumerative Style in Modern German [529]
Poetry," PMLA, LIX (1944), 1111-1155.
REISIGER, HANS, *Walt Whitman*, Frankfurt, 1948; 104 pp. [530]
SCHERRINSKY, HARALD, "Walt Whitman in modernen deutschen [531]
Übersetzungen," NPZ, III (1950), 189-191.
ROECKLINGER, GERTRUDE, *Walt Whitmans Einfluss auf die deutsche* [532]
Lyrik, Diss., Wien, 1951-1952.
MC CORMICK, EDWARD ALLEN, *Die sprachliche Eigenart von Walt* [533]
Whitmans "Leaves of Grass" in deutscher Übertragung...,
Sprache und Dichtung, LXXIV, Bern und Stuttgart, 1953;
118 pp.

WIRZBERGER, KARL-HEINZ, "Ein Hundert Jahre *Leaves of Grass*," [534]
ZAA, IV (1956), 77-87.
J.W.Thomas, JAS, VIII (1963), 351-353.
RIESE, TEUT, "Walt Whitman als politischer Dichter," JAS, IV [535]
(1958), 136-150.
HATFIELD, HENRY, "Drei Randglossen zu Thomas Manns *Zauber-* [536]
berg, Hans Castorp und Walt Whitman," *Euphorion*, LVI
(1962), 365-368.
PREUSCHEN, KARL ADALBERT, "Zur Entstehung der neuen Lyrik [537]
in Amerika: Walt Whitman, 'Song of Myself,'" (1. Fassung),
JAS, VIII (1963), 145-170.
Whitman and Freiligrath
SPRINGER, OTTO, "Walt Whitman and Ferdinand Freiligrath," [538]
AGR, XI² (1944), 22-26, 38.
Whitman and Holz
VON ENDE, AMALIA, "Walt Whitman and Arno Holz," *Poet Lore*, [539]
XVI (1905), 61-65.
Whitman and Mann
HUNT, JOEL A., "Mann and Whitman, Humaniores Litterae," CL, [540]
XIV (1962), 266-271.
RILEY, ANTHONY, "Notes on Thomas Mann and English and [541]
American Literature," CL, XVII (1965), pp. 51-72.

Whitman and Rolleston
FRENZ, HORST, ed., *Whitman and Rolleston. A Correspondence,* [542]
Indiana University Publications, Humanities Series, XXVI
(1952); 137 pp.
For letters to Knortz see H.Frenz, AL, XX (1948), 115-163
and AGR, XII (1946), 27-30.

Whitman and Schlaf
SCHLAF, JOHANNES, "Walt Whitman; zur Einführung: Mein [543]
Verhältnis zu Walt Whitman," *Die Lese*, III (1912), 436-441.

Whitman and Zschokke
GLICKSBERG, CHARLES I., "Walt Whitman and Heinrich Zschokke," [544]
Notes and Queries, CLXVI (1934), 382-384.

ALLEN, GAY WILSON, *Twenty-five Years of Walt Whitman Bibli-* [545]
ography, 1918-1942. Boston 1943; 57H.
—, *Walt Whitman Abroad; Critical Essays from Germany, France,* [546]
Scandinavia, Russia, Italy, Spain and Latin America, Israel,
Japan, and India, Syracuse, New York, 1955.

INDEX OF CONTRIBUTORS

The numbers on these pages correspond to the
bracketed serial numbers in the bibliography.

Castle, E., 112, 129.
Christadler, M., 342.
Clark, E., 300.
Clark, G. D., 522.
Clark, R. T., 42.
Cobb, P., 233.
Cohn, L. H., 357.
Correll, E., 85.
Cronholm, A. C., 77.
Cunz, D., 9.

D

Daiber, H., 492.
Dallmann, W. F., 125.
Damp, 378.
David, A. L., 87.
Demmig, 258, 391.
Descyzk, G., 16.
Dickson, P., 272.
Dietrich, M., 360.
Dilkey, M. C., 150.
Djordjevitsch, J., 124.
Doderer, K., 265.
Doll, E. E., 6.
Donat, A., 413.
Donner, A., 494.
van Doren, M., 512.
Duffy, C., 201.

E

Edener, W., 397.
Edward, G., 223.
Effelberger, H., 257, 243.
Ehle, R. W., 251.
Ehrentreich, A., 432.
Ehrenzweig, S., 309, 321.
von Einsieder, W., 329, 338, 363.
von Ende, A., 196, 539.
Engel, E., 159.
Evans, C., 91, 92.
Ewers, H. H., 224.

F

Fallada, H., 358, 359.
Faust, A. B., 123.
Feldges, A., 444.
Feller, M. K., 23.
Field, G. W., 291.
Fischer, W., 167f., 262, 392.
Fraenkel, E., 17.
Francke, K., 195.
Franz, E. G., 78.
Franzen, E., 334, 370.
Freemantel, R., 263.
Frenz, H., 109, 241, 457, 465, 467,
    474, 480f., 486f., 501f., 507, 542.
Frey, J. R., 277-279, 298, 369.
Friederich, W. P., 7.
Friedrich, J., 509.
Friesé, K., 255.
Fuchs, K., 464.
Fussell, P., 500.

G

Gabrielli, V., 63.
Gärtner, H., 439.
Gaither, M., 467.
Galinsky, H., 485.
Gallinger, H. P., 34.
George, M., 478.
Glicksberg, C. I., 544.
Goebel, J., 15.
Goll, C., 510.
Graewert, T., 121.
Graf, E., 25.
Grames, B. D., 274.
Grande, R., 318.
Gregg, C., 261.
Grenzmann, W., 341.
Grimm, H., 195.
Gronke, E., 373, 459.
Günther, J., 449.
Günther, P. F., 505.
Gurtler, L., 366.

234

235

Tetchmann, E., 212.
von Thaler, C., 161.
Thiel, R., 401.
Thomas, J. W., 534.
Thomkson, G. W., 137.
Thorpe, W., 185.
Thorstenberg, E., 519.
Timpe, E. F., 79, 206a, 207a.
Türk, W., 311.

U

Uhlendorf, B. A., 140.
Uhlig, H., 219.
Urzidil, J., 105, 243.

V

Vagts, A., 55.
Vail, C. D., 97.
Victory, B. M., 52.
Viebrock, H., 504.
Voigt, W., 461.
Vollmer, C., 82.
Vollmer, L., 466.

W

Wadepuhl, W., 96, 97.
Wagner, L. E., 74.
Walter, J., 221.

Walz, J. A., 35, 36.
Weber, P. C., 83.
Wehe, W., 72.
Weisstein, 502.
Wellek, R., 198.
Wellershoff, D., 378a.
Weltmann, L., 308.
Wentz, J. C., 325.
Wertheim, U., 38.
West, V. R., 170.
Wilde, M., 21.
Wille, H. J., 406.
Willey, N., 133, 141, 145.
Williams, A. L., 48.
Williams, B., 246.
Williams, C. A., 371.
Wirzberger, K. H., 208, 322, 324, 405, 534.
Wolfram, K., 423.
Woodson, L. H., 154.
Wukadinovic, S., 186.
Wustenhagen, H., 379.

Z

Zaeckel, E., 183.
Zeydel, E. H., 83.
Zieglschmid, A. J. F., 86.
Zucker, A. E., 9.
Zweig, A., 390.

INDEX OF AUTHORS AND CRITICS

(Translators as such are not included
nor are references in the bibliography)

239

240

Hancock, 10.
Hardenberg, 73, 78.
Harnack-Fisch, 153f.
Harrison, 65.
Hart, 76, 89.
Harte, 62, 111-112.
Hartmann von Aue, 110.
Hauff, 88f.
Hauptmann, C., 164.
Hauptmann, G., 164, 166.
Hauser, O., 61.
Hawthorne, 53, 55, 57, 69, 97, 98, 120, 121, 122, 185.
Heine, 33.
Heinse, 83.
von Heiseler, 150, 153f.
Hellmann, 173.
Hemingway, 8, 117, 121, 123, 124, 144, 147, 150, 153, 157, 180, 186.
Henderson, 114.
Herbert, 171.
Herder, 12, 16, 21, 24.
Hermes, 17.
Herrig, 63, 128.
Hesse, 134, 150, 152, 153, 154, 155.
Hesslein, 101, 102.
Hochwälder, 172, 173, 185.
von Hoffmann, A., 28.
Hoffmann, E. T. A., 55, 65.
Hofmann von Fallersleben, 42f.
von Hofmannsthal, 164f., 181.
von Hohenhausen, 61, 97.
Hohoff, 150.
Hollander, 165.
Holm, 172f.
Holthusen, 175.
Holz, 77.
Home, 7.
Homer, 132.
Hopp, 60, 63, 72.
Howells, 115, 116, 121, 122, 146.
Huber, 37.

von Humboldt, 109.
Hüttner, 86.

I

Iffland, 17.
Ingram, 65.
Irving, 47, 57, 81-85, 88, 91, 109, 122.
Irwin, 173.

J

Jacobi, F., 113.
Jacobson, 67.
James, 121, 122, 157-158, 172, 186.
Jefferson, 8, 95.
Jeffrey, 81.
Jesus of Nazareth, 74.
Johnson, S., 7.
Jones, 124.
Joyce, 154.
Jünger, 126-127.
Jung, 131.
Jürgenson, 132.

K

Kafka, 126, 130, 181.
Kaiser, 164.
Kanin, 174.
Kant, 12, 108.
Karpeles, 63.
Kartzke, 145.
Keats, 52, 53.
Kellner, 57, 128-129.
Kerr, 165.
Key, 63.
Keyserling, 56.
Kingsley, 172.
Kipling, 132.
Klinger, 18, 183.
Klopstock, 10.
Knebel, 24.
Knigge, 28.

Knortz, 47, 49, 60, 61, 62, 64, 67, 68, 72, 74, 77, 112, 113.
Körner, 30, 31.
Korn, K., 144, 154.
Kornfeld, 136, 139.
Korting, 63, 113.
Kreuder, 150.
Krüger, 113.
Krumpelmann, 110.
Kubin, 126.

L

Landauer, 74.
Langasser, 150.
La Roche, 37, 38.
Laun, 60, 62, 121.
Lavery, 173.
Le Breton, 152.
Lecky, 116.
Leixner, 63, 128.
Lenau, 40, 41, 96.
Lenz, 118.
Lersch, 76.
Lessing, G. E., 171.
Lessing, O. E., 17, 72.
Lewald, 95.
Lewis, "M," 65, 123.
Lewis, Sinclair, 121, 124, 135-141, 148, 151, 152, 153, 155, 185, 187.
Liebeskind, 27.
Liebig, 71.
Lienhart, 106.
zur Linde, O., 76.
Lissauer, 76.
Lobetanz, 113.
London, C., 131.
London, J., 57, 80, 121, 123, 124, 130-132, 133, 148, 185.
Longfellow, 39, 49, 50, 53, 54, 57, 61, 63, 64, 69, 72, 122, 186.
von Loper, 110.
Lowell, 8, 48, 62, 97.

Luden, 32.
Lüdeke, 57, 142.

M

MacLeish, 123.
Maeterlinck, 180.
Mager, 63.
de Magny, 152.
Mallarmé, 70.
Malory, 116.
Malraux, 152.
Mann, T., 78f., 128, 130, 158.
Marggraff, 51, 64.
Markham, 63.
Martens, 136.
Marx, 48, 131, 146, 149, 169.
Mather, C., 6.
Mather, I., 6.
Matthesen, 16.
Maturin, 55.
de Maupassant, 112.
Maurois, 180.
May, 90, 120.
Meitner, 137.
Mell, 164.
Melville, 57, 120, 122, 124, 127-130, 156, 187.
Mencken, 152.
Mendelssohn, 109.
Metternich, 27.
Meyen, 25.
Meyer, 110.
Meyrink, 70, 126.
Michaelis, 24, 125.
Middleton, 7.
Miller, A., 173, 178, 182, 185.
Mitchell, 122.
Moeller-Brock, 67.
Möllhausen, 92.
Möllenhoff, 67.
Molière, 139.
von Molo, 174.

REPRINTS FROM OUR COMPARATIVE LITERATURE STUDIES

Through the University of North Carolina Press
Chapel Hill, North Carolina

2. Werner P. Friederich. DANTE'S FAME ABROAD, 1350-1850. The Influence of Dante Alighieri on the Poets and Scholars of Spain, France, England, Germany, Switzerland and the United States. Rome, 1950 and 1966. Pp. 584. Paper, $ 10.00.

10. Charles E. Passage. DOSTOEVSKI THE ADAPTER. A Study in Dostoevski's Use of the Tales of Hoffmann. 1954. Reprinted 1963. Pp. x, 205. Paper, $ 3.50. Cloth, $ 4.50.

11. Werner P. Friederich and David H. Malone. OUTLINE OF COMPARATIVE LITER-ATURE. From Dante Alighieri to Eugene O'Neill. 1954. Third Printing, 1962. Pp. 460. Cloth, $ 6.50.

Through Russell & Russell, Inc.
Publishers, 156 Fifth Avenue
New York, N. Y. 10010

1. Fernand Baldensperger and Werner P. Friederich. BIBLIOGRAPHY OF COMPARA-TIVE LITERATURE. 1950. Pp. 729. Cloth, $ 15.00.

6, 7, 9, 14, 16, 18, 21, 25 and 27. W. P. Friederich & H. Frenz (eds): YEARBOOKS OF COMPARATIVE AND GENERAL LITERATURE. Vols. I (1952) to IX (1960). Cloth, $ 6.50 per volume.

Through Johnson Reprint Corporation
111 Fifth Avenue
New York, N. Y. 10003

4. GOETHE'S SORROWS OF YOUNG WERTER, TRANSLATED BY GEORGE TICKNOR. Edited with Introduction and Critical Analysis by Frank G. Ryder. Cloth, $ 8.00.

5. Helmut A. Hatzfeld. A CRITICAL BIBLIOGRAPHY OF THE NEW STYLISTICS APPLIED TO THE ROMANCE LITERATURES, 1900-1952. Cloth, $ 12.00.

26. DANTE'S LA VITA NUOVA, TRANSLATED BY RALPH WALDO EMERSON. Edited and annotated by J. Chesley Mathews. Cloth, $ 8.00.

28. Haskell M. Block (ed.). THE TEACHING OF WORLD LITERATURE. Cloth, $ 6.00.

30. Oskar Seidlin. ESSAYS IN GERMAN AND COMPARATIVE LITERATURE. Cloth, $ 10.00.